ON DESIGN

ON DESIGN

THEORY, HISTORY, EDUCATION AND PRACTICE

Tevfik Balcıoğlu

BLOOMSBURY VISUAL ARTS
LONDON • NEW YORK • OXFORD • NEW DELHI • SYDNEY

BLOOMSBURY VISUAL ARTS
Bloomsbury Publishing Plc
50 Bedford Square, London, WC1B 3DP, UK
1385 Broadway, New York, NY 10018, USA
29 Earlsfort Terrace, Dublin 2, Ireland

BLOOMSBURY, BLOOMSBURY VISUAL ARTS and the Diana logo are trademarks of Bloomsbury Publishing Plc

First published in Great Britain 2024

Copyright © Tevfik Balcıoğlu, 2024

Tevfik Balcioglu has asserted his right under the Copyright, Designs and Patents Act, 1988, to be identified as Author of this work.

For legal purposes the Acknowledgements on p. xviii constitute an extension of this copyright page.

Cover design: Louise Dugdale
Cover photograph © Burak Özbek, sculpture by Akın Yıldırım

All rights reserved. No part of this publication may be reproduced or transmitted in any form or by any means, electronic or mechanical, including photocopying, recording, or any information storage or retrieval system, without prior permission in writing from the publishers.

Bloomsbury Publishing Plc does not have any control over, or responsibility for, any third-party websites referred to or in this book. All internet addresses given in this book were correct at the time of going to press. The author and publisher regret any inconvenience caused if addresses have changed or sites have ceased to exist, but can accept no responsibility for any such changes.

A catalogue record for this book is available from the British Library.

A catalog record for this book is available from the Library of Congress.

ISBN: HB: 978-1-3503-5931-4
PB: 978-1-3503-5930-7
ePDF: 978-1-3503-5933-8
eBook: 978-1-3503-5932-1

Typeset by Deanta Global Publishing Services, Chennai, India
Printed and bound in India

To find out more about our authors and books visit www.bloomsbury.com and sign up for our newsletters.

This book is dedicated to five people who made me who I am today. They are always remembered with great love and gratitude: my parents, Naciye and Afif Balcıoğlu, my aunt Fahrünnisa, her husband Mustafa Balöz and my other aunt Fatma Moler.

CONTENTS

List of Figures ix
Author xi
Preface xii
Foreword *Jonathan M. Woodham* xiv
Acknowledgements xviii

Introduction 1

Section One Theory 7

1 Original and reproduction: From corporeal to clone 9

2 In search of principles: We have been told that they died long ago 19

3 Problematic of local and global design identity in newly industrialized countries: With special emphasis on Turkey at the end of the twentieth century 33

4 The essential elements: The unity of work and transferability of knowledge 41

5 Research, knowledge and doctorate programmes: Towards the third domain 50

Section Two History 61

6 On transformations of the term design with reference to mass-produced objects 65

7 Mapping the mind: Tracing the mentality change 74

8 Observations on the rise of design historiography by the end of the twentieth century in the UK: A view from 'outside in' with a touch of globalization 86

9 Uncharted territories of transnational design history with particular reference to Turkey 107

10	Turkish graphic design: From the age of the alphabet revolution to the end of the twentieth century	114
11	4T Design and Design History Society: A critical analysis	143
Section Three Education and practice		155
12	Integrated Design Approach (IDeA): Reflections on a new school of design building	159
13	PhD, DFA or both: The protection of identity, nature and the potential power of differences	174
14	Towards an understanding of professional doctorates	178
15	A threshold where theory and practice congregate fortuitously	184
16	Industrial design in Turkey: A new agenda (rewritten with Aren Emre Kurtgözü in 2023)	189
17	Redesigning Turkish cult objects: From traditional to 'modern'?	200
References		209
Index		219

FIGURES

1	Pagoda House designed by Bruno Taut, situated at the Bosphorus in Istanbul	109
2	Propaganda postcard by İhap Hulusi Görey showing old and new marriage ceremonies	115
3	Atatürk introducing the new Turkish Alphabet with Latin script in 1928	116
4	One of the first editions of the new Turkish Alphabet with Latin script by the Language Committee, 1928	117
5	Advertisement for Bank of Agriculture, designed by İhap Hulusi, 1948	121
6	Advertisement for Beykoz Shoes, designed by İhap Hulusi	122
7A–B	Photograph of İhap Hulusi drinking rakı (7A), and the label of Kulüp Rakısı (7B)	123
8A–B	Photograph showing Atatürk teaching the new alphabet to his adopted daughter Ülkü (8A) and the new alphabet book cover derived from this photograph (8B), 1935	124
9	The cover of Edgar Allan Poe's book, *Incredible Stories*, designed by Münif Fehim, 1938	125
10	Münif Fehim's design: the cover of *Amok*, a book by Stefan Zweig, 1939	125
11	Münif Fehim's design: the cover of *The Hungry Stones* by Rabindranth Tagore	126
12	Poster for the play *Amadeus*, designed by Mengü Ertel, 1983	127
13	An illustration by Mengü Ertel	128
14	Poster for Istanbul Festival by Mengü Ertel, 1973	128
15A–C	Logo designs by Mengü Ertel: Logo for a real estate company, 1984 (15A), the Social Democratic Party, 1984 (15B), and the Fair for Affordable Clothing, 1976 (15C)	129
16	Erkal Yavi's book cover design for Tekin Publications, 1984	129
17	Erkal Yavi's poster design for Adam Publications, 1990	130
18	Book cover for *The Iliad* by Homer. Designer: Sait Maden, 1967	131
19	Mengü Ertel's poster design for *Keşanlı Ali Destanı* [The Ballad of Ali of Keshan], a play by Haldun Taner, 1984	132
20	Sadık Karamustafa's poster design for the Eight Istanbul Film Festival, 1989	132
21	Poster for a play by Philip King, entitled *Papaz Kaçtı* [How They Run], designer: Sadık Karamustafa, 1987	133
22	Sadık Karamustafa's poster for the *Mind the Map*, the Third International Conference on Design History and Design Studies, ICDHS, Istanbul, 2002	134

Figures

23	Bülent Erkmen's design for Jan Garbarek's jazz concert, Istanbul, 1998	134
24	Yurdaer Altıntaş's Hitchcock poster for Eighteenth Istanbul Film Festival, 1999	135
25	Poster for International Prison Watch, designed by Bülent Erkmen, 1995	135
26	Bülent Erkmen's poster for the play *Cadılar Zamanı* [The Pope and the Witch] written by Dario Fo and Franca Rame	136
27	Bülent Erkmen's poster design for the film *Arabesk* [Arabesque]	137
28	The sleeve and cover for the book entitled *Benim Tek İstediğim Bir Kitap Yazmaktı* [The Only Thing I Ever Wished was to Write a Book] designed by Sadık Karamustafa, 1999	138
29	Back sleeve of the book entitled *Benim Tek İstediğim Bir Kitap Yazmaktı* [The Only Thing I Ever Wished was to Write a Book] designed by Sadık Karamustafa, 1999	139
30	Esen Karol's poster design for *Macbeth* by William Shakespeare, Istanbul, 1999	140
31	Esen Karol's poster design for an art photography exhibition called *Sokaklardan* [From the Streets] by Şakir Eczacıbaşı, 1996	140
32	Gülizar Çepoğlu's poster for the exhibition *Manuscript*, Istanbul, 1994	141
33	Sunday Supplement of Güneş Newspaper, designed by Gülizar Çepoğlu, Istanbul, 1990	141
34	Faculty of Fine Arts and Design, the building at the opening night, 20 October 2010	167
35	Faculty of Fine Arts and Design building, bridges connecting blocks. A view from the courtyard	168
36	Interior of a typical staff room	169
37	Common design studios	170
38	One of the vast areas of indoor open space and large corridors	171
39	An open office and work area for research assistants	172
40A–B	Traditional coffee pot (40A), compared with Arzum Cezve (40B) designed by Kunter Şekercioğlu in 2005	205
41	Coffee pot made out of glass, designed by Ali Bakova in 2010	205
42	Boiler providing hot water to make tea or coffee in traditional public Turkish tea houses	207
43A–E	A few examples of Paşabahçe tea glasses. From left to right: Aida (43A), Etnik (43B), Heybeli (43C), İncebelli (43D), Samanyolu (43E)	207
44A–F	Tea glasses (from left to right): Ti Te Chai by Ali Bakova (44A), Hisar (two glasses) by Can Yalman (44B), Unnamed by Defne Koz (44C), Dervish (saucer and glass) by Faruk Malhan (44D), İstanbul by Faruk Malhan (44E) and İncebelli (three glasses) by Koray Özgen (44F)	208

AUTHOR

Tevfik Balcıoğlu is a Professor of Design who retired in 2022 and lives in Izmir, Turkey. He received B. Arch (1976), M. Arch (1981) and PhD (1993) degrees at Middle East Technical University; won a British Council research grant and attended the Royal College of Art (1988–1990); and taught at Goldsmiths' College (1991) and Kent Institute of Art and Design (1992–2002), where he established the BA (Hons) Three-Dimensional Design course as course leader. Returning to Turkey in 2003, he founded the Faculty of Fine Arts & Design at Izmir University of Economics. As its Dean (2004–2011), he established five departments, two MA courses and a research centre. He was instrumental in establishing 4T: Turkish Design History Society, which organised annual conferences between 2006–2014. This later became a formal body, 4T: Design & Design History Society. He also served as its founding president (2014–2018). After joining Yasar University in 2011, he worked as Vice-Rector (2012–2015) and Professor of Design until September 2018. Balcıoğlu has organized several international conferences and edited many conference proceedings, some with colleagues. These works include 'The Role of Product Design in Post-Industrial Society', 'Mind the Gap', 'Dancing with Disorder', 'Gender Perspectives in Design' and 'Design and Resistance'. He was a board member of the European Academy of Design (EAD) and the International Committee for Design History and Design Studies (ICDHS) until 2022. He was a design coordinator and member of Izmir Mediterranean Academy's executive board and scientific committee (2012–2018) and initiated the 'Design Corridors' and 'Izmir Good Design' projects.

After buying a 450-year-old Ottoman primary school building in 2005, he restored and converted it into 'Urla Design Library, Faruk Tabak Reading Room', which is open to the public. In 2017, the building received the Izmir Municipality 'Respect for History Local Conservation Award' in the category of 'substantial restoration where original function altered'.

PREFACE

This book includes essays, articles and conference papers delivered in a broad range of geographic locations over the years. They can be classified into four main categories: design theory, history, education and practice. I find this range of subjects rather comprehensive, presenting a fertile ground for generative debate and discussion. Encouraged by the diversity of the ideas and subjects presented in these works, I decided to publish them in a single volume.

Due to the wide range of topics included, I believe that each chapter can attract the interest of different groups of people working in various fields of design. There are chapters addressing pedagogical issues that may interest educationists. There are chapters concerned with theories that may entice academicians. There are chapters on design practice that may draw the attention of designers. Students may find useful information in each chapter depending on their area of research and enthusiasm.

The reasons for and the rationale behind this republication are manifold. When I decided to bring the papers together, the first question I asked myself was what their value and validity in today's world were. Further questions arose: why are they still meaningful despite the contextual differences between their original date of publication and today? Are there books of the same nature available in the market?

I selected the papers with these questions in mind and responded to them one by one. I realised to my surprise that the arguments and the main ideas discussed are still relevant, effective and applicable.

To respond to the second question, we need to look into the characteristics of the essays. I would say that articles on history and theory in Sections One and Two are not – and probably cannot be – time-dependent because the issues raised and the research conducted provide interesting results and valuable information. In Section Three, the reproduction of articles on education has a different purpose. Although the debate on the practice versus studio-based PhD appears to be over in the UK, I think my observations and suggestions may help future discussions and studies when the present situation is reviewed. These chapters also provide alternative views that may be of use to many countries where practice-based PhD programmes have not yet been launched. In Section Three, there is a chapter on integrated design approach that I applied and experienced at the Faculty of Fine Arts and Design, Izmir University of Economics, where I was the Founding Dean between 2004 and 2011. I value this as a unique experience achieved together with seventy-five full-time staff members and about 1,200 students. The lessons learned are prototypical and useable by many schools.

To my knowledge the answer to the third question is negative. Therefore, the publication justifies itself, for there are few design books written by Turkish researchers in English, and there are no collected essays published in the last twenty-five years. What I find most interesting is that this book is a record of an academic journey of a designer/educator who has produced different kinds of work throughout his career. Naturally, the attainments of this journey were not always intentional but emerged gradually in line with the changing academic and administrative responsibilities and duties.

For this publication, each paper was edited, certain parts updated and some papers were subjected to minor amendments and additions except Chapter 16 in Section Three which was completely rewritten. Relying on the quality of papers examined in many academic circumstances and encouraged by their variety, I concluded that this book may make a modest contribution to current global and Turkish design literature and is worth publishing at least to record the design knowledge that I have produced or been involved in. I hope that my expectations will be realised and that this book will fulfil its mission by being beneficial for a broad range of design circles.

FOREWORD
Jonathan M. Woodham

I was delighted to be invited to write the foreword for this absorbing collection of seventeen talks and essays written by Tevfik Balcıoğlu between 1994 and 2023. Grouped in three broad-ranging sections devoted to theory, history, and education and practice, they have been delivered to a wide variety of national and international constituencies. His audiences typically range from those at the Design History Society's (DHS) 17th Annual Conference in Plymouth, England, in 1995; the European Academy of Design's (EDA) conference in Stockholm, Sweden, in 1997; and the inaugural International Conference on Design History and Design Studies (ICDHS) at the University of Barcelona in 1999. He subsequently addressed a spectrum of design-focused audiences in Aveiro, Guadalajara, Havana, Helsinki, Istanbul, Jerusalem, London, Mexico City, Milan, Taipei, Tokyo, São Paolo and elsewhere.

In 1999 Balcıoğlu described himself as 'a foreigner' observing from 'outside in'. This notion of difference is a positive and engaging aspect of this book: audiences will find much of interest in the various lenses through which Balcıoğlu has chosen to interrogate his themes. These include bringing the history and presence of Turkish design to greater international prominence, allowing for greater scrutiny of curriculum initiatives in Turkish design education, and evaluating aspects of the nature and purpose of research in such fields.

The timespan of Balcıoğlu's texts in this book runs from the late 1980s to the present. In addition to the diversity of his research papers delivered in geographically dispersed locations, Balcıoğlu's energy, enthusiasm, and considerable personal involvement in developments in British and Turkish design education, theory, practice, and history shines through. His wide-ranging agenda – as it began to formulate itself – was initially grounded in his direct experience of the Turkish architectural and design education system from the 1970s onwards where he successfully navigated his way through undergraduate and postgraduate degrees at the Middle East Technical University (METU), Ankara. From 1985, at the same institution, Balcıoğlu had also delivered classes in design history to industrial design students. This dimension of his work culminated in the award of a PhD in historiography in 1993, providing an important stepping-stone to his pivotal role in the establishment in 2005 of *4T: Design History Society Turkey* which took on a formal status in 2014 when he was recognized as the Founding President, playing a key role until 2018. 4T annual symposia were established and the proceedings published, several of them in full English editions and thus available to audiences worldwide. In the later 1980s Balcıoğlu was awarded a British Council research grant and attended the Royal College of Art, London, before becoming a lecturer at Goldsmith's College in 1991.

He then spent a decade (1992–2002) at the Kent Institute of Art and Design (KIAD), a Higher Education Institution (HEI) in southern England that had been formed through the slightly uncomfortable amalgamation of three previously independent art schools in 1987. Balcıoğlu was thus thrown into the cut and thrust of British higher education in art and design at a time when there was considerable – often heated – contemporary debate about the nature and structure of doctoral education in the field, accompanied by the emergence of such awards from the early 1980s onwards. Balcıoğlu's evaluations of the pros and cons of Professional Doctorates, Doctorates in Fine Art or Design, or PhDs relating to art and design practices are discussed at some length in this book, especially in Section Three. His direct involvement in such debates reflected his role as the PhD programme coordinator at KIAD between 1998 and 2002. An important footnote relating to his time in British higher education was the fact that the Council for National Academic Awards (CNAA) in Britain had been stressing the importance of establishing research degrees in art and design in the 1980s, a decade in which Polytechnics[1] and Higher Education Institutes prepared for higher level recognition. Polytechnics were recognized by government as 'new' or 'modern' universities in 1992. Consequently, for the first time, these institutions became eligible to bid competitively for significant government research funding and thus raise the perceived status of research in art and design to the highest levels. KIAD went on to become a major constituent element in the University of the Creative Arts when it was formed in 2005. During his time in Britain Balcıoğlu had also aligned himself with notable voices in contemporary discussions of industrial design as, for example, in the conference he organized at the Courtauld Institute of Art, London, in 1995, at which his invited speakers included Ezio Manzini, Dieter Rams, John Heskett and Victor Margolin.

In Chapter 8 in Section Three, 'Observations on the rise of design historiography by the end of the twentieth century in the UK', Balcıoğlu recounts that as a 'foreigner' he 'had an opportunity to look closely into the rise of design history in the UK' and he had identified several possible shortcomings. He gave the chapter a subtitle: 'A view from "outside in" with a touch of globalization'. Whether or not Balcıoğlu was correct or not is open to question: but what *was* important was the realization that, by the turn of the century, a more global critique of design history was 'in the ether'. Balcıoğlu's 'Observations on the rise of design historiography' were presented at the inaugural ICDHS conference convened by Anna Calvera and colleagues at the University of Barcelona in 1999, an event that event presented something of a challenge to a still maturing academic discipline that was increasingly viewed in many quarters as an Anglophone and Western-dominated field of study – academically, museologically, and in terms of publishing visibility. Most delegates at the Barcelona conference were

---

[1] In the 1960s and 1970s, many previously independent schools of art and design were aligned with colleges of technology and colleges of education to form larger, vocationally inclined institutions, the polytechnics. A notable exception to this was the Royal College of Art, London, which received a Royal Charter and university status in 1967.

from Spain and the Spanish-speaking world. This provided a golden opportunity to consider an alternative framework for design history and design studies: the inclusivity of an outlook that foregrounded the many Spanish-speaking countries of the South American continent and elsewhere. Accordingly, a follow-up conference was held in Havana, Cuba, in 2000 and was organized by Lucila Fernandez, a Cuban historian, with Anna Calvera. Balcıoğlu, who had attended and spoken at both events, was persuaded by Fernandez and Calvera to organize the 3rd ICDHS conference in 2002 in Istanbul. This was another venue that would prove attractive to new audiences and thereby have the potential to act as a further stimulus for extending the world map of the history of design and design studies. To effect this Balcıoğlu contacted Professor Nigân Bayazıt, Head of Industrial Design at İstanbul Technical University (ITU) who proved willing to support the proposed conference through the provision of facilities and accommodation. Balcioglu also successfully persuaded his then employers, KIAD, to provide financial underpinning for a joint venture with ITU. In addition to taking on the demanding role of organizer and coordinator of a complex event, he conceived the rather catchy title of the Istanbul conference, 'Mind the Map: Design History beyond Borders', and designed the distinctive conference logo and related ephemera. This major event not only attracted design studies professionals and design historians from Turkey but also from many other countries where networking possibilities were limited and research funding relatively scarce. In passing, it is worth noting that several Turkish design students who had assisted in organizing and assisting delegates at this 'Mind the Map' conference went on to study for doctorates and subsequently became design academics.

In the following year, 2003, Balcıoğlu returned to Turkey, becoming the founding Dean of the Faculty of Fine Arts and Design at Izmir University of Economics (2004–2011). Something of the ideas shaped there are considered in Chapter 12 in Section Three 'Integrated Design Approach (IDeA): Reflections on a new school of design building'. He later moved on to Yasar University, Izmir, as Vice-Rector (2012–2015). Balcıoğlu's insights into Turkish design practices and the country's national industrial design profile are particularly valuable for assisting readers to understand the wider national and international context of such concerns, as in Chapter 3 in Section One 'Problematic of local and global identity in newly industrialised countries'; also, in a considerably updated (2023) co-authored paper in Chapter 16 in Section Three 'Industrial design in Turkey: A new agenda'. The latter concludes with what amounted to a structured manifesto for future action. In these ways *On Design* contributes to our understanding of the characteristics of doctoral research in art and design as contested nationally and internationally in the closing decades of the last century. These early debates, represented in several chapters in this book, have moved on incrementally through the passage of time with increasing levels of sophistication and complexity, as can be observed in the activities of several significant design organizations. These include the European Academy of Design (EAD) with which Balcıoğlu has been closely associated from 1997 to the present day, serving as a member of its Scientific Committee. The EAD held its first conference on doctoral research in design in 1998 and, twenty-five years later in 2023, is mounting a further such conference entitled 'What Got Us Here Won't Get Us There'.

Foreword

This book highlights key elements of the history of Turkish design explored in Balcıoğlu's writings, conference papers, publications, and the activities of the 4T: Design History Society Turkey. He nurtured the latter in its early stages of development through to its emergence as a higher profile organization complete with volumes of proceedings with titles such as *Design in Times of Turmoil* and *Design and Resistance*. As a result of Balcıoğlu's constant interventions in his role as activist, communicator and historian, Turkish design is now far more widely recognized internationally and our understanding of the country's design education much enhanced.

Brighton, England, June 2023

ACKNOWLEDGEMENTS

This book represents research and works developed over the years. Therefore, I would like to thank a number of friends, relatives and colleagues who have encouraged and supported me during all those years. Some of them have made significant contributions to certain articles, and I express my gratitude to them in the acknowledgements at the end of the relevant chapters.

However, some names have never appeared anywhere despite their direct or indirect encouragement. In particular, Bernard Holdaway, Head of School, Rochester College employed me as a course leader and principal lecturer, and was always beside me with brilliant ideas and advice when necessary. A few academicians have inspired me throughout my career. I was lucky to meet them and appreciate their lovely friendship. The late Necdet Teymur, John Heskett, Anna Calvera and Victor Margolin are Four unforgettable figures of whom I always have wonderful memories. Great friends of mine that I feel very close to include Sevil Peach Gence, Gary Turnbull, Claudia Wegener, Emel Teymur, Gülsüm Baydar, Behiç Ak, Ali Artun, Defne Koz, Önder Biçer, Manuela Antoniu, John and Alma Wood, Jonathan Woodham, Helena Barbosa, Pekka Korvenmaa, Oscar Salinas, Priscila Farias, Clive Dilnot, Paul Atkinson, Rachel Cooper, Haruhiko Fujita, Irini Pitsaki and Marinella Ferrara. I am much obliged to these friends for their contributions to my work by means of insightful questions, remarks and comments.

I was fortunate to study and work with wonderful people and colleagues during my educational and administrative experience in Turkey. They have always inspired and motivated me. I would like to thank those who have touched my academic life, enriched it and made it pleasant and enjoyable.

I am deeply indebted to Sinan Niyazioğlu, Ömer Durmaz, Emre Yıldız, Gülsevil Ağca and Ece Helvacıoğlu for providing me with valuable sources, archival materials and images. I have also continuously felt the dear support of Fahri, Tuba and Faruk Öner, Begüm and Gökhan Kılıç, Çiğdem Beyaz, Ceren Aslan, Sevilay Emiroğlu and my close relatives, especially Ekin, Hale, Batu and Melih Balcıoğlu. My brother Melih has constantly been around and helped me generously without hesitation and always with love; likewise, my son Batu, whose existence is the joy of my life.

INTRODUCTION

Metaphorically speaking, I consider each book an unknown box containing its own mystery. You never know what you will encounter until you open the cover and begin to read, turning the pages to discover what it offers. I will tell you straight away that this volume has three sections, consisting of my published articles, conference papers and essays on design theory, history, education and practice. It is a retrospective collection in which each chapter considers a different aspect of design and tries to provide a new vision, knowledge or interpretation, which I believe are all still valid today. One should not look for unity in this book but rather a compilation, variety and diversity of design studies. Each of them, I hope, has merit and provides a fresh spectrum of ideas.

Perhaps the first interesting feature of the book is that I come from Turkey, where I studied design and worked in higher education. Despite growing up in a different culture, I am trying to write on design issues that are mostly questions posed in the West, or at least they often appeared first in the West before spreading to a wider global public. Although I have no particular intention to reflect my background in my writing, this notion of how East sees West is something that the reader should keep in mind throughout the book while evaluating its rationality and legitimacy.

A second interesting feature is the inclusion of chapters specific to Turkish design. This demonstrates the penetration of design into a country facing many dilemmas, such as between new industry and old craft, traditional and modern, secularity and orthodoxy, or progressive and conservative people. These coexist with tensions and conflicts in many situations. I have therefore integrated chapters and cases concerning Turkey into the book to provide an example for other developing or newly industrialized nations.

The book is composed of three sections, namely, theory, history and education and practice. Each section has its own introduction written not for the purpose of explaining the structure but to place the papers into a context since they were published in different years and not necessarily connected to each other. While a general introduction is provided here, the introduction of each section is designed to elevate the discussion to another level with contemporary arguments and references.

The first section of the book focuses on theoretical studies. Chapter 1 explores reproduction, an essential characteristic of industrial design objects and mass production. The relationship between the original, replicas and reproductions is examined in depth, with special reference to cloning as the latest reproduction technique of the late twentieth century.

Objects do change. As we all know, their quantity, quality and variety have been increased and enhanced with enormously accelerating speed since the Industrial Revolution. Objects also have characteristics, which I categorize in terms of their connotative and denotative values, their position as active, semi-active and passive, and according to their tasks as single or multi-functional products. Ultimately, these characteristics are affected when objects are subjected to technological transformation and objects progress in certain directions. For example, the original toothbrush was a passive object requiring human energy to function. However, after the electric toothbrush was invented, it became a semi-active object requiring less human effort to function, thereby evolving from passive to semi-active status. Chapter 2 studies these shifts and attempts to portray the natural evolution of products.

Because industrialization puts pressure on traditional manufacturing systems and replaces them in many cases, it threatens local crafts. In addition, it also generates a design identity problem. Designers of developing countries must come to terms with industrialization, put their signature under new products that they designed and take responsibility for the emergence of new methods, systems, shapes, forms, styles and, thereby, new design identities. Chapter 3 looks into globalization and its impact on design in newly industrialized countries with a special focus on Turkey.

Chapter 4 analyses the problematic relationship between theory and practice, which surfaced when advanced degree programmes, such as practice-based PhDs, first appeared in the UK. The main question is how these art and design practices can contribute to knowledge, which is the essence of any PhD programme. Therefore, the key goal of the chapter is to explain how art and design practices do in fact produce knowledge during a systematic study period and demonstrate how they can make this knowledge transferable and available to the community.

Chapter 5 interrogates the nature of design knowledge. This epistemological investigation goes into the core of art and design practice as they operate at the doctorate level in university departments. The debate is moulded around the following questions: to what extent do design thinking and production processes, and hence the knowledge created, differ from the knowledge derived from art and science? Does this level of knowledge production exalt design and endow it with a special territory of knowledge to form a third domain alongside art and science?

The second section of the book considers design history. Each of its six chapters focuses on a specific subject related to history and historiography. In terms of their ordering, the chapters move from general concepts like the formation and transformation of the term 'design' towards specific subjects like the 4T Design and Design History Society in Turkey.

Chapter 6 begins with the story of the term 'design' in the UK and its transformation over the centuries. The meaning of design has always been an intriguing matter for researchers wishing to uncover the past, understand the present and perhaps to make suggestions for the future. Design is heavily dependent on scientific, technological, social and economic developments, while its content, meaning and direction change and expand rapidly in line as these factors alter. As a result, design is subject to various definitions depending on these factors as well as the aims and objectives of each design area, industry, business, sector and so on. Therefore, tracing the transformation of design is a good start to comprehending its contemporary meaning, position and status. Although the term has its own Latin and Italian origins and different histories in each country and language, as an English word, 'design' has suppressed other similar expressions, dominated the field and became widely accepted and used globally. This chapter reveals how it rose in the UK in parallel with the Industrial Revolution. It also explains why the French word 'dessin' caused misunderstandings in the UK and triggered the invention of several other expressions, especially in the nineteenth century.

Chapter 7, 'Mapping the mind: Tracing the mentality change', proposes a peculiar but perhaps very stimulating way of looking into history. It suggests that researchers should identify a renowned design personality, study their works and trace how their mind has changed regarding a specific subject. The method involves closely analysing various works, especially by examining different editions of the design personality's books to identify what kinds of amendments they made. This enables various questions to be answered: what are the reasons for different ways of thinking? Why did their ideas change at that particular point in time? How many times did they modify, alter or improve their ideas? This method is widely used today by the media, especially by politicians. Journalists are good at digging into files, finding previously published or televised statements and comparing them with what politicians now say to demonstrate contradictions or inconsistencies. Similarly, tracing mentality changes in design could provide a novel view of how ideas mature.

Chapter 8 shows the expansion of design historiography in the UK, which is undoubtedly one of the leading countries on this subject. The abundance of quality British design sources is well known. However, as an 'outsider', I present a different account of history writing and the conditions encouraging the intensification of design literature in the UK. It is rather interesting to observe that this literature has extended far beyond the UK's borders, leading to great books on design in many countries, including Germany, Italy, Spain and Japan. Scholars in the UK have thus played a major role in spreading design interest and knowledge worldwide and hence are instrumental in the globalization of design. This obviously raises the question of patronization and other critical issues as well as initiatives to democratise design, in which the role of UK academics should not be underestimated.

Currently, there is increasing interest in questioning national histories. One reason is the pressure that globalization puts on nation-states as territorially bounded sovereign polities and huge institutional formations formed just a few centuries ago. In fact, all the earth's borders have either been artificially drawn or imposed by wars and mutual agreements. The flow of designs, designers and design ideas naturally extend beyond these borders, so every substantial historiography has to take these dynamics into consideration. Regardless of their writers' own values, neither pure national histories nor comparative studies can provide a sufficiently broad perspective. Accordingly, Chapter 9 explores the concept of transnational design history through an example from Turkey of a well-known German architect, Bruno Taut, who worked in Japan in the 1930s, later came to Turkey, designed several important buildings and died in Istanbul in 1938.

Chapter 10 considers graphic design in Turkey. After the establishment of the Republic in 1923, numerous radical reforms were implemented, such as replacing the Arabic script with the Western alphabet. Building the new nation required powerful devices for education, propaganda posters, advertising and packaging, for which graphic design was an obvious and inevitable vehicle. Turkish designers, whether educated in the West or in schools influenced by modernism, created a new graphic design panorama. This chapter analyses it and categorizes the works produced in terms of their design characteristics.

Chapter 11 offers a brief history of 4T Design and Design History Society, Turkey, which is one of a few design history institutions organizing international conferences and symposia to disseminate design knowledge and encourage young researchers around the world. While this kind of mission was successfully pioneered by the Design History Society (DHS) UK, 4T closely follows its aims and objectives. The inclusion of a short history of 4T in this book could set a precedent for recently industrialized countries considering its role as an international player and the number of proceedings that it has published. This neither means that 4T is exclusive nor that it is problem-free, as it has experienced its own ups and downs due to Turkey's fluctuating circumstances. Therefore, this chapter provides a critical account of 4T by analysing both its successes and failures, and pros and cons.

The chapters in the third section of the book focus on education and design practice. Integrated design approach (IDeA), the topic of Chapter 12, is a method that I developed and applied with colleagues in the Faculty of Fine Arts and Design at Izmir University of Economics, where I served as founding Dean for over seven years. The method requires close collaboration between all design disciplines, common lessons, joint projects, shared studios, offices, tutors and programmes. They must all work in harmony within purpose-built premises that allocates each student year group to the same story of the building and where staff members are mixed without departmental territories. However, this integrative approach only works with dedicated academic members who believe in it and work together in total agreement. The chapter describes the system applied but does not reveal much about the contradictions, internal tensions and other problems which may well be the subject of another article in the future.

The following three chapters, Chapters 13, 14 and 15, discuss various aspects of practice-based PhD programmes, which were the subject of one of the most important academic disputes in the UK at the turn of the twenty-first century. The key dimensions of this debate concern the nature of knowledge produced in art and design practices, the determination of what title to bestow on students who complete the programmes and the relationship between practice and theory.

The penultimate chapter, Chapter 16, provides a list of suggestions for action to develop industrial design in Turkey. The table indicates sensitive areas of design, identifies problems, makes suggestions and shows potential actors. I used a similar table but with fewer items almost 25 years ago for the same purpose, which was published in the catalogue of Turkey's second biggest design exhibition, Designers' Odyssey 98. Revisiting the article and expanding it in accordance with contemporary needs brings a fresh look to the design scene. It is surprising to see how many issues have not been resolved yet and how many new matters have emerged. This inevitably triggers the idea of comparing the two works, which could provide a research topic for a curious reader in the future.

The final chapter, Chapter 17, explores how Turkish design has transitioned from traditional to modern in terms of cult objects, some of which have been redesigned by renowned designers. As mentioned before, design creates an identity problem for newly industrialized countries where many traditional objects are exposed to new substances, shapes and forms thanks to innovations in technology, materials and recent production techniques and methods, such as robots, CNC machines and laser cutters. The tensions between old and new, and the desire of designers to reinterpret cult objects, are perfectly understandable. Nevertheless, the chapter critically scrutinizes the directions that designers have taken, their sources of inspiration and how they are using heritage and tradition.

A legitimate question to ask is what this book aims to achieve. I think the answer is simple and clear: an analysis of various design aspects that first appeared in the West before being reflected overtly or covertly in the East. I hope that the diversity of articles in the book is not a hurdle but an opportunity to address the expectations of various readers with different backgrounds and interests.

SECTION ONE
THEORY

This section has five theoretical chapters related to specific aspects of design. They are independent of each other and attempt to develop theoretical ideas for better comprehension of the design world. This naturally raises the question of what theory is in design. As the first well-established design discipline, architecture provides initial theoretical writings dating back to Vitruvius in ancient times (Kruft, 1994). Various individuals became influential in different historical periods, notably Leone Battista Alberti in the Renaissance, Marc-Antoine Laugier, Giovanni Battista Piranesi and Robert Adam in the Enlightenment, and Augustus Pugin and John Ruskin in the nineteenth century (Pevsner, 1936, 1937).

What I have observed is that 'other' design theories gradually emerged in line with the surfacing of 'other' design fields after the Industrial Revolution in the UK. Theoretical architecture continued to develop thanks to Eugène Viollet-le-Duc, Gottfried Semper, Adolf Loos, Frank Lloyd Wright, Le Corbusier and so on, while industrial design thinking developed with the works of Henry Cole, Walter Crane and particularly William Morris (Naylor, 1971). Naturally, their theoretical writings were based on and related to consumer goods, crafts and mass-produced objects in general. At the beginning of the twentieth century, Hermann Muthesius and the Deutscher Werkbund, William Lethaby and the Design and Industries Association, and Walter Gropius and Bauhaus all contributed to theory strictly related to industry and its relationship with art and design (Naylor, 1985; Woodham, 1997).

What I argue is that the rise of design theory next to architectural theory also marks the beginning of other design theories. Around the mid-1930s, terms like applied art and industrial art were abandoned in favour of industrial design, which initially covered a vast area of various production fields, including tableware, electrical appliances, furniture, vehicles and so on. It was, in a way, an umbrella term embracing all mass-produced things, defining the territory and giving comfort to those who call themselves industrial designers. In the beginning, it was a satisfactory expression for all. However, after the Second World War, specialization and new design practices bourgeoned in a way that made industrial design an inadequate term to cover new emerging subjects, such as graphic design, product design, boat design, interior design, engineering design, visual communication design, experience design and service design. Consequently, these fields have gained their own territories and have become increasingly well-defined, established and theorized. Industrial design gradually became less accommodating and was replaced by design as the term covering all related areas.

It is easy to follow this transformation by looking into the changing names of design associations. For example, the Council of Industrial Design was founded in 1944, but the word 'industrial' was dropped from its title in 1972, when it became the Design Council. In 2010, the Design Council absorbed the Commission for Architecture and the Built Environment (CABE) (Design Council, 2022), which made it explicit that even architecture was now considered part of design.

Another example is the changing name of the International Council of Societies of Industrial Design (ICSID), which was established in 1957. In 2017, it was renamed the World Design Organization. Clearly, 'design' has become the only word that everybody agrees has unifying power for every creative and innovative production activity.

In this respect, two options can be considered regarding theory in design. Either there is a grand theory that explains almost everything concerning design or theories are specific to each design field. Is there a grand design theory that we subscribe to today? If there is, can we say that it explains almost everything? Is there such a thing in design? Probably not. And, even if it exists, what is a grand theory in design anyway?

The concept of grand theory was coined by American sociologist C. Wright Mills in reference to Talcott Parson's work, which he found so general that it was useless. An analogy with design may not be completely appropriate. Nevertheless, if we borrow the term and look into history, we can say that major styles and movements may be considered in this category, such as Gothic, Baroque, Rococo, Arts and Crafts, Futurism, Art Nouveau and Art Deco. During the twentieth century, we have experienced Modernism, Postmodernism, Structuralism and Deconstructivism among others. Thus, today's design world apparently has no single dominating grand design theory but many proliferating ideas operating simultaneously. These theories are based on semantics, environmentally friendly approaches, human-centred design, user experience, recycling and other factors.

During the 1960s, design research was an important issue in the search for a scientific method. Herbert Simon's book, *The Science of Design* (1998), was very enlightening as well as expanding the territory of design into everything. Since 'everything is design' (borrowing the title of Paul Rand's 2015 exhibition at the Museum City of New York) theories of design appear to be the deux ex machina for many fields thanks to 'design thinking' that became popular in recent years. Design thinking comprises five fundamental stages (empathise, define, ideate, prototype and test). It is now used by businesses and recommended for everybody, not just designers. A comprehensive list of theories and models of design is available today. It shows us the wide variety of design theories we encounter (Chakrabarti, 2015; Rodgers, 2021).

The chapters in this theoretical section draw on this background to investigate various aspects of design, particularly theoretical topics that are considered less often. Chapter 1 questions the relationship between the original and its copies, which is an issue in multiple production. Chapter 2 tries to identify a general pattern or direction in the development of products. Using Turkey as an example, Chapter 3 focuses on local design identity in relation to globalization. Chapter 4 considers transferable knowledge and the relationship between theory and practice in education. Chapter 5 examines the nature of research in design and questions how it differs from scientific and artistic ways of producing knowledge.

CHAPTER 1
ORIGINAL AND REPRODUCTION
FROM CORPOREAL TO CLONE

This chapter is based on a paper delivered at the 17th Annual Conference for the Design History Society, 15–17 December 1995, University of Plymouth, UK.

There are many phrases in English to describe production: repetitive production, multiple production, quantity production, volume production, mass production, serial production, batch production, flexible production, electronic production and so on. These names are based on the outcome and technology employed or coined in terms of how the production was organized and managed.

1.1 Reproduction

This chapter investigates the reproduction process from the viewpoint of industrial design to develop a coherent perspective. It also identifies the distinct stages of reproduction historically. Here, it is useful to distinguish between production and reproduction.

Production refers to a wide range of fields of activity, from agriculture to manufacturing. In this chapter, reproduction is used specifically for objects, implying that there is an original, a product or a thing to be reproduced, while also referring to the processes dealing with re-creating and re-making. The concept of reproduction entails that something already exists or has been produced, such that the issue is its *re*-production. This interpretation of the concept forms the backbone of my principal argument. If reproduction is accepted as an umbrella term, one can fit many versions or variations beneath it: copies, replicas, fakes, counterfeits, duplicates, facsimiles, imitations, simulations, clones, models, prints, photocopies and so on. Each has its own characteristics, function and relationship with the original. In this chapter, I prefer to ignore them in favour of surveying the relationship between original and reproduction within the context of industrial design specifically. The reproduction of two-dimensional works is also beyond the scope of this chapter.

1.2 The original

The key to the analysis, however, is the concept of 'original', which is crucial both for thinking about and producing designed objects. The attributes of reproduction with respect to the original were studied first by Walter Benjamin ([1936] 1977), who, according to Jean Baudrillard, 'showed that reproduction absorbs the process of production, alters its goals, the status of its product, and the producer. He [Benjamin] established this on the terrain of art, cinema, and photography' (Baudrillard, 1988: 138).

In order to investigate reproduction systems, I apply a method inspired by Benjamin and based on the concept of 'original'. Two meanings of the word 'original' will be the subject of our inquiry. The first is the use of original in the discourse of reproduction, while the second refers to the original as an object of design or work of art.

1.2.1 Original in the discourse of reproduction

Any work to be produced in quantity requires a reproduction system. Any work to be produced in quantity is an 'original'. A reproduction system requires an 'original', for an original is the initiator of reproduction. Without an 'original', there cannot be a reproduction. Reproduction is thus the production of a 'thing' that has already been produced. Hypothetically, anything that has already been produced can be reproduced. By the same token, as an initiator of reproduction, an original can be anything.

The outcome of reproduction varies according to the technique employed, as the end product can be copies, replicas, imitations, prints, counterfeits, simulations and so on. The initiator is called the 'original' simply because the end products originate from the original. In other words, the reproduction process attributes the status of original to anything from which copies are derived. What makes it original is the existence of its copies, duplicates, multiples and so on.

1.2.2 Original and uniqueness

The second meaning of the original refers to its status, which has a relationship with 'uniqueness'. An original can be a work that is unmatched and not identical to any other similar thing in its category or nature. This could be an 'original' created by people – most likely an artist, architect, a designer or a craftsperson. In this sense, a sculpture, painting or design is an original and a unique piece of work.

What makes it unique is the nonexistence of its copies, duplicates and multiples. Yet, paradoxically, what makes it original is the existence of its copies, replicas, duplicates, counterfeits and so on. We call it the original when we know that there are copies and to differentiate it from its copies. Hence, an object is unique unless a similar one is unveiled, discovered or disclosed.

The uniqueness prevails in the absence of the other. The presence of the other jeopardizes, invalidates and eliminates its uniqueness. The uniqueness then bids for the state of 'original' when a ground for commensurability and comparison is established by the existence of the other. The other evokes the question: Which one is the original? Therefore, once an object is known as unique, it ceases to be unique and can only be original when its copy is found. Ironically, the 'copy' discovered might well be the original. In this case, the object known as unique not only loses its status of uniqueness but also the chance of being original.

The motivation for differentiating the original from its copies stems from the belief that originals are more valuable than reproductions. As Lewis Mumford puts it: 'Though here, as in many other places, I shall be grateful for the mechanical reproduction, I shall never deceive myself by fancying that it is more than a hint and promise of the original work'[1] (Mumford, 1960: 108). Throughout the text, the word 'original' will be used in both senses, as an initiator of reproduction and as a work of art or design. To understand the position of the original in the production process, a framework for the analysis is needed. The criteria for this are explained below.

1.3 The criteria

Two criteria are used to reveal differences between reproduction systems with respect to industrial design.

1.3.1 The first criterion: Involvement of the original in the reproduction process

The prime concern of the analysis is to figure out how the original is involved in the reproduction process. Theoretically, this means to question the function of the original with respect to the reproduction process. The way in which the original activates and contributes to reproduction is directly related to the nature of the original. It is therefore the principal criterion for classifying reproduction systems.

1.3.2 The second criterion: The relationship between the original and its reproductions

The second criterion concerns the relationship between the original and its reproductions. The degree of resemblance and identicalness is the battleground where reproductions challenge the original. The closer reproductions are to the original, the more one questions the role, position, status and form of the original. The quality of technique is also tested in terms of the degree of resemblance between the original and the reproduction. Reviewing reproduction systems with these two criteria suggests four distinctive historical stages: repetitive production, multiple production, mass production and electronic production.

1.4 Repetitive production

Historically, the Stone Age is the earliest period when simple tools and techniques were employed. Its products include stone implements, bone needles, handmade clay

---

[1] I find a strong influence of Benjamin's article in this work. The way Mumford uses the word 'reproduction' and the way he describes the invention of print directly recall Benjamin's work.

objects, early glass pieces, hand-woven fabrics and carpets. A master with appropriate knowledge, experience, skill and possession of or access to the means of production, materials and tools can make similar objects. Each is made individually by repeating the whole process again and again. Thus, independent repetition forms part of the production process whereby all activities for creating an object are repeated from the original or another copy. Repetition happens in every reproduction and is a necessary factor. What is interesting here, is the detachment of each unit from others and from the one that inspired imitation or copying. To depict this particularity, I call this first period of reproduction 'repetitive production'.

1.4.1 Involvement of the original

Applying the first criterion, we see that the original has no active role in the reproduction process. Its physical entity is not involved in the production at all. Yet, knowledge about or of the original is utilized. Knowledge of similar objects and the prefiguration of what the final reproduction should be are essential theoretical elements derived from the original. Knowledge of the object is thus an inseparable part of production. However, it is not the real, actual object but its image, represented by a model, a plan or a scheme, that participates in reproduction.

Prefiguration is the advance comprehension of the final form in the maker's mind through invoking memory or studying the original. Memory is the accumulation of past experiences, while the original is the real thing facing the maker. The original may stand before the master or apprentice to be observed and, if necessary, measured, imitated or copied.[2] The function, form, pattern, texture and colour of the original remain a source of inspiration or imitation. For instance, a Palaeolithic scraper made by the Levallois technique is undoubtedly a designed object and certainly carved on the basis of prefiguration, accumulated knowledge, experience and talent (Childe, [1942] 1964; Cipolla, 1979). One can assume that the Palaeolithic craftsperson had an image of the final form in mind, and probably an example in front of him, before starting the act of cutting, scraping or carving. Obviously, since the technique applied is not sufficient for perfect duplication of the original tool and the material property of every stone is different, each piece can be similar but not exactly identical. A potter, on the other hand, can achieve a higher degree of resemblance to the original and make copies of it rather easily because of the elasticity of the material and the consistent power provided by the turntable.

---

[2]'Imitation' and 'copying' are terms to pinpoint the spectrum of resemblance. Of course, one may propose using 'duplication' and 'replica' as well. Since in these terms, respectively, the exaltation of the original and the denigration of copies is visible, it seems that they should not accompany the term 'reproduction'.

1.4.2 The original and its reproductions

The second criterion enables us to compare the end product with the original. Ultimately, many similar objects are made as derivations of and deviations from the original. Variations in the degree of resemblance of the objects depend on the techniques mobilized and display a historical trajectory of evolution in conjunction with the development of social formations.

Each product is different from others to different extents. Similarity is the common feature. The level of resemblance changes with the skill of labour, the source and quality of materials and conditions. In other words, no objects are entirely identical, neither to each other nor to the original. This situation may create a dilemma: Is every single work produced through repetitive production an original, for they are not identical and made separately? It is neither easy nor straightforward to answer this. For instance, can we say that a Roman sculpture is an original until we discover that it is actually a copy of a Greek work? What seems not new is the idea, form and composition of figures. However, the material, technique, artistic skill and interpretation are perfectly Roman.

1.5 Multiple production

The second stage in the historical development of reproduction techniques goes back to antiquity. In this period, we come across the discovery of moulds and mould-related techniques like stamping and casting. In addition, there is extensive use of new materials like metals and, later on, the emergence of auxiliary equipment, such as templates. Clay, glass and metal are the materials used in moulds. While probably not the earliest examples, Greek red and black figure vases, the famous Arretine vases and the minted coinage of the Macedonians are certainly some of the best examples of their kind.

1.5.1 Involvement of the original

In contrast to repetitive production, here we witness the direct participation of the original in the production process because moulds require an original. The original may also be in the form of a prototype or a one-to-one scale model around which the whole production process revolves. Moulds, which are of a reverse form to the prospective product, are shaped in several ways, such as carving and casting, by using guides or samples. In an extreme case, a maker prepares a mould without an original and actually makes an original in the form of a mould. Hence, the mould itself could be an original actively participating in production through both its physical entity and information.

Moulds and their relationship with reproductions have an interesting dimension in that moulds themselves are also reproduced after reaching the end of their life span.

There is thus an anachronistic repetition of two cycles of reproduction: the first is concerned with the duration of reproduction for each item, while the second relates to the duration of renovation for each mould. Since a mould can cast many objects, the frequency of repetition for moulds is low. Therefore, these two cycles of production are completed in different time periods. This non-parallel rotation of each cycle is termed anachronistic repetition.

1.5.2 *The original and its reproductions*

Regarding the resemblance between the original and reproductions, the similarity is so close that one can consider them the same. As opposed to 'similarity' in the previous phase, 'sameness' here refers to a very strong resemblance.[3] There are two aspects of sameness.

The first is the sameness of each single item produced. In other words, we can question to what extent they look like each other. We know that moulds are subject to deformations, deflections and fatigue due to their intensive use, which may create differences between products, even if minute. Ultimately, therefore, each item may possess a barely discernible difference, which sometimes provides objects with particular characteristics and value. This is the case with textile products like carpets and kilims. In other words, accidental differences may increase or decrease the value of certain items.

The second aspect is the degree of sameness between the original and the reproductions. Obviously, the above argument is also perfectly valid for the relationship between the original and reproductions. One substantial distinction is that reproductions are checked and tested against the original, which constitutes the basis of comparison. The quality control process takes the original as the reference and monitors production accordingly. Success is proportional to the degree of resemblance.

This reproduction process includes a multiplier, namely the mould itself, which gives its form to and leaves traces on the reproduced objects. Given this role, this phase is called multiple production. Multiple production involves the use of moulds, templates, stamps and so on, which determine the final form of the object and are the fundamental elements in the production process.

As one might expect, multiple production raises the quality of products and labour productivity through the use of moulds. In multiple production, a copy may well overshadow the so-called 'original'. An ideal example is Josiah Wedgwood's attempts to make a copy of the Portland Vase, a Roman cameo glass. According to Adrian Forty: 'The point of the reproductions was not just that they were as good as the original, but that they demonstrated the sophistication of contemporary manufacturing techniques better than any new and original designs could have done' (1986: 16). It is obviously a matter

---

[3]There are three levels of resemblance, each of which points to the different modes of reproduction. These levels are indicated by three concepts, namely similarity, sameness and identicalness. In this particular context, 'sameness' refers to a certain degree of resemblance between 'similarity' and 'identicalness'.

of discussion whether Wedgwood's version is more valuable than the Roman Portland Vase. The reason why an original can sometimes be challenged by its copy is that value judgements are involved in the evaluation. These concern both age and historical value. In this case, value attribution mechanisms play a significant and rather complicated role, but this goes beyond the scope of this chapter.

Both multiple and repetitive production are essentially pre-capitalist and pre-industrial, besides being craft-based techniques. Usually, the major source of quality is skill. The number of items generated by these techniques is limited because production capacity relies on human beings and their abilities.

1.6 Mass production

Mass production is the third period in the evolution of reproduction systems. This crucial break in history corresponds to the Industrial Revolution, when technology gained a significant momentum and incentive. The late eighteenth and nineteenth centuries witnessed new manufacturing techniques, production machines and numerous inventions. Steam, iron and coal constituted the backbone of the societies of the era. The driving forces of the American system were standardization, interchangeable parts, assembly lines, substituting manpower with machines and new energy sources. Frederick Klem, the writer of *A History of Western Technology*, observes: 'At the end of the nineteenth century the Americans began to plan mechanized production by accurate time and motion study. Especially Frederick W. Taylor from the turn of the century led the way with his scientific and rational system of works management' (1964: 331).

The core of Taylorism is to free production from skill and replace labour with machines wherever possible. Where workers are irreplaceable, Taylor suggests treating them as machines: 'Under our system the workman is told minutely just what he is to do and how he is to do it; and any improvement which he makes upon the orders given to him is fatal to success' (Taylor, 1906: 26–7). The result of mass production was the remarkable escalation in the variety and number of commodities and the consolidation of consumption culture.

1.6.1 Involvement of the original

What is new in comparison to multiple production is the introduction of mechanization and precision. In terms of the role of the original, production is not drastically different from the previous phase since moulds, stamps, templates, presses and so on continue to be the main elements of production. Instead, the most significant change is the mechanization of almost all processes, such that even originals and moulds begin to be generated through appropriate mechanical tools, instruments and other relevant equipment that also benefits from automation.

In the end, it is the nature of original that slightly changed rather than its necessity. Models are found sufficient to provide the form required for industrial moulds.

Prototypes are now essential to test new designs. In this sense, originals are no longer distinct objects. Instead, they result from research, projects and design activities. In the realm of industrial design, we utilize the results of reproductions in the form of consumer goods, everyday used objects, gadgets and so on, while the original may not exist anymore in the form that we are familiar with. There could be more than one mock-up, while the final product may incorporate elements that did not exist in the test models. Therefore, the original of, let's say, the Fiat Panda is the Fiat Panda that we know, rather than the one created through projects, models, mock-ups, prototypes and so on.[4] In mass production, the involvement of the original requires not only the knowledge and presence of the original or its models, prototypes and so on but also the knowledge of its elements, parts and components with all their complexities.

1.6.2 The original and its reproductions

As mentioned above, in analysing the resemblance of reproductions to the original, we should bear in mind that the original may not exist in the form of an original. Probably, the most appropriate word for expressing the likeness of reproductions is 'identicalness'.

In almost all cases, the identicalness of the reproductions is taken for granted due to the precision of the manufacturing process. One factor supporting this is the use of advanced quality control systems to identify anomalies and discard substandard elements, pieces and components – that is, not identical to those aimed at. Despite these efforts, researchers have demonstrated various differences in quality if not in form. In the automobile industry, for instance, cars produced on mid-week days tend to be better quality than those produced on Mondays and Fridays. Therefore, identicalness can still be questioned at various levels despite the extremely high precision achieved through modern technology.

1.7 Electronic production

Increasing production and productivity is one of the main motives of the entrepreneurial system and the direction of improvement in technology. The introduction of computers and computer-aided design (CAD) in industry has contributed immensely to achieving this goal. Computer numerical control (CNC) systems, for instance, incorporate a microcomputer loaded with information to control and direct machine tools 'to produce a part according to pre-recorded, coded numbers, letters, and symbols' (Lindbeck, 1995: 290). Increased use of automation, computer-guided machine tools, robots, flexible manufacturing systems and other advanced technologies has shifted technological development towards electronic production.

---

[4]For the detailed story of the Panda, see Edward Lucie-Smith (1983: 133–40).

1.7.1 Involvement of the original

Obviously, these systems operate with electronic information. Consequently, the original often no longer needs to be three-dimensional. Instead, it can be created on a screen with various views and wireframe representations from which solid models can be produced for design trials and possibly consumer tests. This process allows designers to make alterations to their design easily and get models for new variations quickly if they wish to proceed with the images on the screen. According to Lindbeck, 'These new technologies, whereby CAD plans are quickly transformed into solid objects and not merely 3-D drawings, are variously referred to as rapid prototyping, free-form manufacturing, conceptual modelling, and desktop fabrication among others' (Lindbeck, 1995: 281).

Through electronic production, the original gains a new form, shifting from concrete to abstract, from real to representation, and from physical to hypothetical. The original of this chapter does not exist. Instead, what exists is its representation in an electronic configuration on my screen. The models produced from the screen are models of thoughts, ideas and designs but not the original, which is not present. Its representation leads to production, such that we have no originals for some products. Since the invention of electronic reproduction, the status of the original as well as its uniqueness are now under threat for the first time in history.

1.7.2 The original and its reproductions

The absence of the original makes it impossible to compare it with the reproductions. The models, mock-ups and prototypes are not the original but rather its representation and substitute. Nevertheless, one should not think that the original will disappear immediately. As discussed earlier, there is a factor of coexistence that implies a pattern of substitution and replacement. In addition, there is no rule that early versions, or old techniques, production systems and products will instantly disappear. Even the developers of computer modelling warn us: M. Evans, M. Veveris and P. Wormald underline that the range of modelling techniques continues to increase and stress that it is necessary to carefully consider the relative merits of 'conventional' approaches before changing to computer-based modelling (Evans, 1994). No doubt, their role in production will inevitably be reviewed in light of recent innovations. A comparison between reproductions will show a higher degree of resemblance and, on many occasions, identicalness.

1.8 Conclusion

Several points can be made about the relationship between these four reproduction systems. First, they evolved historically in the chronological order presented here, that is, repetitive, multiple, mass and electronic productions. The first two emerged in the pre-capitalist era, while the latter two flourished in the industrialized and capitalist societies.

This order of appearance does not imply that later systems superseded previous ones in every field of production. Not at all. They have all survived to operate in particular industrial and geographical domains. Thus, the invention of new production techniques does not necessarily annihilate or replace the prevailing ones. Instead, they can coexist and serve together for a certain period of time, although this coexistence may vary from place to place and from one field of production to another.

There are composite reproduction processes benefiting from several different processes of reproduction to produce certain objects, especially those with many complicated components. A sophisticated manufacturing process utilizes various reproduction techniques, such as artificial intelligence and robotic systems, which require further investigation.

There is also a general tendency to reduce the size of products. Tomás Maldonado interprets the miniaturization of components as dematerialization: 'Miniaturization of this sort may appear to upset the material reality of objects as we know them today by cancelling their physical identity, or indeed contributing to their actual disappearance as technical objects' (Maldonado, 1993: 3).

Electronic production enables us to create imaginary environments and objects for which the original does not exist. Virtual reality promises to furnish us with the appropriate equipment to experience these at full scale.

I am not a great believer in linear development. Discontinuities, epistemological breaks and paradigm shifts form the other face of what one may dare to call progress. However, when the story of the original is reviewed in terms of reproduction, it reveals an interesting pattern of transformation. In the first phase, the original enjoys a status of uniqueness and independence from reproduction. Its image and knowledge contribute to the making of things, similar to that of the original. The second phase requires more involvement of the object, which physically participates in production. During mass production, the complexity of products means that the original is designed and subject to testing through its representations as models, mock-ups, prototypes or computer-generated images. That is, the unity of the 'original' is composed of these fragmented experiments. The original drives from a process and continues to be a part of the process of research and trials. Thus, in one sense, the disintegration of the 'concept' of the original as much as the original itself reaches another level with electronic production, where it is subjected to perpetual alterations and negations. If this is the current direction, the question is then what the future of industrial design will be. Is designing for virtually real environments going to be more challenging than designing for the real one?

CHAPTER 2
IN SEARCH OF PRINCIPLES
WE HAVE BEEN TOLD THAT THEY DIED LONG AGO

This chapter was first presented as a paper at the international conference, 'Contextual Design – Design in Contexts', organized by the European Academy of Design, at the Swedish Industrial Design Foundation, Stockholm, between 23–27 April 1997.

2.1 Introduction

I would like to begin by making comparisons between different design practices and cultures and finding out what we have in common. Generally speaking, what different societies have in common regarding design cannot easily be abstracted from what they have in common regarding socioeconomic and technological systems. Dominant factors, such as the market economy and technological development, have a considerable impact on design, independent of the cultures within which they operate. This chapter looks at this commonality from a global point of view rather than a contextual perspective.

First, one has to ask what commonality means. In practical terms, it is something shared by all parties. If references are being made to understandings, values, forms, functions and so forth, and if a common ground is found, especially a strong one, wouldn't we be facing a question concerning the nature of design? Again, if these common features exist despite cultural obstacles, and exist for certain periods of time, wouldn't they go further, beyond the limits of the word commonality, and be perceived as the natural attributes of design? If these commonalities depict the nature of design, aren't they forming the principles of design? The question that I am asking indeed concerns the extent to which commonalities lead to principles, that is, principles of design. By searching for common aspects, and widespread, ubiquitous and universal values, aren't we in fact investigating possibilities for principles, that is, principles that govern the realm of design? Ultimately, if commonalities are the source of principles, then we need to be aware of what principles mean today.

Given that the word 'principle' is forceful and powerful, one may prefer the modesty of the word 'commonality'. In addition, principle does not happily fit into the agenda of the late twentieth century, which tends to be critical, cautious and sceptical of any definitive statement. For example, Odo Marquard's book has a stimulating and provocative title representing the critical spirit of the era, the *Zeitgeist: Farewell to Matters of Principle* (1989). Keeping this suggestion in mind, I will look at the transformation of products, objects and artefacts to find a common ground for various fields of design and design practices in context. Certainly, if there is a commonality among design objects independent of their cultural presuppositions, this should be traced not only within their form and function but also within the progression and advancement of products. In other words, the purpose of this inquiry is to find common attributes, particularly certain directions occurring during the development of products, which are intrinsic to, embodied in or anticipated by design processes. To that effect, I will scrutinize two aspects of these changes. The first is the oscillation between the denotative and connotative values of objects, while the second is changes in formal qualities.

2.2 The oscillation between denotative and connotative values of objects

Before proceeding further, I would like to explain two concepts essential for the 'reading' of objects: denotative and connotative values. Briefly, the denotative value of an object corresponds to its functional value only. For example, a pair of scissors is made to cut; as long as they cut, they fulfil their function. Hence, denotative value is determined by a) how successfully the purpose is achieved (for example, how sharp the scissors are, how easy to handle, how efficient to use); and b) to what extent meeting this function is important. The connotative value of an object corresponds to its symbolic, ideological, reflective, communicative, aesthetic, ethical, environmental and other subjective aspects. Going back to the same example, scissors designed by David Mellor, scissors having an ivory handle or scissors belonging to Queen Victoria have many qualities apart from their normal function of cutting. The connotative value is thus created: a social, historical, psychological, ideological value and so on.

The correlation of denotative and connotative values of objects and the transformation of this link with respect to time reveal the original history of products. In other words, a social history of objects reflects the displacement of values from the connotative realm to the denotative one or vice versa. Let us have a look at Rolex watches: they gained their reputation initially due to their reliable performance and fortified it with their classic, aesthetic features. Today, although many other technically perfect watches are available, Rolex still retains its fame independent of its initial credentials. In other words, possessing a Rolex watch is so important that it probably doesn't make much difference whether the watch fulfils all expectations of users concerning functions properly. It is likely that consumers take its functional qualities for granted. In this particular case, it is also clear that the introduction of other factors considerably shifted the significance of the object from denotative to connotative value.

The determining essence of this reciprocal relationship is tangible. I think a product can exist without denotative values but never without connotations. Religious, ideological and cult objects are examples of things with no direct function, such as a medal awarded to a war veteran or a crucifix worn by a Catholic.

The status of objects in a society and their denotative and connotative values are closely allied with the prevailing cultural and socioeconomic climate. Thus, they are formed under the influence of current circumstances. The ruling market economy and its crucial tools, such as advertisements and promotion campaigns, have a substantial impact on the consumption of products. The media is another giant agent promoting the proliferation of both values, no matter how artificially boosted.[1]

If we return to our main point of investigation, we see that the common denominator is the oscillation between denotative and connotative values that occurs everywhere, independent of culture or time. For example, let us take a lemon squeezer. As a contemporary cult object, a lemon squeezer by Philippe Starck is much more than a lemon squeezer. It is so popular that you can find it both in quality high street shops worldwide and in design museums. The question is to what degree its function is eclipsed and subordinated by its connotative values created within a few years and to what degree you would like to buy it for its potential to define your social status rather than its practical use in the kitchen. Thus, normal traditional glass lemon squeezers, which fulfil the same function – probably better than Starck's – can be turned into an object, a wall lamp doing an entirely different job, as we see in the work of Michael Marriot who inserted a bulb into it and transformed it to a lighting apparatus.

2.3 Transformations in formal qualities

Throughout history, objects with more or less the same function have varied and evolved greatly in shape, size, form, texture, function, material and so on. Although it is hard to identify the dominant factors that determine the transformation of objects, it should be accepted that it is mostly due to technological improvements alongside other social and cultural elements. This is the situation we encounter today, especially in contemporary industrialized societies. I shall try to develop a conceptual framework for detecting, understanding and analysing the direction and logic of this transformation. Before commencing, let us focus our attention on a few points that need further explanation.

The direction in the transformation of objects can be formulated roughly as follows: from *easy* to *difficult* within the range of *optimum* and *reasonable*, conceived and set up, in relation to socioeconomic aspirations as well as scientific and technological constraints. The direction follows the challenge. For example, if making an object smaller is difficult to achieve but offers a benefit, then research is encouraged in this direction, not because of its size, of course, but because small means less space, weight and material, and in many cases makes the object more mobile, practical or portable. Conversely, if it is advantageous to make the object bigger, then efforts are channelled towards that target. Targets, that is to say, directions, are determined by a much more complex mechanism, such that, in many cases, it is easier to discern and follow their route rather than the reasons.

---

[1] W. F. Haug takes the role of the media further by speaking of manipulated needs and their repressive satisfaction ([1971] 1986 and 1987).

However, there are cases in which the motivation and impetus determining the design of objects are self-evident. When the first cars were produced at the beginning of the twentieth century, one of the prominent objectives of manufacturers was to increase their velocity to keep pace with contemporary society and its rapidly growing expectations. These had already been identified with speed, as in the Futurist movement. A few decades later, it reached an optimum. In the early seventies, however, the unexpected oil crisis rendered fast cars redundant as speed limits were introduced for highways. Moreover, rising costs were forcing manufacturers to build smaller cars. Of course, other factors supported this trend, such as parking difficulties in metropolitan areas and the possibility of selling more small cars. Aerodynamic forms became popular, not only because of stylistic interest but also because less wind resistance saves fuel. Thus, design criteria keep changing due to the different trends created by media, fashion, tradition, and socioeconomic and technological aspirations. Unsurprisingly, commentators on design make similar observations in terms of changes:

> Three clear cultural changes are encouraged by the new technology in the late twentieth century. There is a move away from heavy to lightweight and sometimes invisible infrastructures. And there is also more perplexing change: the narrowing of the gap between what looks like nature and what looks manmade. A third trend, a move away from non-renewable resources, is also beginning to flourish in the form of research into re-usable materials.
>
> (Dormer, 1990: 62)

When we compare Dormer's trends with those employed in this chapter, we notice that his first and third observations, 'a move away from heavy to a lightweight' and 'from non-renewable to re-usable', correspond to what I call 'from large to small' and 'from non-renewable to renewable', respectively, as we will see below.

The following observations on changes to products indicate the directions that mostly fluctuate between opposite poles. Therefore, rather than represent a complete list or mark out one direction of progress, they present a foundation, an initial view, a potential framework for further analyses. For the sake of the argument, 'developments' concerning the nature of objects can broadly be classified as one- and two-directional.

2.3.1 One-directional transformation

I assume that designed and produced objects generally improve over time. I call this one-directional progress since there is a linear course from one pole towards the other. However, even if this presupposition is correct, objects and their production techniques from earlier categories or stages do not necessarily disappear. Instead, in most cases, they continue to exist alongside the new one or in a different location.

This situation also begs the question of domination. Can we assume that objects produced more recently are superior to previous ones of the same kind in terms of quality, quantity, technical and aesthetic aspects and popularity? My answer is no, not necessarily! To be new does not always mean to be better. Goods just introduced to consumers may not necessarily be better than previous ones of the same kind. Vance Packard,[2] an American journalist and consumerism expert noticed this more than thirty years ago:

> Karl H. Nagel, head of Consumers Union television testing division, told me that despite all the miraculous claims made in television advertising a television set made in 1952 offered a 'nicer picture' than sets made in 1959. He said: 'There has been no major advance in terms of the quality of the received picture since the early 1950s.' And he felt that sets made in 1947 were better constructed than those being offered for sale a decade later. In 1947, television sets were able to reproduce all the picture components contained in the 'signal' sent out by a broadcasting station. In 1956, not a single one of the sets tested could reproduce the transmitted picture!
>
> (1964: 106)

The technological myth that 'the newest one is the best one' is not as persuasive as it once was. Regarding technology, people have adopted a cautious approach. Years after Packard's investigation, Peter Dormer, a design consultant and interpreter observes:

> In 1989, following incidents and a crash (in Britain) involving Boeing aircraft (not 747s), the aviation authorities in the USA and Britain ordered special wiring checks on new Boeings. Faults were found. What is surprising is not that faults were found, but that the world expects their total elimination. Of course, manufacturers and service industries must aim for perfection, but they and we, as the consumers, make mistakes more rather than less likely by believing in the myths of technology, rather than in what common sense and common experience should teach us. To demand perfection is sensible; to expect it can be fatal.
>
> (1990: 18–19)

These reservations regarding the idea that technology can achieve perfection make it clear that the future may not always bring better things than we have already. Old objects can be as valuable as new ones – perhaps even more so. Besides, there are other demands that encourage the consumption of different goods, prevent earlier goods and their production techniques from vanishing, and provide us with a variety of objects, occasionally even enriched with an antique style.

---

[2]Packard worked on human behaviour, advertising, consumerism, planned obsolescence and briefly on objects and their reflections on our lives. He highlighted the confusion of 'the possession of goods with the good life', publishing a trilogy on the subject: *The Hidden Persuaders* (1957), *The Status Seekers* (1959) and *The Waste Makers* (1960).

There is another important aspect worth mentioning: being one-directional is not a destiny, verdict or eternal attribute. Over time, the direction may well swing to the opposite pole. For instance, electrical appliances have brought comfort and ease to kitchen work, which was sometimes considered rather monotonous and unexciting by working people. Now, with changing attitudes, the kitchen is becoming the central living area in the house. In parallel, not only our cooking and eating habits but also our taste in kitchen appliances is altering. Energy consciousness and the rediscovered aesthetic of metal and authentic forms are encouraging us to use traditional kitchen tools.[3] For example, the Aga Cooker, first manufactured in the nineteenth century, is now a very popular and expensive cult object.

2.3.1.1 From passive to active

We are surrounded by three basic types of objects: passive, active and intermediary or transitory which can also be seen as semi-passive or semi-active. Passive objects never bear signs of movement and never act by themselves, while active objects move, operate, act or at least have the potential for motion due to some mechanism like a machine, electric or electronic circuit and so on.

Passive objects are mostly household items: kitchenware, silverware, tableware, furniture (urban, office and domestic), garments (regular, official and casual), packing materials, furnishings, and almost all ceramic, glass or textile objects. There are two kinds of passive objects, classified according to their performance and energy requirements.

The first group comprises entirely passive objects, which do and need nothing but function as they are, such as containers, furniture, mirrors, ceramic and glass objects. I call these immobile passive objects.

Objects in the second group require human touch and energy to operate and perform their function. They are mostly basic tools that do not incorporate any machine within themselves, such as simple knives, forks, screwdrivers, gardening and agricultural tools. I call these mobile passive objects

Active objects include mechanical, electrical and electronic devices. They include production, transportation, communication (audio-visual), scientific, technical, medical and educational instruments, domestic appliances, agricultural machinery, and some sports and hobby equipment. Fully automatic robots with artificial intelligence represent the cutting edge of this group. In many cases, these objects require no human energy to function beyond a touch. Of course, the level of human interaction required varies with their level of sophistication. For instance, a great majority of aircraft still need a human touch despite their complex and refined systems although fully automatic electric cars are on the agenda today.

Finally, semi-active or semi-passive objects lie between passive and active ones, as they contain elements with the qualities of both groups. Examples include tools that are

---

[3] These kitchen tools, having traditional forms are, of course, still available. However, in some circles where design is highly popular and prestigious, their new and modified reproductions as well as replicas are desired.

not active alone but participate in an action as auxiliary members and require human energy to some extent, such as electric toothbrushes, lawnmowers, torque screwdrivers and power drills.

Before dwelling on the justification of this tripartite scheme, it is time to turn to its source of inspiration from Lewis Mumford's *Technics and Civilization*, in which he sets out the distinction between tools and machines:

> In general, the machine emphasized specialization of function whereas the tool indicates flexibility; a planing machine performs only one operation whereas a knife can be used to smooth wood, to carve it, to split it or to pry open a lock, or to drive in a screw. The automatic machine then, is a very specialized kind of adoption, it involves the motion of an external source of power, a more or less complicated inter-relation of parts and a limited activity.
>
> [1934] 1947: 10)

Here, the horizon of the notion of machine was enlarged in the light of contemporary technological developments and was substituted not with a concrete entity but with an abstract concept like action, which always consumes energy. The properties of objects regarding energy sources can determine the tripartite classification: active objects require sources of energy whereas semi-active ones require both external energy (electricity, battery spring and so on) and human power. Container-type, immobile passive objects need nothing; they serve as they are. However mobile passive objects require human touch and energy.

This crucial categorization takes into account the objects' historical mission. In many cases, the invention of passive and semi-passive/semi-active objects was followed by active ones. The juxtaposition of active and passive objects corresponds to certain historical periods. Although this can be different for each particular item, the Industrial Revolution is the turning point for the great transformation from passive to active, and since the mid-eightieth century, the balance has changed in favour of active objects. In other words, since the Industrial Revolution and across all countries, the production of active objects has increased significantly along with a shift from passive to active.

This shift – the invention of the active versions of previously passive objects – does not necessarily eliminate passive objects. Instead, they coexist most of the time. For example, the mechanical (semi-active) toothbrush did not supersede the passive, traditional one. Rather, they continue to appear next to each other in department stores.

What we observe in this process of transformation is an inclination towards much more complex structures. For example, the electric shaver is undoubtedly more complicated than a disposable razor, which is in turn already more advanced than a traditional razor blade. This exigency of transition also indicates the degree of specialization. While objects become more and more complex, they also become specialized and the number of their variety increases immensely. One should think about the multifariousness of electric shavers that we have in the market today as well as the complexities and varieties they present.

No doubt, the classification and categorization of objects in terms of the three distinctive positions intrinsic to their very nature should be further studied, detailed and illustrated. This chapter draws the basic framework, and I hope it prompts interest for further research.

2.3.1.2 From functional to multi-functional

Maximum utilization of goods is obviously for the benefit of users. Increasing the range of use of an object helps to reach this target. If a minor modification is sufficient to enlarge the capacity of a product, why should it not be realized? Production-wise, saving materials, energy, labour and time will lower the cost. From the owner's viewpoint, it should in theory save money and space.

The application of these ideas to production has been widely visible in furniture since the eighteenth century. A chair designed for sitting is made convertible into a table when necessary. A bed combined with a wardrobe can serve as a bed at night and a wardrobe during the day. As books by Sigfried Giedion and Edward Lucie Smith show, this process has sometimes gone too far with exaggerated designs like a combined piano, bed and drawer (Gideon, ([1948] 1955).

Nevertheless, the aim was achieved by bringing together at least two items of furniture, regardless of the weight and bulk of the resulting product. This was very rightly called 'combination furniture'. Another approach was also possible: the functions of two different things could be the starting point to design a new item of furniture. However, this was not the case in the earlier examples, which involved combining two items together with their functions. The bed was still a bed; the wardrobe was still a wardrobe; and the result was a 'wardrobe + bed', not an integrated unity. It was not an amalgamation of functions but objects with their functions. The first step had been completed.

The second step deals with functions only and unites them so successfully that totally new products appear on the market. The emergence of many contemporary goods is based on this policy of production.

If the first step was a 'combination of objects', this second step can be called a 'unification of functions' or rather 'multi-functional'. Here, it is worth noticing two points. One, the transition from the first to the second does not necessarily occur for every object and in the same manner. Second, the existence of the second step does not necessarily correspond to a replacement of the first. Both can overlap and juxtapose.

One simple example incorporating all these processes is the music centre more than 40 years ago. Initially, two objects, a record player and a radio, were combined to form one piece of music furniture. Later, a tape recorder was added and fused into a new body, for which a new term is coined: the music centre. The addition of an amplifier created an inseparable trio. At the end of the twentieth century, the compact disc (CD) player joined them. Music centres then became portable with a proliferation of combinations:

radio + tape recorder, radio + alarm clock, CD player + tape recorder + radio, TV + radio + video, TV + radio + alarm clock, and so on.

In the twentieth century, this strategy of production (combining objects and unifying functions) was widely accepted implicitly or explicitly, and applied by companies' design research and development departments. No doubt, producers and salesmen were very happy with this, as it was a magic key for re-opening saturated markets. Consumers have become accustomed to buying the same thing in different forms and with slightly different functions. However, 'multi-functional' does not necessarily mean 'multi-purpose'. What I understand from the former is that a product includes many functions in its body and that we can benefit from the combination of them in most cases. A telephone answering machine, for example, is basically a tape recorder connected to a telephone. It answers the phone and records messages, while more advanced types provide other functions, such as hands-free calls, call screening, day/time stamp, memos, mute and remote-control facilities. Certainly, it is multi-functional.

However, all these functions are bound to one purpose only, which is to communicate with whoever phones if the phone user is not available or does not wish to reply. In other words, all of these functions are centred around this one, single purpose and cannot be used for other goals. For instance, the answer phone's tape recorder cannot be used to listen to music since its sound quality is poor and the whole machine is not designed appropriately. Especially in compact models, the recorder is integrated with the telephone and cannot be separated for use as an independent recorder. Unfortunately, therefore, these apparatuses are single-purpose objects despite all their multi-functional features.

Secondly, various functions compounded in one body are very often used singly. In some pieces of equipment, these various functions are adjacent and may perform with the advantage of this expanded capacity achieved by a harmonious interconnected network. However, it is more likely the functions do not all perform simultaneously. If one is switched on, then the others are most probably off, as with a Swiss pocket knife: when the can-opener is in use, the knife cannot function. Similarly, while listening to a record on a music centre, one cannot also listen to the radio or the tape recorder. Even if technically possible, it would be nonsensical. Thus, when one part of the music centre is functioning, the other parts are usually useless and cannot be used by others.

The consequences of these strategies in the production of commodities are devastating if seen from the customer's point of view. First, the user is entirely alienated from the mechanisms of these high-tech, compact devices. Neither repair nor maintenance is possible without specialist services. Indeed, they are usually not designed to be repaired but to be replaced. If one attempts to get the device repaired, it does not take long to realize that it costs almost as much as buying a new piece of equipment. On the other hand, when one of the parts irreparably breaks, the other working parts are immediately affected negatively and often become useless since the functional and perhaps aesthetic unity is destroyed.

Nevertheless, the number of multi-functional objects will continue increasing as this is inevitable within the logic of consumer-oriented economic programmes. The market keeps demanding new consumer goods, and the easiest way is to create 'unified functional objects' with newly invented or merely fabricated purposes.

These strategies are obviously familiar to anyone living in neoliberal economies, and this undoubtedly considerably influences the design and formation of new products. Perhaps the best example is smartphones, which replace cameras, video cameras, tape recordings, video players and, in many cases, table and laptop computers, thanks to the abundance of new software they contain.

2.3.1.3 From common to personal

Considering the above framework, we can observe that another policy that the industry strongly approves of is to support the expansion of personal territory by providing people with a wide spectrum of goods. Items that were once introduced for the family, a group of people, large companies and even for public use now became personal property. The most dramatic example is one of the pioneering technological achievements: the clock. When mechanical clocks were first invented, it became a widespread practice to build clock towers in the main square of towns. Only rich people could afford to buy one for domestic use. Public clocks, as well as church bells in the West and calls to prayer from minarets in the East, used to contribute to the organization of daily life. By the late nineteenth century, however, mass production in America made clocks available and inexpensive so that almost every family could afford to buy one. At the beginning of the twentieth century, the 'one-dollar watch' campaign was aimed at individuals within the family and furnished many people with a new gadget (Heskett, 1980).

The following pattern of progress in time measurement seems very useful for illustrating the expansion of objects from public to private, from common to personal, and from space to objects. Initially, clock towers served the public while mass production later furnished houses. Soon, every man had the privilege of enjoying his own personal watch, while watches for women followed later as did watches for children. In the meantime, the clocks' areas of use extended from space to objects. Cars, refrigerators, ovens and radios were decorated with them. Thanks to developments in digital technology, even a simple fountain pen could include one.[4]

Similar chronologies can be given for many other technology-based, industrial products: radios and televisions (from grandiose items of home furniture to the pocket-sized Sony Walkman and Sony Watchman[5]), calculators, cameras, computers and so on. All these articles have become personal. In the early decades of the twentieth century, 'one car per family' was considered an ideal match. Later, however, this changed to 'one

---

[4]Simply to satisfy my curiosity, I calculated how many time measurement systems there are in my home, where two people live. I found ten: two personal watches, one alarm clock, one small plastic digital table clock (a free promotional gift), one in the oven, two in mobile phones, one in the alarm radio, one for the automatic hot-water heating system and one in the computer.

[5]The Sony Walkman is a portable, small cassette player that emerged in 1979 and revolutionized the way people listened to music. Sony Watchman is again a pocket-size television that was available in the market in the early 1980s.

car for each parent' followed by 'one car for everybody' and nowadays 'a car for every age'. The message is clear: please keep replacing your car according to your changing age and status.

From this, we can conclude that a common tendency in the development of technologically intensive objects is from mass consumption towards personal use. This is achieved by making products more advanced, cheaper, smaller scale, with a bigger capacity, or more efficient.

It is high time we remembered that individualism is the keystone of the capitalist system. It is bolstered and stimulated both philosophically and theoretically, and thereby ideologically, and by a physical environment stuffed with a plethora of goods that display both advantages and unbearable attraction of personal objects. Without doubt, the technological and ideological products of the system are working in compliance with each other: what you hear is being consolidated by what you see.

2.3.1.4 From single to various
Another change in the world of commodities is more variety. Once, only one or two objects were used to execute the same job. Today, many kinds of artefacts are available for the same or very similar purposes. Mass production, which aims at gigantic consumerism of goods, has introduced the idea of a proliferation of functions whereby new fields of use are opened for more specialized products. Examples are evident in many areas. Let us take a very simple one: toothpaste. Even an ordinary corner shop stocks many varieties produced with mint, menthol, fluoride and so on. Similarly, thinking of the wide selection of chewing gums is sufficient to realize how the variety of goods has increased and has poured into the market again and again.

Product variety is another strategy used by companies. Consumers are bombarded by new items or by new looks for old ones. Thus, the apathy of users is minimized; visual fatigue caused by repeated appearances of the same product is cured by the use of brand-new labels, packaging and forms that demand close attention rather than a single glance. If customers are dissatisfied with one product, they do not get particularly upset but try a different one next time. Alternatives are always being presented. Customer discontent is thus eliminated by purchasing the other product, at least until that one is used. Products that do not sell well enough are removed from the shelves, their ingredients slightly modified and their packaging redesigned before eventually being presented as a *new* product for the attention of users. Of course, it is not just company policies that create a variety of goods; there are many duplicated companies operating in the same field, thereby providing competition and the emergence of countless new articles.

2.3.1.5 From non-renewable to renewable
A perceivable change in the strategy of current technology occurred thanks to the rise of environmental consciousness. Since the late 1960s, alternative technology groups have warned that natural resources are not infinite and that the appropriation of the world's non-renewable sources should cease. In the early 1970s, the petrol crisis showed how right they were. The calculation of the earth's oil reserves indicates that non-renewable

energy sources, minerals and other raw materials would be exhausted in the foreseeable future.

The environmentally friendly approach encourages the use of replaceable materials, energy sources and recycled components. This attitude towards nature is mostly a phenomenon of the twenty-first century and finds its reflection in objects in a material sense. The sustainable world is the ultimate aim, while design is one of the crucial means to this end as expressed in a project called The Solid Side (Manzini, 1995).

2.3.2 Two-directional transformation

The basic feature of this group is that transformation occurs in both directions, from one pole to the other and vice versa. Both objects and some production techniques follow this line.

2.3.2.1 From simple to complex or vice versa

As with arguments concerning passive and active artefacts, parallel progress can be observed in the structure of objects. The more technology is introduced to an object, the more complex it becomes. The transition from passive to active involves the inclusion of sophisticated mechanical equipment, electrical devices, electronic circuits and so forth. Each stage of development corresponds to a higher level of sophistication. Two kinds of sophistication can be distinguished: process and product-oriented. The former refers to sophistication in production processes due to using more complex technologies. The Wassily chair designed by Marcel Breuer is a classic example. At first glance, the chair does not show any interesting features, being made out of tubular steel and leather with remarkable simplicity. However, the achievement behind this simplicity comes partly out of the design and partly out of previously impossible technical progress that opened up ways for making tubular steel, bending it without distortion, perfect welding and chromium polish. In this kind of example, the production hardware becomes more and more sophisticated although it is not so clearly reflected in the manufactured objects themselves.

Product-oriented sophistication refers to products with more complex or high-technology hardware. The signs are often visible through a series of knobs, lids, control systems and so on. For example, we can see how complicated things have become by comparing the number of buttons on a CD player remote-control device with a hand-driven gramophone of the early twentieth century. Such changes have not only occurred in the world of electrical or electronic objects. Tools have developed as well. Even a simple pocket knife has been transformed into a portable workbench as with the famous Swiss Army knives. In the case of tools, there are two ways of becoming complex. One is the transformation from passive to active, as in the case of the toothbrush. Here, the main function of the tool is retained in a new object that includes an electrical device or circuit.

However, objects can also become more complex by keeping their original characteristics while adding new elements and functions to become more complex than ever. The Swiss Army knife, for example, is still a pocket knife; it still retains its own identity and mechanism despite these new features. What makes it more complex is combining extra functions.

2.3.2.2 From large to small or vice versa

Size is another variable. Objects that are highly subjected to technological innovations may change size over time. The ultimate objective is to reach the optimum size for the function alongside other limiting factors. If the prototype or early version of an object is clumsy, it is most probably due to the technical material used in it. Later versions are developed by removing these obstacles and to give a 'better' look as well as to make it more practical. Almost all electrical and electronic devices fall into this category. The radio, television, telephone, tape recorder, record player, computer, camera and many other commodities share the same history in terms of the larger sizes of their predecessors. For some design objects, the target is to be larger. Efforts are focused on achieving an optimum feasible capacity. Transport is a good example.

Mass transportation requires more effective vehicle systems, particularly by accommodating more passengers by enlarging the vehicle. Buses, for example, reached an optimum capacity of forty to forty-five people before their volume was reconsidered. One solution was to introduce double-decker buses while another was to attach a new articulated section to the rear, rather like adding another carriage to a train. However, here the constraints are visible: a third level cannot be built on top of double-decker buses since the physical balance of the structure does not allow it; a third coach cannot be added to buses because driving would become impossible in city traffic where the curvature and slope of roads are not designed for such long vehicles. Of course, the larger space needed for more powerful engines, high running costs, management problems and efficiency are other reasons, to name a few. Therefore, the optimum is not always determined by technical factors.

Consequently, increased efficiency is a constant objective, with greater size being one way to achieve it. Here, two points are worth mentioning. First, smallness does not necessarily correspond to reduced capacity. Theoretically, smaller but technologically new and recently designed products should perform at least as well as their predecessors. Secondly, largeness definitely means greater capacity. No objects are made larger without introducing some new aspect.

2.4 Conclusion

The observations in this chapter are indicative rather than conclusive. Undoubtedly the factors affecting the transformation of products are influencing how new-generation objects are being designed, whether noticed or not. Are they hidden principles of design or some commonalities that we share? I would be cautious in responding to this question. According to Necdet Teymur, 'a pure principle is a pseudo-theoretical structure defined by a homogeneous field. It is assumed to be the property of the 'essence' of the phenomena.

As such, it is a 'unique internal principle" (Teymur, 1982: 100). This definition is rather precise and leaves no room for manoeuvre. Therefore, I would prefer to highlight the strong commonalities regarding the development of products, independent of their contextual existence, and to leave the question of whether they are principles for my readers to decide.

CHAPTER 3
PROBLEMATIC OF LOCAL AND GLOBAL DESIGN IDENTITY IN NEWLY INDUSTRIALIZED COUNTRIES
WITH SPECIAL EMPHASIS ON TURKEY AT THE END OF THE TWENTIETH CENTURY

WHERE DOES HOPE LIE?

THE EXPLOITED PROMISES OF GLOBALIZATION AND LOCAL HEROES

A version of this paper was presented at the Third European Academy of Design Conference, Sheffield Hallam University, Sheffield, UK, 30th March – 1st April 1999 and published in its proceedings. (Balcioglu, 1999)

3.1 Introduction

I would like to begin with certain aspects of globalization that affect local design cultures. The purpose is to develop short but general perspectives that will provide important clues about where local design practices arise. The second part of the chapter will look into a newly developing country, Turkey, and the state of design at the end of the twentieth century. I would like to share some observations regarding the impacts of globalization as an external factor on the one hand and changing social, economic and technological internal factors on the other.

3.2 Aspects of the theses of globalization concerning local design

3.2.1 Economics

Marx's rallying cry from 1848, 'Workers of the world unite! You have nothing to lose but your chains!' is remembered as the last sentence of the Communist Manifesto. Now, over 150 years later, it reads slightly differently: 'Capitalists of the world unite! You have a lot to gain with no pain!' – and probably deserves to be remembered as the first declaration of globalization. This is to say that the economic aspect of globalization makes the rich richer and the poor poorer. As Bauman (1998: 70) notes, 'the total wealth of the top 358 'global billionaires' equals the combined incomes of 2.3 billion of the poorest people', that is, '45 percent of world population'. Eighty per cent of the world's population owns 22 per cent of global wealth whereas, 'in 1991, 85 percent of the world's population received only 15 percent of its income.' Bauman (1998: 71) continues, '2.3 percent of global wealth owned by 20 percent of the poorest countries thirty years ago has fallen now still further, to 1.4 percent.' The World Bank's World Development Indicator 1997 gives a similar impression: 'More than 1.3 million people live on less than a dollar a day, and 2 billion more are only marginally better off' (The World Bank, 1997: 22).

While the financial situation of the world's poorest is not improving, cash flow clearly represents the globalization of economies.[1] According to The World Bank, 'net private capital flow to developing countries has soared – from $44 billion in 1990 to $184 billion in 1995 – outstripping official flows' (26). However, this does not mean equal distribution of investment, as '78 per cent of this private money has been going to only a dozen or so countries' (26). It is thus fair to claim that while globalization has produced undeniable economic growth in recent decades, only some countries, and mostly their higher and upper middle classes, have benefited. Given that most designers are likely to be situated here, I believe they belong to a category that has benefited from the ever-increasing opportunities offered by economic globalization.[2]

3.2.2 Communication

Probably the least disputable attribute of globalization is what has been achieved in communication (Jameson, 1998). The triumph of communication networks and the rise of the media have made the world smaller. Consequently, economic, political, ideological and cultural issues have become more transferable and accessible to the public. Designers are one group enjoying this rapid advancement of information technology, as international links and joint projects and schemes with overseas companies became easily realizable.

3.2.3 Awareness

I would argue that the most paramount, but ironically less visible, impact of the globalization debate has been a rising awareness of the world. Roland Robertson, who coined the term, emphasizes the importance of awareness in his definition: 'Globalization as a concept refers both to the compression of the world and the intensification of consciousness of the world as a whole' (Robertson, 1996: 9). People begin to realize that we are all on the same small planet: so much so that a fire on one side may easily spread and burn others. For example, the unexpected and sudden fall of East Asia's so-called

---

[1] Woudhuysen reaches a similar conclusion from his analysis (1998).
[2] For a wider discussion of globalization from the viewpoint of design and designers, see Aldersey-Williams (1992) and Margolin (1998).

Asian Tigers threatened the world with a new wave of recession. This issue dominated the G7 meeting of 1998, and the news broke on newspapers' front pages. The first sentence of a *The Guardian* report on 31 October 1998, reflects the spirit of those days: 'A global action plan to rebuild shattered confidence in the international financial system and to shore up failing economies in the developing world was yesterday unveiled by the Chancellor, Gordon Brown.' The acting chairman of the G7 meeting, Brown made a statement on the matter with a vision of the world: 'A new age requires a new approach. Ministers agree that in this new inter-dependent and instantaneous global market place we must now create systems for supervision, transparency, regulation and stability that are as sophisticated as the markets they have to work with' (Gordon Brown. *The Guardian*, 31 October 1998).

Consciousness of globalization raises hopes of realizing the dream of 'a better world' possible, simply by encouraging us to make plans for the future. However, this optimistic view has not got much ground for the main impetus towards globalization. This mostly stems from economic and political advantages as well as the need to collaborate against natural disasters to save the world, such as measures to protect the ozone layer (Martin, 1997).

Clearly, it is not sufficient to analyse how globalization occurs but essential to propose what it should be. A similar observation is valid regarding the relationship between nature and human beings. We interfere more and more every day. Desirable or not, I suspect, one day someone will notice that *the world is revolving on its own and we still do nothing about it!* Is it not true that the entire history of human beings is the history of gradual emancipation from an unknown destiny towards a known destination? In this respect, designing the future or designing for the future is indeed an indispensable part of design as a discipline and congruent with creative design practice. It explains why designers more than welcome the idea of a wider perspective.

Not every professional is as lucky as a designer since some other fields have fewer prospects than others. Take literature for example. How many poets can produce a global product written in a global language to sell around the world? Not many I guess! This, of course, does not mean that literature has not benefited from electronic information flow and the internet. However efficient it is, we cannot expect everyone to utilize globalization to the same degree due to the nature of their professions. Since designers create objects for global markets, speaking a relatively more common global language, such as need, function, aesthetic, meaning and so on, they thus have many opportunities to serve internationally.

3.3 Culture and its infiltration channels

The dominating factor for local design is undoubtedly cultural flow and its irresistible force. For many theoreticians, modernization, equipped with a vigorous concept of Americanization, appears to be the driving force towards a global culture. Featherstone (1993: 170) writes that 'a global culture was seen as being formed through the economic and political domination of the United States which trusts its hegemonic culture into all parts of the world' Fredric Jameson does not disagree with this view:

A great Indian filmmaker once described the ways in which the gestures and the allure of walking of his teenage son were modified by watching American television: one supposes that his idea and values were also modified. Does this mean that the rest of the world is becoming Americanised? and if so, what do we think about that; or perhaps one should ask, what does the rest of the world think about that, and what might Americans think about it?

(Jameson, 1998: 58)

We all experience how quickly branches of McDonald's, Kentucky Fried Chicken and Starbucks are opened everywhere; how Hollywood penetrates our domestic privacy through the black hole in the living room; how CNN turns facts into fiction and wars into electronic games. Under such a bombardment, it is rather difficult to witness the transformation of what we have as remnants of cultural heritage.

Assuming that each society is influenced by others, I would like to make some observations on the particular domains where we are subjected to the notions, norms and values of other cultures in relation to design. Technology is one of them. As Arjun Appadurai notes, technology 'moves at high speeds across various kinds of previously impervious boundaries' (Appadurai, 1990: 297). It is easily disseminated widely and receives the least cultural resistance, except in those cases where it clashes with ideological values or beliefs – as in internet prohibitions in China for example.

Foreign food and cuisines also do not recognize boundaries as long as they do not hit high costs or quota barriers, or require complicated and less familiar cooking techniques. Fruits, prepacked and ready-to-eat products are cautiously welcomed as an exotic addition to domestic cooking but without radically changing entire eating habits. In Turkey, for example, kiwis and avocados were introduced approximately fifteen years ago. While they have increased variety, they have won only limited acceptance. Foreign restaurants are likely to develop rapidly in metropolitan areas as it becomes more and more popular to try ethnic cuisine. A Thai, Italian, Vietnamese or Chinese restaurant next to a Greek taverna is not an unusual sight in cosmopolitan districts. The lesson we learn from this culinary mosaic is that ethnic cultures can coexist within a given urban fabric. Does this not provide us with an excellent example of concurrent cultures where different backgrounds, races, and ethnic, religious, and ideological groups live together in harmony, providing that no group attempts to subordinate the others and they respect the rules and rights of coexistence?

When France's film industry was shaken by Hollywood, the government protected this cultural production with subsidies. Yet is this the way to preserve local cultures against the global one? Can it be a solution to accept the dominance of the latter while supplying a lifeline for the former? How realistic a policy is this when the other local industries under threat also demand subsidies? Protection of an industry as such is nothing but the protection of the industry only, which does not ensure absolute immunity against the interventions of alien cultures. Let us think of Turkish cinema for a moment without underestimating the international reputation of its directors and the popularity of its TV series. Many directors who have been abroad, some of whom have studied there, inevitably and understandably admire particular foreign directors, such as Fellini,

Wenders and Tarkovsky. Likewise, we can sympathize with Turkish scriptwriters who are influenced by European writers or actors who follow the same path as Hollywood stars. How then can we claim that a film shot in Turkey with Turkish crew and personnel is purely Turkish once we know about the complicated intellectual backgrounds, desires and aspirations of those involved as well as the imported techniques and equipment? Creating a cultural identity with mostly foreign methods, techniques and technology and a determined subscription to modernism probably results in global more than local values. Nevertheless, operating mostly with global values does not mean that these works automatically reach a global standard or quality.

If we draw an analogy with product designers in Turkey, we may come to the same conclusion that they are aware of contemporary developments and have similar design tools as their counterparts in other countries. Cultural infiltration is most difficult if not impossible ideologically. For example, you can eat Chinese food and read Chinese literature every day without changing your image in society. However, the day you wear traditional Chinese clothes in your country, you make a statement. Such visible cultural interference and identity markers probably face resistance more often than not, while for most consumer products that leave no traces of visible identity change, social approval is easier with no objections.

The ideological elements of cultural infiltration are probably the hardest to accept without confrontation, which may even escalate to war. History is an excellent collector of wars caused by the manipulations of ideological differences. Therefore, regardless of whether it is right or not, I would suggest that the introduction of Western ideology and thinking process is a minefield of cultural infiltration. One can anticipate that establishing a common ideological ground is the most formidable task to be completed for the sake of a 'united globe'.

3.4 Turkey: Where does it stand?

Over the years, Turkey has undeniably progressed despite its political and economic instability, as clearly demonstrated by these figures.

	1973	1977	1993
Annual income per capita (USD) *(Source: Macrotrends.com)*	490	1,427	3,180
Urban population (%) *(Source: Macrotrends.com)*	40.3	42.51	65.6
Fertility (%) *(Source: Macrotrends.com)*	5.39	4.83	2.89
Life expectancy (years) *(Source: Macrotrends.com)*	53.75	56.39	65.49
Infant mortality (%) *(Source: Fred Economic data)*	116	101.2	47.6

Having reached 4,500 USD by 1998, per capita income grew over tenfold in twenty-five years. Although Turkey's inflation and state debt are both rather high, overall, the figures indicate a shift from a poor rural state to a relatively better-off urban society with half the infant mortality and higher life expectancy than before. Is this a tangible sign that Turkey is now a newly industrializing country (NIC)? Although I would prefer economists to answer, I am content to portray how Turkey is participating in the globalizing world and radically intensifying its international links.[3] Outgoing phone calls totalled 130,205 minutes in 1989, rising more than three and half times to 473,433 minutes in 1996. The number of foreign tourists almost doubled from 4,516,077 in 1989 to 8,536,778 in 1996.[4] Likewise, the number of Turkish citizens travelling abroad increased at a similar rate from 2,590,844 in 1989 to 4,309,606 in 1996. Over recent years, there have been similar increases in private TV and radio channels, mobile telephones sold and purchases of new cars. These are concrete indications that Turkey is eager to plug into international networks.

3.4.1 Local designers

Creative designs based on ideas inspired by local cultures may revitalize ossified thinking and bring a distinctive flair for internal markets as much as the potential they have for international clients. In recent years, Turkish product design has been documented, published widely, reasonably exhibited and its discourse was elaborated thanks to dedicated academics and successful designers (see Asatekin (1975, 1976, 1994, 2006), Bayazıt (1984, 1987, 1996, 2006) Bayrakçı (1996), Er, A (1995, 1997, 2003), Er, Ö (1997, 2006) Küçükerman (1978, 1996, 1997, 2021), Hasdoğan (1994, 2009, 2021) and so on). I will try to explain the advantages and opportunities of globalization for designers working in Turkey.

What I notice is how the gap is closing between developing and developed countries. Indeed, there is no single gap as such; rather, there are qualitative and developmental differences that vary between sectors. While Turkey might have been in the Champions League with its leading football teams, its high-tech industry definitely remains in the second division. Likewise, communication technology may have reached an acceptable level, but the quality of Turkish TV programmes has a long way to go. The reasons are manifold and vary accordingly. Each sector requires detailed scrutiny to identify which one has more potential and a tendency to globalize. For instance, we all know that Turkey's furniture industry is rather advanced and already participates in the international market, even if its share remains small.

Here, however, I will focus on small design offices and freelance designers rather than the industry overall. Within this framework, their positions in the global market clearly reveal the possibilities:

---

[3] It is interesting to note that the development of design in Turkey resembles in many aspects the pattern followed by other NICs (Ghose, 1995).
[4] The number of tourists is still rising. According to the Turkish Statistical Institute, more than 29 million people visited Turkey in 2021.

1. Design is not a mega, technology-based industry; hence it does not require a great deal of unsustainable infrastructure.
2. The overwhelming majority of design activity and practice does not require advanced scientific knowledge or high technology that an NIC could not afford.
3. Design does not demand large capital investment; hence many design companies are small with few employees.
4. Design education in Turkey perfectly meets Western standards despite criticisms of it. Foreign languages are widely spoken, and many designers take the initiative to pursue lifelong learning even if this is rarely organized institutionally.
5. The sudden rise of design publications in Turkey provides concrete evidence of public interest as well as a growing domestic market.
6. Many practitioners and academics are well connected to the design world through media, publicity, information technology, international fairs, exhibitions, institutions and so on; hence the intellectual level of the field is never inadequate.
7. The workforce, including design labour, is generally economically viable in Turkey, which may easily attract foreign investment and collaboration.
8. Local designers have the significant privilege of unprecedented creative designs inspired by Turkey's culture, which is understandably not well known in the West. Given that design perpetually insists on and instigates novelty, unknown territories always promise serendipity. The potential of local design is within its hidden capacity and its ability to produce new designs.

3.4.2 How does local culture work for new design? (Does it really work?)

I doubt there is a simple answer to this question although speculation is possible. Based on the interviews I conducted for design research in Turkey, I observed various ways of exploiting culture with different levels, aims, intentions and implications. Their success or failures could be evidence of justification. Rather than making judgemental remarks, I offer the list below as indicative, suggestive and never complete – and may never be completed.

1. The neologistic approach: design objects are commonly named after a Turkish city, hero, location and so on, including battleships and aeroplanes, many of which have nothing to do with Turkish design. However, the title of the object rather than the making of it is the signifier that tries to position 'a modern and global' product within a national context by naming it.
2. Morphological application: here, a cultural, historical, traditional or even popular 'shape' is picked up and bestowed on objects for decorative purposes. Such utilization may alter the 'original' size, colour, texture, meaning and function. Above all, the shape becomes a symbol representing common values as well as establishing a missing link between users and their identities.
3. Topographical execution: forms can also be generated by bequeathing three-dimensionality through a function to a two-dimensional 'shape' or fragment of

a pattern derived from historical ethnographical or architectural sources. This strips the shapes of their context and attributes a use value to their new three-dimensional configurations.

4. Formal interpretations: occasionally, a new form or product is created from a known item by developing, mutating, distorting, altering, modifying or adjusting it. The major issue in such interpretations concerns the relationship between the previous and subsequent forms, regarding the dominant element of identity. Products falling into this category continue to reflect the main form with some degree of respect.

5. Allegorical interpretations: another way of benefiting from our living memory and material archive is to give a new function to an old object and modify its known features. These alterations may employ new, sometimes metaphorical, allegorical and/or ironical depth that may subordinate the original function by imposing new meanings. In other words, a source of inspiration, such as the original form, may not retain its prime characteristics after introducing entirely new functions or meanings. Although the main source is still the recognizable 'original' form, the imposed attributes hijack the former ones – hence my term, allegorical interpretations.

6. Conceptual inspirations: probably the most sophisticated and stimulating sources for designing new products are ideas originating from cultural norms, beliefs, social behaviours and actions rather than concrete objects. In this age of mass communication, emphasizing the semantics of objects and making them more than what they are strongly represent the Zeitgeist.

3.5 Conclusion

Needless to say, the level and variety of Turkey's design industry determine the experience of designers, whose possibilities of new fields of expertise are increasing rapidly and confidently. The global market is certainly a magnificent opportunity that local designers are successfully penetrating, albeit slowly. Designers in Turkey are no less creative than their colleagues in other countries. Although their number remains small, they are producing high-quality, world-standard work. This is, in fact, the new feature of globalization: the highest quality design work is no longer produced in just a few developed countries. Instead, you may come across remarkable design projects anywhere in the world, realized and executed with refined ingenuity, although they may be limited in numbers. The West retains an advantage in having more good quality designers, a wider variety of design fields and greater experience. Therefore, successful, creative and intellectually well-equipped local designers always have a chance to go beyond their borders. Bill Gates, one of the world's richest men, would not have employed Indian software designers if he had not seen the right capacity and had not had the right strategy.

CHAPTER 4
THE ESSENTIAL ELEMENTS
THE UNITY OF WORK AND TRANSFERABILITY OF KNOWLEDGE

This chapter was first presented as a paper at a conference entitled 'Practically speaking: The relationship between theory and practice'. It was a two-day national conference on practice-based research in Art and Design at Wolverhampton University, 14–15 December 1998.

This chapter analyses the relationship between theory and practice within the context of advanced study programmes. Later, in light of this analysis, I offer some suggestions on the issue of studio or practice-based doctorates. There are a few characteristics within the reciprocal relationships of theory and practice concerning practice-based doctorate schemes. This paper studies some of them and concentrates on certain concepts, such as timing, unity, permanency, balance, individual identity and transferability.

4.1 Timing and sequence of realization: Theoretical and practical work

The timing of the execution of each work is the first consideration. Why one part will be realized before the others needs explanation:

1. The theoretical part is developed first before practice is used to prove, support, explain, explore or exemplify the thesis generated in a classic scientific approach. You develop the theory and then go to the laboratory to test and prove it.[1] I can imagine a study where, say, constructivism is theoretically explored, its contemporary interpretation is drawn out and then the artwork, in line with these findings, is produced to realize the points made. Thus, in a successful study, one part of the work completes the other and presents a consistent body.

2. The practical part is realized first, theorized and put into an historical, philosophical, theoretical, conceptual and/or contemporary context so that the portion of the practical work is defined in relation and with reference to the

---

[1] A research student makes a clear statement on this issue: 'Practice is absolutely the real test of research' (Macleod, 1998: 33)

others. Practical work incorporates practices and embodies physical works, performing arts, composing music and so on. This process enables the student to contribute to the development of knowledge, as is the case in art criticism, where theory may be derived from existing practice. Equally, existing practice may be inspired by the theory available. Practice may involve exploration of new material or even its invention. In that case, the theory incorporates the knowledge derived from the process of making. A very typical example is material science in which a candidate develops a new material in workshops before writing about the process and explaining how it was obtained. This, ultimately, forms the thesis. This is probably acceptable for scientists and designers but not for artists. There is a paradox here, which I will try to explain. Recording and documenting the process and the result may well be sufficient for some disciplines to award a doctorate degree where there is an assumption that the final product is something useful and will be reproduced as necessary.

Recording and documenting is a kind of log that describes the process so that whoever follows it may produce and realize the new material or product as it was discovered, designed, manufactured or invented during the original research. In art, however, if the recording and documenting of the process result in the form of a thesis, anyone applying it as described will end up producing the same artwork. This is neither meaningful nor desirable. Of course, I do not deny that there might be other useful information in the records and documentation. If the main purpose of a dissertation is to contribute to knowledge, it should clearly communicate and argue in depth the theoretical context of the work in line with the research undertaken. The records and documentation are part of the practice and must represent the practical work accordingly unless they are deliberately linked to the theory for justifiable reasons.

3. Theoretical and practical work are conducted simultaneously, creating a mutual and interactive relationship that brings a new perspective as well as unity. Each part influences the other reciprocally and the development of research accordingly. Findings in practice re-shape the theory and the re-shaped theory re-forms the practice. This impact has its own creative and destructive tension, with the danger of bringing one part of the work to the fore in place of the other. It may also build a consistent unity between theory and practice; as Hanrahan explains 'the relationship between the two modes of communication can involve the equal participation of equals in investigating a common concern' (Hanrahan, 1998: 31). I wish the relationship between theory and practice was as simple as I have described so far. Unfortunately, it is not so explicit. In many cases, these three forms of realizing theoretical and practical research may overlap or correspond at certain stages of the process. Regarding the composition of theoretical and practical elements, other concepts are involved, among which unity becomes an absolute necessity for the coherence and completeness of the ultimate work.

4.2 Unity

In principle, the work produced for a doctorate must have a coherent body, which is the key factor when it is composed of practical and theoretical elements. The relationship between these two parts is the first potential question a candidate may face in the viva voce. In the extreme case of a relationship forming a unity, one could say that neither of these works can stand on its own without the other. This may create a problem, particularly at the examination stage, as indicated in the booklet of the UK Council for Graduate Education (UKCGE) on Practice-Based Doctorates.

> It has been noted that examiners still receive the written thesis in advance and, whilst this should include photographs, drawings or other representations of the exhibition, this is not the same as viewing the genuine artefact. One institution, recognising this, stated that the examiners should not come to, or record their decision until they had experienced the creative work.
>
> (UKCGE, 1997: 36)

Initially, this argument seems fair regarding the assessment of the work. However, reading between the lines, it becomes obvious that attributing great importance to the ephemeral part of the final submission undermines the permanence of accessibility to the knowledge produced, as explained below.

4.3 Permanency

If the contribution to knowledge is being made with the entirety of the project including an exhibition, how can we claim that the remaining parts can continue to fulfil their function after dismantling the practical work? What the examiners judge would be different from what the public would find on the library shelves. I do not think that it is satisfactory if a work contributes to knowledge at a particular point during the examination and exhibition period but later ceases to do so.

Where the completeness of the work entirely depends on its unity, both parts must be available for public scrutiny since the entirety of the work contributes to knowledge rather than either part alone. Therefore, I suggest we must secure the permanency and unity of the work contributing to knowledge. I believe temporary elements must be well recorded through films, videos, photographs, catalogues and so on. This would then be presented in a completed form with the written work to leave no gap in the final submission.

This does not mean that only the permanently available part of the work should be assessed; rather, it means that what is permanently archived is the part contributing to knowledge. As the contribution to knowledge is not the only criterion to look at, the assessment process should also consider other requirements as appropriate in awarding the degree.

4.4 The individual identity of each part

At the other extreme sense of relationship, the theoretical and practical parts may stand on their own as a piece of design or artwork on the one hand and a thesis on the other. Additionally, when considered together, a third option, another reading and unity of self-standing pieces may occur at another level. The integration of each part with or without losing its individual strength must bring a clear insight, a strong statement of its own that adds value to both the practical and theoretical sections.

Noticeably, this is a highly sophisticated relationship. Projects anticipating a structure as such need to elucidate the justification and reveal how the unity is being constructed. This will undoubtedly form the introductory and methodology section of the dissertation.

4.5 Balance

This raises the question of the balance between theory and practice. In an ideal world, both have equal weight in forming the final product. However, one element of the work tends to subordinate the other due to the candidate's main interests, background and research findings. If the theory dominates the artwork, the final outcome may well be a conventional PhD.[2] If the practical part dominates, the result may be a design of an object, an artistic performance or an exhibition. Although this may be perfect in its own right, it is unlikely to fulfil the requirements of the research programme.

Here we come across one of the main arguments regarding the position of practice-based doctorates. The UK Council's booklet implies that the focus of such research is not 'to advance the knowledge *about practice*, or to advance knowledge *within practice*. … The practice-based doctorate advances knowledge partly *by means of practice*' (emphases in original) (UKCGE, 1997: 18). Of course, there is no problem in advancing knowledge through practice.[3] However, the question is how to make this 'knowledge' generally accessible: a knowledge that is indeed intrinsic, embodied and integrated within the practice itself as experienced by its author. The final product may reflect these qualities. However, in the absence of a thesis contextualizing the creative work, it is exposed to all too superficial judgements. This brings us to the issue of transferability of knowledge.

---

[2] An example is the work of Claudia Maria Wegener, an artist who graduated from the RCA printmaking department in 1991, attended a practice-based PhD programme at the Fine Art Department of Goldsmiths' College and ended up submitting a 'normal' PhD dissertation without any significant practical work attached (see *The Last Monument*, 1998, unpublished PhD Dissertation, London: Goldsmiths' College).

[3] The ways of advancing knowledge through practice have been well illustrated by Frayling (1993, 1998), who examines the differences between research into art and design, research through art and design, and research for art and design.

4.6 Transferability

How can we find out what the contribution of an original practical work to knowledge is? Some may think that the work speaks for itself. However, it speaks to a Chinese person differently than it speaks to a Saudi as much as it speaks differently to anybody. Frankly, the work does not speak at all. It is we who make it speak, and undoubtedly in our own language. This is the inspirational and subjective power of the work, which is open to interpretation. Texts are also interpreted as studied by hermeneutics. However, the reading of texts is identical, while the reading of practical works is not. Once written, texts do not normally change over the centuries; if they survive, they survive as they are. Our spectacles change, yes, but not the texts. We often explain a text with another text using excerpts while operating within the same realm and medium.

The unfortunate destiny of practical work is that it conveys knowledge to us in a very different way. 'Us' is the receiver, the audience, the viewer before the work. We do not make an artwork to narrate another one. The medium is replaced by words, images and secondarily representative vehicles rather than an original language. It appears that the textual narrative is sine qua non. That is how the relationship between theory and practice is cemented.

4.7 Other aspects of the relationship

In a practice-based doctorate, I believe, a theoretical text is an arena where the practical work is emancipated from its subjectivity by being exposed to critical inquiry, put into a wider context and related to contemporary or other relevant literature. Kate Macleod describes this eloquently:

> Artists undertaking higher degrees need to identify the position of their art practice, not through historical research, in the sense that this dictates the methodology but through a knowledge of what their practice is and what it does and this, I have to say, is dependent on knowledge of other practices, of artist precedents, of other artists' judgements, of the discourse of art to which they are contributing.
>
> (1998: 36)

It is an amalgamation of practical and theoretical research, a testing ground for ideas, hypotheses and findings. These require the skill to analyse and process the results of the research conducted. Here, we arrive at an often forgotten and omitted aspect of the debate, which is the study.

Let's remember that doctorate programmes are advanced studies developing the intellectual perceptions of students among other things. The period of study equips students with research skills, techniques and methodologies, with abilities to collect and analyse data and work under supervision. They also experience argument development, academic paper writing and presenting and gain expertise within a particularly well-defined domain of their subject. Vital though it is, research is just one of the aspects of the study. Without other elements of the programme, no completion of the degree should be expected. Hence, not every research project is a PhD, and a PhD is not research only. Not every PhD holder is an excellent researcher, just as not all excellent researchers are PhD holders.

After looking into the complexity of theory and practice, I realized the potential embedded within the scope of practice-based doctorates for the future of art and design in general. It is not a matter of finding an appropriate niche within the conventional PhD to implement practical work and receive a title. I am aware that the UK Council booklet advocates another direction by calling it an 'inclusive model'. Understandably, it warns us against the increasing number of titles and supports a simple and unique PhD to avoid such complications. 'It is arguable that more flexible, inclusive and nationally agreed regulations for PhDs could extend to all such professionally-oriented study and activity, and avoid further proliferation of titles' (UKCGE, 1997: 26). Visibly, another concern of this approach is to eliminate the possibility, image or notion of second-class doctorates by only offering an inclusive PhD programme. At first sight, this looks refined, workable and lucid. It also suits the personal aspirations of many practitioners. However, I believe that this strategy can be risky in the long run. New research degree programmes emerge from the needs of people, society, industry and technology. Establishing programmes without investigating these needs thoroughly may lead to undesirable consequences. I have a few observations regarding what the framework of such a programme should consider.

4.7.1 The demands of the artists and designers

The first question is why the practitioners need a research degree. Responses may vary but I can list some:[4]

1. Professional development: advancement of personal skills, professional knowledge, research techniques and problem-solving ability.[5]
2. Career development: increased the probability of employment and the area of job opportunities at higher levels including universities.
3. Intellectual development: intensive academic discussion on wider issues and feedback on personal work.
4. Profile development: wider audience, networking, contact and publicity.

---

[4] There are other reasons causing a rise in the numbers of postgraduate students in general, including 'economic recession' and 'the attractiveness of postgraduates to higher education institutions themselves' (UKCGE, 1995 & 1996).

[5] Expectations regarding doctorates have gradually changed as in other fields. As one education supervisor noted, 'The people who come for our doctorates don't want that (an academic career). They want to do a doctorate because they are interested in a problem. We're in a different ball game' (Hill, 1994: 61). The expectations sound different in scientific circles:

> Our informants assumed that PhDs will provide for the replenishment of the UK academic community and, despite the state of the academic labour market in most subjects, that most PhDs would want jobs in higher education. The assumptions among scientists were broader: that the PhD was a licence to do research but that many students would be recruited to industry as researchers.
>
> (Becher, 1994: 58)

4.7.2 The demands of the changing nature of professions and practices

We live in an information era where the production and circulation of knowledge are growing exponentially. Research skills are essential to keep up with the growth in knowledge, progress in technology and overwhelming availability of information. Current art discourse is characterized by a sophisticated and highly elaborate nomenclature derived from contemporary philosophy. Art with a capital A does not exist anymore without its discourse, at least in certain circles. Therefore, artists very rightly wish to be equipped with theoretical tools for further understanding, interpreting, presenting and developing their work.

4.7.3 The potential of a new professional degree

An advanced study and research programme incorporating theory and practice will inevitably and proactively explore the relationships of its components in depth. This initial debate about the programmes themselves has already interacted with, instigated and accumulated a considerable body of ideas and literature in the last few years. It would be naive not to imagine that a new form of art, design and theory alliance would flourish from these programmes, contributing not only to knowledge but also to motivate each of the participant disciplines enormously. A separate degree structure has more potential than the established PhD tradition because a specialized, dedicated and well-defined advanced professional study and research programme would be purpose-built as opposed to the general structure of PhD programmes.

4.7.4 Jeopardizing the established concept of the PhD

Despite variations between each university's PhD regulations, there is some sort of consensus on what a PhD consists of. The sciences, social sciences and humanities each have their own traditions and systems in place, namely an academic research degree mostly based on theory presented in the form of a thesis. When the practical element constitutes half of the final work, the nature of theoretical participation and the essence of the final products differ radically from a traditional PhD. Given that the number of words required also changes drastically, it becomes hard to define what a PhD consists of, if the 'inclusive model' is adopted.[6] The term 'practice-based PhD' has already become popular to mark these differences, which are rather clear, as argued above. The problem, however, is to coin the right term for the right activity. If a practice-based PhD is different from a traditional PhD, why do we not name it differently? This will give a

---

[6] The 'inclusive model' is developed and suggested in the UK Council pamphlet. It reads: 'This inclusive model would involve either demonstrating/accepting that the activities and outcomes outlined ... could reasonably be seen as consistent with a traditional scientific model, or broadening the model so as to encompass the entire continuum from scientific to practice-based research' (UKCGE, 1997: 20).

distinctive character and mission to the programmes without jeopardizing the existing conceptualization of PhDs.

4.8 Conclusion

My argument is that the so-called practice-based PhD has its own attributes, potential and strengths that are sufficiently dissimilar from the traditional PhD that it deserves to be named independently. This will give a new identity and power to such programmes regarding further exploration of the fertile soil of the theory–practice duality. Degree titles such as Doctor of Art (D.Art), Doctor of Fine Art (D.F.A.) and Doctor of Design (D.Des) awarded by Harvard University, clearly demonstrate the area and the level of specialism. I have noticed the implication that separate titles prefaced by the word 'Doctor' may be treated as second-class degrees. I disagree with this view because I think that they are equal to PhDs but with different expertise (which conventional PhDs lack). I can think of the extreme benefit of this level of expertise within education. Take BA art or design studio teaching: would it not be ideal to have a practicing artist or designer, someone with a D.Art or D.Des, and another tutor with a PhD teaching various aspects of the subject with a greater balance of theory and practice embodied within the expertise present? In other words, one could anticipate the alleviation of the theory–practice controversy within art colleges by employing tutors with D.Art or D.Des qualifications.

Some may feel that it is rather tiring and an unnecessary battle to raise the status of these new degrees instead of taking refuge in the easier solution and enjoying the existing prestige of the PhD. If this approach achieves a consensus, then I am worried that the concept of the PhD may soon become misleading with all these options included within it. This may even cast a shadow on the quality and substance of the title, both nationally and internationally, not due to the standard of the work but due to inconsistency in the inclusiveness.

If, however, we argue that D.Art and D.Des are dissimilar to PhDs in nature, then let's face the fact and work for it. When prestige is concerned, we should remember that the relationship in question here between a practice-based PhD and a PhD somewhat resembles the statuary relationship between design and art at the turn of the century: Although the recognition of the design profession had been on the agenda, many people continued to prefer the expression 'industrial art'. *Moot points: friendly disputes upon art & industry between Walter Crane & Lewis F. Day*, a book published in 1903, is an ideal example to re-discover this (Crane, 1903). The designers used to call themselves 'artists' to benefit from the existing prestige, status and protective umbrella of art.[7] According

---

[7] I encountered this desire of being or being considered an artist during my research on design concepts. Those who we confidently call 'designers' today were far from naming their activity 'design'. Instead, they insisted on terms containing the word 'art'. Commercial art, industrial art, applied art, practical art, art manufacturers and art applied to industry are some of the expressions employed in the nineteth and early twentieth centuries (Balcioglu, 1993).

to Noel Carrington, 'Lethaby managed to avoid the dangerous word art almost entirely from the start to finish in the pursuit of the recognition of "design" in the inaugural pamphlet of the (DIA) Design and Industries Association in 1915' (1976: 30).

I do not think that history repeats itself. However, some social and human attitudes do. In this particular case, I would like to believe in the lessons learnt from history to avoid repeating what has turned into a deviation from the identification process.

CHAPTER 5
RESEARCH, KNOWLEDGE AND DOCTORATE PROGRAMMES
TOWARDS THE THIRD DOMAIN

This paper was first presented at a conference in Milan and then published in its proceedings. Pizzocaro, S., Arruda, A. and de Moraes, D., eds, (2000), Design Plus Research: Proceedings of the Politecnico di Milano Conference, *321–329, Milan: Politecnico di Milano.*

Two prevailing aspects of the debate regarding research in art and design concern me: the epistemological and the educational. This chapter undertakes an epistemological investigation of the nature of knowledge in art and design, while its reflection on the educational perspective is traced through research-based education at doctorate level.

5.1 Background

At the turn of the twenty-first century, a debate regarding research has become dominant within art and design. Among the many reasons why research has been praised are the following – in no particular order:

Research Assessment Exercise was introduced to UK universities and art and design in 1992. As the ranking of departments, schools and colleges intensified competition, institutions rushed to establish research centres, programmes, fellowships, research assistants and studentships, motivated primarily by the funds given to higher education institutes based on their rating. Depending on size, it was not unusual for a higher education institute with a 'five-star' ranking to receive up to one million pounds. Earlier, the majority of UK art and design courses were delivered by polytechnics and institutes. However, in 1992, polytechnics became universities or began operating as part of the university sector. Art and design education was thus subjected to a more academic and structured approach, within which research is paramount. Within curriculum design, unitized or modular systems gained recognition. In parallel, vocational training courses like the Higher National Diploma (HND) have lost popularity, whereas BA and master courses are in the ascendant. Certainly, the prevailing climate is increasingly aspirational, with rapid growth in taught master courses, research degrees and MPhil and PhD programmes.

There are, of course, other factors. Higher education in the UK is an industry.[1] It is known that 'whatever their slant on postgraduate work, all institutions will have to come to terms with the increasing internationalisation of the postgraduate market as part of the liberalisation of world trade' (Bone, 1999: 59).

This transposition is particularly noticeable in newly developed countries, where once there is reasonable provision of undergraduate courses and universities, the main interest in advanced study focuses on education abroad. Demand from overseas countries is thus shifting towards postgraduate courses, which has encouraged the rise of research in the UK. Postgraduate programmes need to be delivered by academically qualified teachers. However, supervisors with doctorate degrees are still rare in design, and particularly art. Although more scholars are now researching the history and theory of the subject, they often operate in academic environments while few conduct practice-based tutorials. This niche encourages the ambition to teach in higher education, thereby motivating some practitioners to equip themselves with the requisite qualifications. In comparison with the vagaries of the art market and art business, a teaching career appears an attractive proposition.

There are complex and diverse reasons why artists and designers require advanced research degrees. The hiatus between their expectations is also visibly widening. Designers are often interested in a specific problem and wish to direct their research abilities towards its solution. More often than not, these solutions are product-oriented and applicable to industry. This is attractive to businesses, companies and industries, which are likely to provide funds and financial support for prospective or present staff members wishing to undertake a project-related research degree. In theory, the hopes of higher education institutions have been realized, as there are qualified and experienced applicants, funding is available and collaboration with industry is being intensified. It looks like an ideal situation! However, it is not so straightforward because conventional programmes such as MPhil/PhD are often unsuitable for industrial projects. This is because they are usually theoretical, require full-time involvement and are structured to produce academic researchers and scholars rather than practitioners with advanced applied research skills. Although applied research is not alien to scientific disciplines like physics, chemistry and anthropology, this question needs to be addressed within art and design education.

Artists' mounting interest in research degrees is likely to be linked to personal, professional, intellectual and career development.[2] In other words, the research problems

---

[1] The number of international postgraduate students rose by over 300 per cent from 25,000 in 1988 to almost 78,000 in 1997 (Watts, 1999: 17). Over the same period the number of international students in the United States grew by approximately 20 per cent from 123,000 to 147,000 (Watts, 1999: 17). These figures demonstrate the rise in the popularity of English-medium universities. Given the average annual cost of a postgraduate science course was £14,800 in 1998 (Watts, 1999: 16), such students obviously provide millions of pounds per year.

[2] There are other reasons for the general rise in postgraduate students, including 'economic recession' and 'the attractiveness of postgraduates to higher education institutions themselves' (UKCGE, 1995 & 1996).

they intend to tackle have probably emerged from their individual work. No doubt, a creative and responsive milieu in academic circles could be a source of inspiration for many people. The establishment of the Art and Humanities Research Board in 1998 notably encouraged research through funding research projects with a budget of approximately 50 million pounds dedicated to art and design, and its practice. All of these issues have propelled the debate on research and research degrees. Many questions were asked and considerable advances were achieved. Arguably, however, a consensus has yet to be reached about the nature of the PhD and its difference from studio or practice-based PhDs.

5.2 Epistemological aspect

When artists and designers want to do a research-based PhD for their own reasons, they encounter the basic principle of the degree: 'A PhD dissertation must contribute to knowledge.' This argument of 'contributing to knowledge through art and design practice' raises the question of what knowledge fundamentally is. The Rector of the Royal College of Art, Christopher Frayling, summarizes it succinctly and effectively:

What we actually do:
- Research into art and design
- Research through art and design
- Research for art and design (Frayling, 1993: 3)

The first two are relatively uncomplicated. Historical, aesthetic and theoretical research falls into the first category, whereas material and technical research, development work and action research are covered by the second one. But the third category is what Frayling calls 'thorny': 'Research where the end product is an artefact – where the thinking is, so to speak, embodied in the artefact, where the goal is not primarily communicable knowledge in the sense of verbal communication, but in the sense of visual or iconic or imagistic (sic) communication' (Frayling, 1993: 5).

When we enter the domain of action within which an art or design object is created, the place of knowledge becomes elusive. What motivates artists and drives the creative action is not essentially knowledge but a composition of subjective decisions, ideas, feelings, expressions, exploration, intuition and so on. Within this process, the position of knowledge, its weighting and its determinative role, is questionable and varies in each case. What is certain, however, is its uncertainty, as Clive Dilnot notes.[3] In his Ohio (1999a) and later Helsinki Paper (1999b) he examines the issue further, focusing on

---

[3] I do not know at this stage what Heisenberg's theory of uncertainty may offer to design, but if 'uncertainty' is further studied and accepted as intrinsic to design knowledge, a visit to Heisenberg may be inevitable. (Theory of uncertainty: the impossibility of determining the exact position and the momentum of a moving particle simultaneously. Chambers, 21st Century Dictionary).

the concept of knowledge and its validity in design. 'A third way of knowing' is the precept which permeates his investigation: 'Because design cannot be accommodated satisfactorily within either the model of the sciences/technological sciences or within the humanities/social sciences, then design sets up "an-other" model of knowing and doing; instantiates a particular form of praxis or phronesis' (1999a: 67). Dilnot approaches the concept of knowledge from a 'language' perspective, through which knowledge develops and is communicated. Without communication, knowledge does not exist. Communication is not limited to one or two particular ways of conveying knowledge. Indeed, there *must* be different ways of communicating knowledge. There are different languages. The development, generation and production of knowledge is also dependent upon communication. Language within a given discipline is the medium through which the knowledge of that particular discipline is advanced. Different languages and ways of communication may thus be instrumental in the emergence of different kinds of knowledge. Once the vital link between knowledge and language has been perceived, the unique characteristic of knowledge can be better comprehended – if, of course, it exists as such. This at least is my reading of Clive Dilnot's account.

His analysis of knowledge highlights an interesting association: 'Science numbers the world and the humanities narrate it.' He continues: 'design neither narrates nor numbers.' If so, the logical conclusion is that art operates audio-visually and/or sensorially while design does so artifactually. Thus, artefactual and sensorial knowledge need to be defined. Furthermore, the formation of artefactual and sensorial knowledge, its accumulation and progress should be discernible, as should its mechanisms and *raison d'être*. The exigent task of developing design knowledge, as described by Dilnot, is rather new to us.

However, what I am concerned with here is not to develop a language of objects and thereby knowledge particular to the artificial but the concept of knowledge as articulated in science. I believe that the concept of knowledge borrowed by many design theorists and historians belongs to certain schools. One of them is Justificationism, which believes in proven knowledge and is the source of post-Enlightenment rational thought (Lakatos, 1970). It is not difficult to predict how design operates within this premise: identification of a design problem, developing a project (a proposition), designing, testing, observing failures, getting feedback, redesigning, re-testing, market research, users' and consumers' response, alterations in design and so on.

Another trend subscribes to Karl Popper's explanation of knowledge within the school of Falsificationism, whereby a proposition remains valid unless it is refuted. Before formulating the systematic application of Falsificationism or Justificationism to design, we should note criticisms of these theories. Any theory imported into design should also give an account of itself within its own context. This is what I see missing in the relationship between design and knowledge. What both proven knowledge and non-falsified knowledge impose is that what is proven is valid forever, and what is non-falsified is valid unless it is refuted. In both cases, time and space are not specified. Once accepted, that particular item of knowledge is valid everywhere on earth, independent of location but confined to the time period between when the proposition first emerged and its falsification (if it ever occurs). This notion of knowledge – spatially independent but temporally bound – is not valid for either art or design because their knowledge is strictly bound to both. Therefore, what constitutes art knowledge and design knowledge has to be explored with surgical precision. The relationship between science, art and design also needs to be portrayed in context because, if the concept of knowledge is only developed by scientists, its application to art and design remains undifferentiated.

5.3 Science, Art and Design

If any single work defines the polarisation and split between art and humanities and science, it is *The Two Cultures* by C. P. Snow (1995). First published in 1959 after the annual Rede Lectures in Cambridge, it initiated a public debate that still resonates. Snow observed, analysed and compared the two cultures to develop 'a brilliant delineation of divide' (1995). Although he mostly referred to the humanities and literature, he nevertheless fomented the art and science controversy. Since then, however, the contemporary understanding of interdisciplinary approaches has removed many of these boundaries, although the belief in the oppositeness of art and science has not diminished.[4]

Design was not part of this polarization, at least initially. Various propositions situate design in relation to art and science. Philosopher Vilém Flusser has made observations similar to C. P. Snow's: 'Modern bourgeois culture made a sharp division between the world of arts and that of technology and machines; hence culture was split into two mutually exclusive branches: one scientific, quantifiable and "hard", the other aesthetic, evaluative and "soft"' (Flusser, 1999: 18). He demarcated a region for design between art and technology.

> In the gap design formed a bridge between the two. It could do this since it is an expression of the internal connection between art and technology. Hence in contemporary life, design more or less indicates the site where art and technology (along with their respective evaluative and scientific ways of thinking) come together as equals, making a new form of culture possible.
>
> (Flusser, 1999: 18–19)

Earlier attempts tried to secure space for design within science rather than claiming a zone of its own. These efforts included Bauhaus, Hochschule für Gestaltung (HfG) Ulm,[5] Herbert Simon's *Science of Design* (1998) and Bruce Archer's attempts to introduce scientific methods into design processes in the UK. Educationally, design in the UK lined up with art as a traditional ally. This is probably because, at least until recently,

---

[4]For me, the question is not whether it exists but what the relationship is within the unity and diversity of scientific, artistic and design thinking.
[5]Richard Buchanan (1995) gives a good account of the endeavours connecting design with science.

art and design education has often been established under one roof, thereby bolstering the image that they are inseparable. With the raising of the question of knowledge, science, art and design (SAD) require repositioning in relation to one other. However, this chapter does not risk undertaking this task. Instead, it is worth looking into the use of knowledge in science, art and design as an initial criterion for comparison in the context of research. In science, knowledge forms the basis of research and development. Observation, experiment, rational and abstract thinking, logic, creativity and so on are all important. Scientific knowledge forms the basis of scientific research, pursued intrinsically and perhaps solely to expand the frontiers of knowledge. That is, knowledge is the main motivation, stimulus and outcome.

Art, however, benefits from knowledge differently. History, theory and knowledge of materials, techniques and processes are all useful intellectual backgrounds for artists and for producing work. However, when it comes to contemporary artistic activity, other forces predominate: ideas, intuition, creativity, meaning, subjective decisions and plans, aesthetic and expressive concerns and so on. The role of knowledge in the act of producing an artwork is 'uncertain' and not easily definable for many, if not all artworks. Therefore, it is probably right to say that the main personal drive in creating art today is the idea, meaning and communication.[6]

A major conflict, however, emanates from what I call 'the challenge of uniqueness'. In principle, an artwork should be unique, except for manual, mechanical or electronic reproductions. Even then, these reproductions are numbered and signed separately to ensure that they too are endowed with a degree of uniqueness. Therefore, the art knowledge leading to the creation of a particular and unique artwork is destined to be unique itself. Whether artists use the same knowledge to produce the same work again is another matter. What matters is that the knowledge of each work is embodied within itself and remains with the artist (or designer) unless conveyed to others. While the production techniques, materials, forms and experience gained can be shared and may lead to other works, the uniqueness of the artwork and its embodied personal knowledge remains intact. Although the end product can be multiplied, the uniqueness of the design experience for each single project is identical to that of art. Under normal circumstances, an artist does not use the same knowledge to produce the same work again. If the knowledge is not shared and remains possessed only by the artist, its validity as knowledge becomes questionable. On the other hand, if the artist reveals the knowledge of that particular work – whatever that knowledge might be – this knowledge will be useless because it can only lead to the reproduction of the original work. This is the challenge of uniqueness in the context of knowledge.

Personal knowledge, on the other hand, is the kind of knowledge we try to formulate for art and design. Michael Polanyi, a distinguished philosopher of science, has already eloquently articulated the notion in a way that is perfectly applicable to art and design.

---

[6]Artistic action and its main drive are not fixed but subject to changes, altering historically and culturally between eras and locations.

> We may distinguish between the personal in us, which actively enters into our commitments, and our subjective states, in which we merely endure our feelings. This distinction established the conception of the personal, which is neither subjective nor objective. In so far as the personal submits to requirements acknowledged by itself as independent of itself, it is not subjective; but in so far as it is an action guided by the individual passions, it is not objective either. It transcends the disjunction between subjective and objective.
>
> ([1958] 1974: 300)

Commitments are crucial for personal knowledge and instrumental for demarcating its differences from subjective knowledge: 'commitment is a personal choice, seeking, and eventually accepting, something believed (both by the person incurring the commitment and the writer describing it) to be impersonally given, while the subjective is altogether in the nature of a condition to which the person in question is subject' ([1958] 1974: 302). I believe that his explanation of discovery is also applicable to art and design: 'From a first intimation of a hidden problem and throughout its pursuit to the point of its solution, the process of discovery (or art or design – my addition) is guided by a personal vision and sustained by a personal conviction' ([1958] 1974: 301).

The knowledge I have talked about so far is the knowledge of the artist while creating an artwork. Once created, however, the artwork itself generates its own discourse, hence its own knowledge. The value and knowledge of a given artwork are not determined by scientific tests and experiments but by consensus, probably formed by artists, critics, audiences, dealers and so on. Although the mechanisms of what constitutes consensus are complicated and may not even be impartial, it is obvious that the value and thereby the validity of an artwork is determined through these mechanisms, which are in a sense verification devices.

Comparing the use of knowledge in design to its equivalent in art and science helps make the relationship between them clearer. Certain elements of design require scientific, social, economic, ergonomic, cultural and technological knowledge that is very solid or 'hard', as Flusser described it. In contrast, despite all the attempts outlined above, creative processes are not accessed through scientific methods but via an approach similar to that of art. The designer's philosophy, interpretation of the subject, creative instinct, feelings, principles and so on may also play a role in forming the product. However, the key player and determining factor for which the knowledge is employed is satisfying needs and requirements by producing products and environments with strong functional characteristics.

By identifying the main use of knowledge in scientific, artistic and design research as a knowledge-oriented, idea-oriented and function-oriented activity, I am trying to underline one of the major aspects defining science, art and design. I would predict that design will become an issue in the coming years. Indeed, a few scholars, such as Victor Margolin, Clive Dilnot and Nigel Cross, have already initiated the debate: 'There has been a growing acceptance of design on its own terms, a growing acknowledgement and articulation of design as discipline in its own right. We have to come to realise that we do not have to turn design into an imitation of science, nor do we have to treat design as a mysterious, ineffable art' (Cross, 1999: 7).

Let us be clear about the relationship of science, art and design regarding the use of knowledge: rather than representing three monolithic domains, the trio are all interrelated and inter-penetrable to various degrees. Science is not devoid of art: a mathematical formula, DNA helices and images of the nucleus of an atom or from space can be more than an excellent aesthetic. Similarly, design is becoming gradually integrated into science as in bioengineering and cloning. Conversely, artworks benefit from science and technology while modern design has been an integral component of modern art. In short, every work receives a certain input from other domains. For instance, designing a lancet or surgical knife may require scientific knowledge of the latest materials, ergonomics and function, although no art is involved; nothing should distract attention in an operating theatre, only design, science and technology. In contrast, Swatch is more successful through its artistic appeal than technological expertise. Design knowledge has explicitly contributed to producing unusual watches for different age groups while the environment has something to do with the Zeitgeist rather than any proven knowledge. Taste, style, manner, popular culture, tradition, fashion and many other social and cultural ingredients determine the success of a design. Here, we encounter the problem with the concept of proven knowledge mentioned above. Understandably, proven knowledge is needed to design a product, yet not every product is successful as many disappear as rapidly as they appear. Does this mean that the design knowledge has failed if a product does not survive? Is the market a verification mechanism for design knowledge *per se*? Can we ask the same question about artists by claiming that only those who are established and known by the public are endowed with art knowledge? Can success be tied to the justification of knowledge? What can we say of those who are not successful and whose work is not known? Ultimately, what does success have to do with knowledge?

All these unanswered questions tell us something, namely that the deciding agent in art and design is consensus. This consensus is constituted by a comprehensive mechanism that probably comprises various powers, such as the market, media, culture, custom, ideology, tradition and so on. If consensus is the key to the substantiation of art knowledge and design knowledge, we can look to existing theories to determine whether consensus-based knowledge is legitimized.[7]

Imre Lakatos explains the same situation in science. 'For centuries knowledge meant proven knowledge,' he says, 'proven either by the power of intellect or by the evidence of the senses' (1970: 91). Although sceptics questioned the power of intellect

---

[7] This approach does not rule out what Dilnot suggests: an understanding of design knowledge with its own means of communication and justification.

and sense, the success of Newtonian physics prevailed and added another keystone to the Enlightenment's foundations. According to Lakatos, 'Einstein's results again turned the tables and now few philosophers or scientists still think that scientific knowledge is, or can be, proven knowledge' (Lakatos, 1970: 92). One of the strongest arguments is truth by consensus. If the truth is constituted by consensus in science, why would not this be applicable to art and design? This question is perfectly legitimate considering that discourses determine the aura of art and design works and form the consensus within communities. Therefore, consensus-based knowledge is perfectly suitable for art and design, even in the form discussed by scientists. This definition of art and design knowledge is crucial for doctorate-level research, for which 'contribution to knowledge' is an indispensable condition. To this end, it is time to review the structure of advanced research programmes with all these concerns in mind.

5.4 Educational aspect

The debate about art and design doctorates has generated great enthusiasm and interest. Particular attention has been directed towards practice-related doctorate programmes. Artists and designers who believe their practice is research, or incorporates a great deal of research, question the nature of PhDs. They demand academic recognition for their practice as the core aspect of art-based PhD programmes.[8] In other words, the theory and practice duality and their balance or proportional representation appear to be the key issue dominating the dispute.[9] The relationship between theoretical and practical work, their composition and weighting raises the question of whether they are PhDs or professional doctorates.[10] This division has emerged in the last decade. Some PhD programmes have reduced the number of words required for the dissertation while incorporating a substantial amount of practical work for submission. As a result, practice-based, practice-led and studio-based PhDs have appeared.

Other universities have preferred to award a separate title, such as professional doctorates (PD), for similar kinds of work. Practice-based learning and cooperative education are phrases used in Australia, where they are now considering 'work-based learning programs at the doctorate level' (Caban, 1998).

These schemes are not only confusing but also considerably damaging to the concept of the PhD. Trying to introduce practice as the basis of research while redressing and renaming the existing PhD is problematic. Instead, clarification and simplicity are needed. I therefore argue that a doctorate level of both PhDs and professional doctorates

---

[8]Katy Macleod's paper reveals these. She states, 'What this study uncovered was the postgraduate Fine Art student's anxiety about centring the research firmly within his/her art practice' (Macleod, 1998).
[9]For a detailed articulation of the argument, see Hanrahan (1998).
[10]This question is described as a contentious issue in the UK Council for Graduate Education, Practice-based Doctorates in the Creative and Performing Arts and Design (1997).

offers a good combination of degrees from which to launch a variety of research projects. PhDs can be allocated mostly to those who wish to pursue an academic and research career and mostly for theory-based research aiming to contribute to knowledge, the advancement of the discipline and its theory. Professional doctorates can be directed at those who wish to improve their subject specialism and practical research skills, pursue educational and professional careers, and contribute to knowledge, the advancement of the profession and its practice.

Having these two programmes does not prevent the assimilation of the two different notions of knowledge discussed above. Proven knowledge or unfalsified knowledge, or other notions of knowledge discussed and employed in science, can serve the same function for theoretical research in art and design within PhD programmes. As I argued before, artefactual language, personal knowledge, design knowledge and art knowledge are likely to be consensus-based and inseparable from practice. The duality at the doctorate level is thus congruent with the kinds of specialist knowledge functioning in each programme. No clear-cut division is suggested here, except an attempt at demarcating zones.

These concise definitions of the two doctorate programmes give critical importance to the threshold where theory and practice merge. If theory, theoretical research and the thesis form the main body of work, a PhD is the right programme. Within this spectrum, work comprising substantial theoretical research appears adequate for PhD programmes whereas work balancing theory and practice is an ideal duality for professional doctorates.

I think that allocating the PhD mostly for theoretical, academic, knowledge-oriented, discipline-related research and the PD scheme mostly for professional and practice-based research with an identified subject specialism, draws a clear line between the differences. It also incorporates many contentious areas within a simple and coherent structure. However, there are a few points to stress. First, while both degrees are equal at the doctorate level, they are designed to serve distinct functions as required by various bodies. This equality is an important issue, and the worry that one might be superior to the other is actually groundless, for each one is distinct and serves a different purpose.

Second, both degrees contribute to knowledge in their own direction and with their own means. I think, to ensure quality, one should not sacrifice the principle of contributing to knowledge and originality of work at doctorate level. Third, there has been concern about the proliferation of titles. Although I sympathize with this, I do not worry about the number of qualifications providing that the resulting works are high quality and of the required standard. No doubt, a proliferation of titles will attract more people to apply for doctorate programmes. This does not mean that standards will be lowered. However, it does necessitate that the areas of interest defined by the new titles be carefully tailored to the needs of industry and people – more people than those who are already involved. Hence, the real question is not qualification inflation but the quality of qualification, which is not to be compromised at all. This is why I insist that 'originality and contribution to knowledge' should remain two of the main criteria and defining factors at the doctorate level.

PhDs and professional doctorates operating at the threshold of theory and practice, exploring the potential of design knowledge, developing the language and knowledge of the artefactual for the third domain and searching for possibilities of personal and consensus-based knowledge promise new perspectives in art and design. They will probably lead towards work that is not only new but also full of promises.

SECTION TWO
HISTORY

Design history has developed immensely in the UK thanks to the annual conferences of the Design History Society, its journal and works of distinguished scholars such as Adrian Forty, Clive Dilnot, Gillian Naylor, Grace Lees-Maffei, Guy Julier, Hazel Conway, John Heskett, Jonathan Woodham, Judy Attfield, Kjetil Fallan, Penny Sparke, Tim Putnam, Tony Fry and so on. Therefore, the chapters in this section are nothing more than a modest contribution to the field from an outsider who gives examples of design history research, methodology and historiography with a different view.

Chapter 6 explores the term 'design' and its transformation in the UK. This provides a useful perspective regarding its development and the emergence of various design-related professions and disciplines. Chapter 7 proposes another way of looking into design history by tracing mentality changes. For this purpose, it focuses on the writings of John Gloag to show how his ideas improved over time and how these changes in his thinking furnished us with new knowledge about the perception of design in society.

Chapter 8 focuses on research concerning the rise of design historiography in the UK, which is a continuation of the previous two in providing insights and presenting how British design history flourished. Chapters 9, 10 and 11, however, consider Turkish design. Thus, this history section contains research about both the UK and Turkey, reflecting the author's Turkish origin and his extensive research activities in London. Since the examples come from both the UK and Turkey, it inevitably raises issues regarding the relationship between British and Turkish design, and two significant current debates: decolonising and transnational design history. Where should we place these chapters in this context?

The relationship between British and Turkish design is not new. Its early culmination goes back to the 1851 Great Exhibition, where the Ottoman Pavilion was one of the centres of attraction. Although this relationship requires further detailed study, there are a few points worth underlining. For instance, Sir Alec Issigonis, the designer of the Morris Mini-Minor was born in Izmir, Turkey, while the first mass-produced Turkish car, the Anadol, designed by Reliant and Ogle, arrived in Turkey in 1966. Rıfat Özbek, Bora Aksu and Hussein Chalayan are famous names in the UK fashion world while the British designer Ross Lovegrove is responsible for many products of the Turkish company VitrA.[1]

---

[1] The Turkish company VitrA is different than the other similarly named furniture company Vitra which gives a brief explanation in its website about this coincidence:

> VitrA is a company that constitutes part of the Turkish Eczacibasi Group which has produced tiles and sanitary ceramics and distributed these globally since 1942. The name similarity with the brand name vitra is coincidental; both companies developed entirely separately from one another. A friendly exchange presently exists between both companies, but there are no commercial links. http://www.vitra.com.tr/

Regarding the academic relationship in design, the author had the opportunity to meet Sir David Carter, Prof Frank Height and Prof John Heskett in the UK in late 1987 thanks to Michael Preston, who was a senior member of the exhibition department of the Science Museum, London. These well-known figures were invited to Turkey and delivered a series of lectures that had a considerable impact on industrial design students at Middle East Technical University in late 1987 and 1988. Later, Prof Bruce Archer was involved in design research activities in Istanbul and Ankara. Thanks to the strong networks established over the years, many Turkish professors of design completed their PhDs in the UK, and some are now heads of university departments and have published well-regarded academic papers.[2]

At the end of the 1990s, the author was instrumental in organising a conference on Turkish Design at the Architectural Association, where Marco Susani, Defne Koz and John Langrish delivered speeches. The British Council had organized similar activities in Turkey. Nowadays, there are so many British and Turkish architects and designers operating in both countries that it is a hard task to list them. The relationship between British and Turkish design and its effects have become rather complicated, which needs further exploration, perhaps in a comparative study. When the papers in this section were written, a comparative study was never on the agenda, as Turkish product design was still in its infancy and globalization was a mainstream matter preoccupying intellectuals as decolonizing and transnational history do today.

In a broad sense, colonization probably started in ancient times when a group of people migrated and occupied the lands of the indigenous people. We witness this in each period of world history. Perhaps the word gained its current meaning after Columbus's discovery of the New World, which enabled European countries to establish colonies in America, Africa, the Far East, Australia and New Zealand. As a result, local resources were exploited, and Western values were imposed on indigenous cultures. Such anti-democratic and imperialist moves are criticized today while decolonizing design has been introduced as a vehicle to appreciate local values, products, techniques, experiences, views and so on, and to incorporate diversity and inclusion. The term decolonization itself is also problematic and widely discussed. As Dori Tunstall, Dean of Design at the Ontario College of Art and Design University, puts it, 'Diversity is getting the invitation to the party. Inclusion is if someone asks if you want to dance. Decolonizing is allowing the most vulnerable to choose the music, plan the food, etc. for the party' (Tunstall, 2020).

In this respect, it would be rather interesting to read some chapters in this section with these debates about decolonizing in mind since Turkey was never colonized and the Ottomans had not colonized at all. That is, although the Ottomans occupied huge territories in Europe, Asia, North Africa and the Middle East, they mostly retained local systems and were satisfied with governing the people and collecting taxes.

---

[2] I would like to list a few holders of PhDs from the UK who serve in academia in Turkey: Alpay Er, Özlem Er, Naz A. G. Z. Börekçi, Gülay Hasdoğan, Bahar Şener Pedgley and Harun Kaygan.

If, however, decolonizing design means removing white or Eurocentric thinking in design, this is another issue. Westernization was introduced to the Ottomans in the nineteenth century, with all kinds of styles emerging in architecture, including Baroque, Rococo, eclecticism and Art Nouveau. The question is the extent that Westernization overlaps with colonization in a country that was never colonized. If a country's leaders decide that Westernization provides a means to progress and therefore adopt and apply its various institutions, systems, sciences, technologies and values, can the result be considered indirect colonization or a new state with its own structure and merit? The latter is the case for Turkey.

Thus, it is neither reasonable nor possible to connect the following chapters on Turkish design with decolonization. Furthermore, decolonization design has never been a focus of discussion within the Turkish intellectual milieu. What surfaced instead as a consequence of Westernization is the question of design identity and its link with heritage, tradition and local culture. The first and second national architectural design movements in Turkey are two examples while design identity remains an issue, particularly among product designers.

While in my experience, decolonization is not applicable to Turkey, transnational history is essential to understand design developments in depth. Considering how cosmopolitan the Ottomans were and how Turkey exists at the crossroads of many cultures and under the influx of immigrants today, transnational historiography is becoming essential. To this end, Chapter 9 considers examples from architecture while encouraging new researchers to take transnational historiography seriously.

Chapter 10 studies Turkish graphic design in the republican era, categorizes works in terms of their style and characteristics, and analyses some to justify the argument. Finally, Chapter 11 narrates the story of the 4T: Design and Design History Society in Turkey in which the author played a major role. At first sight, these last three chapters are not directly linked – in contrast to the first three chapters on UK design, which were derived from the author's PhD and subsequent research work. The last three chapters in this section, which surfaced out of distinct interests, touch on different aspects of Turkish design while giving key information and introducing new insights into three diverse areas.

CHAPTER 6
ON TRANSFORMATIONS OF THE TERM DESIGN WITH REFERENCE TO MASS-PRODUCED OBJECTS

The first version of this chapter was published in Design, Industry and Turkey. *See: Balcioglu, T. (1994), 'On Transformations of the Term Design with Reference to Mass Produced Objects', in* Design, Industry and Turkey, *253–263, G. Hasdogan (ed), Ankara: Middle East Technical University*

In this chapter,[1] I will first present the crucial elements of this analysis. There will be two arguments: a) the impossibility of reaching an agreed meaning of design because of the term's very nature and, consequently, b) the transformation of design in line with technological change and in relation to the development of other design fields.

Using this initial framework, I will then scrutinize the term design in the context of mass-produced objects. I will introduce three phases of the term design. The first corresponds to the period when design has a broad content. The second describes a period when design was misinterpreted under the influence of the French word *dessin*. The third concerns the rise and absolute dominance of the word design over other expressions in the field.

To begin, I would like to look at the design concept first since, without having a view of design, it is impossible to perceive the transformation. To understand design is also to set the parameters and describe the fluctuating boundaries of the field. However, this is not as easy as it looks due to the lack of consensus on what design is. This surfaces immediately in texts dealing with the subject. Writers are aware of it and quick to draw our attention to the matter.

For example, Clive Dilnot offered what is probably the first critical analysis of design history decades ago in an article entitled 'The State of Design History'. He pointed out the difficulty: 'design has acquired several different, often seemingly contradictory, meanings and associations' (Dilnot, 1984a).

Five years later, in 1989, John Walker published a book entitled *Design History and History of Design*. He claimed that 'there is not yet a consensus concerning the meaning and scope of the term/concept "design"' (Walker, 1989). In 1993 Paris witnessed a comprehensive exhibition with a substantial catalogue offering a 100-year account of

---

[1]This chapter is an extension of ideas developed in my PhD dissertation presented at METU in 1993.

industrial design history. The author of the forward written for the catalogue was Sir Terence Conran, the design guru of the 1970s and 1980s, the creator of Habitat and Mothercare, and the founding figure of the Design Museum in London. He made a very similar statement. After asking what design is, he responded that it causes confusion to many people and means different things to them. He underlined that a great deal of people had tried to define its meaning and according to him, some attempts were made with great erudition, some with simple good intentions and some with malice (Conran, 1993).

These quotations are sufficient to show that there is still no agreed definition and conception of design. Why are we deprived of a common perception on this matter? What are the reasons for the lack of consensus? What are the particulars of the concept that stop us from finding a common ground for a definition? Despite widespread complaints about the lack of consensus, these questions can hardly find convincing answers. Dilnot, in his aforementioned article, tried to provide an explanation. According to him, it was 'because of its [that is, design's] refraction through the still incompletely chartered and understood industrial, economic, and cultural developments of the past 200 years' (Dilnot, 1984b).

Victor Margolin, an American scholar and editor of the journal *Design Issues*, has made similar observations. He writes that 'Designing is an activity that is constantly changing' (Margolin, 1992).

I think these points are important and need to be explored. Several factors contribute to the formation of the profession we call design today and any changes within them affect its meaning. First, design consciousness – that is, a systematic way of looking at the subject, its education, professional bodies and literature – was developed mostly in the West, at a certain cultural, socioeconomic and technological level. Hence, design has always remained dependent upon these levels and has varied with respect to them. Later, when design was introduced to other countries in the same way that had allowed it to flourish in the West, it took on a different shape and was interpreted according to these countries' needs and means. It became a political and ideological term as well as an economic one.

Technological progress is undoubtedly the dominant cause of the proliferation of new design areas. The variety of objects produced during the twentieth century is so vast that, with the introduction of new objects, the field of design expands naturally. When these new objects are accepted and established in society, their continued production, together with the expertise and specialism they offer, is guaranteed. It is normal to expect that these design specialisms may define their own area of operation in due course and have their discrete title as a discrete profession. It is also normal to expect that, with the annexation of new design areas, the design concept develops new meanings and is subjected to change. The widening of the areas where design operates means broadening the content of design and thereby modifying the term. Since both the understanding and developments of industry and technology vary, their intervention and impacts on design alter accordingly. Hence, different definitions are inevitable and seem intrinsic to the characteristics of the term.

Although the West is credited for the rise of design awareness, one should not assume that the design concept and the term have identical connotations in all Western countries. *Formgebung* (that is, 'form giving' in German) is not the same as *disegno* in Italian or *esthétique industrielle* in French. Jacques Guillerme, in his article 'Design in the First Machine Age', accentuated that the word design has been used recently for what was earlier known as *esthétique industrielle*, and he claims that these terms do not mean the same thing (Guillerme, 1993). Therefore, it is logical to conclude that what we understand by design has a different etymology and history in each country or even in every design circle. The concept's dynamic and dialectic kernel thus avoids any generalization by not referring to a specific time and place. Having recognized this, we can now talk about the word transformation regarding design.

The abundance of meanings and changing interpretations of the term design encourage us to investigate it from a historical perspective. Examining its patterns of variation from past to present shows not only changes in meanings but also its ramifications and the proliferation of new design vocabularies, terms, expressions, areas, activities and professions. All these aspects of design have a mutual and interactive relationship with design and within themselves. It is this web of lineage and its changing fabric that forms the transformation of design. Within this framework, transformation means converting various sets of relationships with and within design and design-related fields over time. In this particular sense, transformation neither corresponds to development nor to progress or linear evolution. Rather, it is just a change in the pattern of a set of relations and meanings.

After this somewhat lengthy introduction to the key elements of the subject, it is time to review the transformation of the design concept in Britain. From my reading of literature, I identify three easily discernible phases. The first is the period when design accommodates comprehensive and spacious meanings. In the second, there is a withdrawal, a pullback, a reduction in content, limited use and subordination. The third phase is when design comes to the fore to cover a wide area and dominate as a ruling term. Obviously, this is the panorama when one views the past from the perspective of the present. That is, I wish to reconstruct a story of how design acquired the meaning it has today.

The first phase corresponds to the early use of design. In his book *Design*, Anthony Bertram confidently proposes a date and a clear meaning: 'by 1588 the word "design" had the meaning "Purpose, aim, intention": by 1657 the meaning "The thing aimed at"' (Bertram, 1938: 12). In the sixteenth century, the word was employed by Shakespeare.[2] In *Love's Labour Lost*, he uses the word in the last sentence of a love letter written by Don Adriono de Armado: 'Thine, in the dearest design of industry' (Shakespeare, 1988: 142). This probably means something like 'yours, with best intentions at your service'.[3]

---

[2]'Shakespeare also used the word 'design' in his other plays, such as in *The Tragedy of King Richard II* and *Macbeth*. What I find alluring here is the coincidence that design and industry, two inseparable words of contemporary design literature, were actually uttered together, centuries ago, in such a different context.
[3]Here, design reads as intention, purpose and aims. Industry, according to commentator Richard David stands for 'assiduity in ladies' service' or 'careful and kind diligence' (1966: 69).

From our point of view, probably the most interesting contribution to the content of the term was made by Jean-Jacques Rousseau, the famous French philosopher of the eighteenth century. Rousseau published *A Musical Dictionary* (1768) in which he defined design as 'the invention and conduct of a subject, the disposition of each part, and the general direction of the whole' (Rousseau, 1779: 116).[4] Rousseau was thus highlighting the significance of part-whole relationship to achieve a unity in a subject:

> It is not sufficient to compose beautiful airs [that is, melodies][5] and a pleasing harmony. All this must be conjoined by a principal subject, to which all the parts of the work must be connected, and by which it may become one. Thus unity should reign in every air [that is, melody], in the movement, the character, the harmony, and the modulation. The whole must have reference to one general idea, which unites it.
>
> (Rousseau, 1779: 116)

His description of design was a theoretical enterprise rather than an attempt to attribute a new meaning or introduce a new application. Rousseau converted the term into a concept by analysing what constituted design and by proposing principles for its formation. In 1771, the first edition of the Encyclopaedia Britannica presented a variety of meanings and situations in which design was used. (Rousseau's interpretation was included later in the second edition.) It described design as 'the plan, order, representation, or construction of a building, book, painting, etc.' (EB, 1771: 418–419). The figures applied to fabrics, carpets and so on were also called design as well as contours or outlines of the figures in painting, which owe much to the interpretations of *disegno* in the Italian Renaissance.[6]

All these meanings referring to various fields of production enriched the content of design in the late eighteenth century. From today's vantage point design in this era was a broad term, mature enough to cover several aspects of the subject. One might assume that design would have become the leading term in the following century, when the fruits of industrialization began reaching the people, mainly as mass-produced objects. This is the corollary I deduce after reviewing the first phase of design.

However, the second phase of design is full of evidence that challenges the impression given in the first. That is, the term design is stripped of its potential power, loses its strong

---

[4] I quote from: Monf. J. J. Rousseau, *Dictionary of Music* (trans. by William Waring) London: Printed for J. French, 1779 (?), 116. The original: J. J. Rousseau, *Dictionnaire de Musique* Paris: M DCC LXVIII (Chez la VEUE DUCHESNE, Libraire, rue Saint Jacques, au Temple du Gout).

[5] My addition.

[6] Baxandall expresses clearly that 'disegno' has also caused theoretical confusion for Italian artists. According to him, Leon Battista Alberti, the great architect of the era,

> was trapped with the ambiguity of the term disegno'. Piero della Francesca, a well-known painter, approached the problem by surveying the principles of painting: 'Painting contains three principal parts, which we call disegno, measurement and colouring. By disegno we mean profiles and contours which enclose objects. By measurement we mean the profiles and contours put proportionally in their proper places. By colouring we mean how colours show themselves on objects, lights and darks as the lighting changes them.
>
> (Baxandall, ([1991] (1972): 141)

position and is subjected to limited use. Throughout the nineteenth century, its low profile remains in the background of a debate concerning art and industry.[7] The idea that the word design was not at the axis of discussions in the nineteenth century contradicts the common belief of today. Nevertheless, it is true that the controversial terms were art and industry while the other terms created and involved in the debate were fine art, decorative art, ornamental art, art manufacture, commercial art, industrial art, applied art and so on.

Why was design as a term deprived of its leading role in the nineteenth century? Why was it ignored as a major term despite being available with its full capacity and potential? Most likely these questions have several answers. However, the one I would like to highlight here is the misleading and confusing meaning of design, which was imported 'successfully' from France. The confusion lies with the French word *dessin*, which then only meant drawing. I believe that this association and identification of design with *dessin* (that is, drawing in English), created a minefield for the term and led people to use it cautiously.

Historically, the French connection has always existed, with well-known figures of the time expressing their admiration of French products. For example, the distinguished eighteenth-century painter William Hogarth wrote to a member of parliament in 1735 to express his concern about the aesthetic qualities of British products in comparison to those of France.

> That this is not merely a Romantic Notion, will appear from the remarkable Preference which is given to the French in everything of this sort they send over to us. Our own Furniture, our own Silks, our own Manufacturers are as useful as theirs; but not so elegant, not so well fancied, nor our patterns so well Designed.
>
> (Hogben, 1983: viii) [8]

In 1766, architect John Gywnn made a similar remark:

> Happy would it be for this country if we imitated the French in that patriotic prejudice for their own productions which has rendered them the arbiters of taste to Europe, the rewards and honours paid to the artists of their own nation, have been the great incitement of every work of genius for which they are distinguished.
>
> (Gwynn, 1766: 32)

The issue of British products' quality continued to be discussed, with Sir Robert Peel raising the same argument in the House of Commons in 1832. A few years later, in 1835,

---

[7] In an article published in *Journal of Design History*, v: 4, n: 4, 1991, David Irwin prefers to name the art and industry debate as 'Art versus Design: The Debate 1760–1860'. However, he accepts the 'imprecise meaning of a modern term such as "industrial design" when used in the period under discussion'. In my reading, he studies the debate using the modern concept of design rather than the actual terminology used in those discussions.

[8] This quotation from Hogarth was cited by Carol Hogben, in the 'Introduction' to *British Art and Design*, London: Victoria & Albert Museum, 1984 (Catalogue, first published in 1983) viii.

a Select Committee was formed under Mr Ewart 'to examine the state of art in this and other countries as manifested in their different manufacturers. To see how a knowledge of the arts and the principles of design might best be spread among the people. And to find the best ways of advancing the higher branches of art at the same time' (Hogben, 1983: viii). The Select Committee's report opened the way for the establishment of the Normal School of Design in London in 1837. William Dyce was appointed its director following his visit to several European cities, including Paris, Lyon and Berlin.

All these examples show that links were already established and that there were good grounds for allowing the word design to be translated and thereby confused with *dessin*. According to Quentin Bell, the writer of *The Schools of Design*, a misleading parallel between the word design and the French *dessin* occurred when the school was founded. The performance of the school may have influenced the use of this misleading image of design. Nikolaus Pevsner writes that, in 1848, a Parliamentary Committee investigating the system introduced by the school concluded that it was 'an utter and complete failure' ([1940] 1973: 248). They reported critically that the main exercise seemed to be copying drawings.

Under those circumstances, it would have been very peculiar to advocate a new image for the word design. When Henry Cole, founder of the *Journal of Design and Manufactures*, was asked to organize a new school after the closure of the Normal School of Design, he proposed that the name should be changed to provide a clearer definition. His concern was made explicit in a letter he sent to the Board of Trade in 1852. 'I would venture to suggest that the name of the "School of Design" which is subjected to misinterpretation, should be altered to one more nearly expressive of the objects in view. Such a name as the "Department of Practical Art" would, I think, be well understood and appropriate' (Cole, 1884: 296). He was absolutely right to indicate the risk of employing a confusing term. An essay published in The Gentlemen's Magazine in 1856 included the remark that government drawing schools had been a 'facetiously styled, "School of Design"'.[9] It appears that the confusion between *design* and *dessin* stayed for a long time in the public domain. The following text from the Times, published on 7 October 1876, tries to separate design from *dessin* by differentiating the two meanings:

> All the drawing schools in France were called 'Ecoles de Dessin' which, as is well known, means 'Schools for Drawing' and not necessarily 'Schools of Design'. However, the justification of the Board of Trade's inquiring into these schools, was that information as to 'design' – an important element in the commerce of fancy articles – was required in England.
>
> (Cole, 1884: 281)[10]

---

[9]Later, the essay also claims that the schools failed to create 'an English school of ornament, or, probably an English Style'.
[10]The last sentence is notable for its somewhat archaic description of design as 'an important element in the commerce of fancy articles'.

To conclude this description of the second phase, when design was often confused with *dessin*, we should mention briefly the other terms that proliferated to address the problematic marriage of art and industry. Henry Cole claims that he invented 'the term "art manufacturers" meaning Fine Art, or beauty applied to mechanical production' and that Prince Albert coined the term 'Fine Art applied to Industry' (Cole, 1884: 104). Applied art, industrial art, decorative art, ornamental art and so on were popular and widely used terms, especially after the Great Exhibition of 1851. In 1886, in a lecture entitled 'Of the Origins of Ornamental Art', William Morris, after describing 'a mass of wealth-producing labour', said 'this labour is called what I should almost venture to name in our modern jargon the Industrial Arts' (1969: 137–138). A year later, in 1887, Walter Crane listed them: 'We have "industrial", "decorative", or "applied art", as we call it, and "fine" art' (1887: 717). There is no need to prolong this lexicon, but what is worth emphasizing is that almost all art and industry debate was conducted using this terminology, which rarely included the word design.

In the third phase, we see the triumphant return of design and its overwhelming domination, which grew steadily during and especially towards the end of the twentieth century. At the beginning of the twentieth century, design was far removed from any association with *dessin*, and no reference was made to it, thanks to writers, theorists and 'designers' such as William Morris, Walter Crane, Lewis Day and W. R. Lethaby. However, by the time the Design and Industries Association had been established in 1915, its credibility had already been restored. That is, design had begun to enjoy its pre-nineteenth-century rich content and came to the fore while its meaning began to be explored. The stylish expression of art and industry was gradually losing its place to design and industry – although there was resistance. The problem was the difficulty of abandoning the banner of art as artists have always enjoyed the high status of their field while 'designers' were used to calling themselves artists not designers. Thus, when Lethaby presented a complex notion of design at the Design and Industries Meeting in 1915 he faced a reaction from the audience. He 'had sometimes defined design as "the arranging of how the work is to be done" but this annoyed the people who loved to be told that design is the organization of beauty, embodying style by creative genius e.t.c.' (DIA, 1915: 5). Beauty, style, creative genius and so on, that is what some people wanted to hear – an obvious reference to art. In the inaugural pamphlet of the Design and Industries Association (DIA), entitled *Design in Industry*, 'Lethaby managed to avoid using the dangerous word art almost entirely from the start to finish,' as Noel Carrington (1976: 30) spotted. Actually, Lethaby distanced the DIA from the traditional art and industry dispute, which had strong links to the Arts and Crafts Movement. By doing so, he not only endorsed the word design but also attributed to it a new identity and status, independent of that of art.

These pioneering efforts needed time to develop. Furthermore, two popular terms survived from the jumble of nineteenth-century vocabulary: industrial art and applied art. Both terms were widely discussed. 'There has been much talk in recent years of *applied art*' said Serge Chermayeff (1982: 24) in 1933 while the writer Arthur Pulos commented that Robert W. de Forest, President of the Metropolitan Museum of Art in the 1920s, 'felt that although industrial art was not quite appropriate title, it might have to be used' (1983: 318). In England, the Committee on Art and Industry under Lord Gorell prepared a report in 1932 that expressed concern about the terms ornamental art and applied art since both 'gave colour to the pernicious notion that Art is something superficial and extraneous to be "applied" to an industrial product, instead of being an essential and organic element in the article itself' (Read, ([1934] 1956: 192–193).

While these two terms were being worn out through these discussions, a new one found relatively quick acceptance among the public: industrial design. Industrial design gained respect in the United States in the late 1920s thanks to some flamboyant designers, such as Walter Dorwin Teague, Raymond Loewy, Norman Bel Geddes and Henry Dreyfuss. Obviously, the British public was not unaware of the expression, which was used occasionally. However, I have not come across any argument about this term in British literature before the 1930s. American scholars believe it was developed in the United States. However, the oldest text I have found referring to industrial design is a British book from 1894.[11] Whatever its origins, the term's practical consequences remain the same: it was recognized in the United States and known in the UK as early as the mid-1930s. The literature has since gained impetus, with books using industrial design as the title and subject published in both the United States and the UK.

Design also became a very popular expression. It already had its own area of dominance in the realm of architecture and architectural texts but soon became an expression linked with the objects of daily life. In Britain, it was also promoted by the magazine *Design for Today* and on design programmes on the radio and became common parlance. However, industrial design was initially the winning term, leaving behind the two worn-out expressions of industrial art and applied art. American influence may well have encouraged the acceptance of industrial design in the UK (Gloag, 1946). This acceptance also reflected the establishment of professional associations, including the Industrial Designers Institute and the Society of Industrial Designers in the United States and the UK's Council of Industrial Design, formed in 1944.

To cut a long story short, I would say that industrial design has enjoyed its popularity for a few decades more. Another sign of change was detected at the beginning of the 1960s, when the Society of Industrial Artists changed its name to the Society of Industrial Artists and Designers (MacCarthy, 1982: 149) Over the course of time, several fields of what was once referred to as industrial design gained recognition under discrete titles because of the inevitable and rapid growth of specialisms, such as furniture design, vehicle or transport design, and packaging. After all, the emergence of the term product design not only created confusion with industrial design but also somehow ended its

---

[11] The writer, Frank G. Jackson, employed the term industrial design in the book, *Theory and Practice of Design: An Advanced Text-Book on Decorative Art* where he explains novelty in design: 'Industrial designers are so accustomed to the elaborate decorative objects which are current, that the reasons for the particular forms they have assumed are rarely sought after; and, if a new design is wanted for an old purpose, a mere alteration or rearrangement of part is held to be sufficient to effect a new pattern' (1894: 3).

dominance. These specialisms obviously already incorporated the word 'design' in their titles since they were all part of a general design discipline. That is, design is an umbrella expression covering all these fields.

The official leadership of design was declared when the UK's Council of Industrial Design was renamed the Design Council in 1973. What has happened since then is another story.

CHAPTER 7
MAPPING THE MIND
TRACING THE MENTALITY CHANGE

First presented at 'No Guru, No Method', International Conference on Art and Design Research, 4–6 September 1996, University of Art and Design, Helsinki.

Do not ask who I am and do not ask me to remain the same

Michel Foucault ([1969] 1974: 17)

7.1 Introduction

Concepts have their own history. During the process of emergence, development, maturation and fatigue, they are subjected to various interpretations, descriptions and definitions. It is probably fair to say that the history of a concept mostly comprises the history of its transformation and the consensus formed. Both transformations and the forming of conceptual consensus within a community endure for a period of time during which the process itself gains importance, and becomes significant and revealing. Accurate dating is neither possible nor desirable because events have yet to be defined but remain as a flow of thoughts, opinions, ideas and understandings spread over a time span. Therefore, studies dealing with the development of concepts need to focus on the processes of mapping. These, I think, require theoretical tools devised for this purpose.

What I attempted to do was to look at one particular person's understanding of one particular subject and to observe how this view was altered, and/or modified over the years. The first task is to identify an institute, an association, a group or an individual involved in the subject who has made many statements on the issue. We are seeking gradual variations in the view of this particular institution or person. It is therefore essential to locate as many written or recorded sources as possible to make a fair comparison. These include films, speeches, statements, notes, letters, interviews, papers, books and articles, wherever possible in translated versions and, the different editions – especially those with differences – because they are the prime sources to trace changes in an author's thoughts.

7.2 A survey: John Gloag and the concept of industrial design

Before going into the details and analysing the use of the method and its pros and cons, I would like to begin with a short case study. I have chosen John Gloag (1896–1981), who was a prolific writer and had an opportunity to witness the rise of design culture in the UK from the 1920s. In 1947, he introduced himself in his book, *Self Training for Industrial Designers*:

> Here are the facts: I studied architecture in 1911–12, went into business as a junior draughtsman in a studio in 1913, changed over to the selling side of the business which interested me more, and after service in the 1914–18 war, I went into advertising and technical journalism. I also taught myself how to write books, because I wanted to write books, both technical books and novels; I was also interested in organization and in industry and educational propaganda. This sounds like the set up for a jack-of-all-trades: but I have become a writer: between 1921 and 1945, I published thirty-six books, fourteen of which are works of fiction, the rest dealing with such technical subjects as architecture and industrial design.
>
> (1947a: 22)

John Gloag continued to write, producing over ninety books in the following decades. I will probe the ideas of John Gloag on two subjects: first, the formation of the concept of 'industrial design' in the UK; second, the British intelligentsia's understanding of industrial design and designers. Let us begin with the meaning and definition of industrial design and follow its progress through his eyes.

7.3 John Gloag: The meaning of industrial design

In 1934, Gloag writes in *Industrial Art Explained*:

> The growth of mechanised industry during the last hundred and fifty years has affected our surroundings and the articles we use every day. It is the purpose of this book to show how design has affected:
> 1. The accommodation of industry
> 2. The products of industry, and,
> 3. The distribution of those products to the public.
>
> The term *industrial architecture* will be used for the first category; *industrial art* will apply to the second, and *commercial art* will cover the third. Reference will also be made to the nature and the development of what may be called *machine design*.
>
> (1934: 33)

Here, Gloag uses the term industrial art to indicate what we nowadays call 'product design'. It is worth remembering that, at the beginning of the twentieth century, industrial art was the popular expression to represent the area we currently name industrial or product design.[1] Therefore Gloag's definition was not unusual. Yet the third edition of *Industrial Art Explained*, published in 1946, has significant revisions and enlargements. Gloag writes:

> The term *Industrial Art* is used throughout this book to describe the visible results of our industrial civilisation which have been or could be affected by the operation of design. It is a comprehensive term; but it covers a subject which may be conveniently divided for study, such divisions being determined by the character of industry, its service and its needs. Three main divisions are thus suggested:
>
> 1. Industrial design.
> 2. Commercial art.
> 3. Industrial architecture.
>
> (Gloag, 1946: 17)

Comparing this passage with the previous excerpt, we discover that the term 'industrial art' is now interpreted as having a higher status in comparison to his first edition. According to Gloag, it covers great variety of design activities and appears as an umbrella term with three subdivisions. Industrial design, commercial art and industrial architecture. 'Machine design' is withdrawn.

The following amendments are discernible. (a) Industrial art has been elevated to the level of a main concept covering all other three divisions. (b) Where 'machine design' disappears, 'industrial design' is introduced. (c) The order of subdivisions is also modified: 'industrial architecture' moves from the first to the last and 'industrial design' proceeds to the first rank in the list. What interests us here is the recognition and the use of the term 'industrial design', its position among the others and if there is a sense of priority in the list. This was not the first time Gloag acknowledges the term 'industrial design'. Two years before, when he published *Plastics and Industrial Design* in 1945, Gloag gives his own account of what it is:

> Industrial design becomes a basic operation in the production of goods when trained imagination is introduced to secure the most efficient, agreeable and inventive use of appropriate materials and processes. The industrial designer is the man with the trained imagination; he is a technician, and his work is just as basically important as that of the research chemist or the production specialist. Omit the designer, and you have omitted imagination, and very often lost the chance of gaining a new market or reviving and extending an old one.

---

[1] The difference between industrial design and product design is a matter for another discussion. I try to avoid it here for it does not directly relate to the subject and is not relevant to those years mentioned.

There are two divisions of industrial design, and I put them in this order of importance:

1. Design which is concerned with the *form* and *function* of a manufactured object and which determines the selection of materials and fabricating processes. It is for this division that the industrial designer works primarily, though his interest and activity are often carried into the second division
2. Industrial decorative art, which is concerned with the creating of *decorative patterns* and the use of colours and textures in relation to such patterns.

(Gloag, 1945: 46–47)

There is no doubt that, by the mid-forties, Gloag was already preoccupied with the concept of 'industrial design', reflections of which can easily be traced in his subsequent publications. The status of 'industrial design' changes soon after this time to reach a more prestigious position in Gloag's understanding, as presented in *Self Training for Industrial Designers*, published in 1947. He explains the term with a new insight: 'Industrial design, or, as it is sometimes more loosely termed, industrial art, may be classified under these divisions: – (1) Industrial design and (2) Commercial art' (1947a: 16).

Here, he has begun to associate industrial design more closely with industrial art. The former acquired an increased popularity whereas the latter lost ground. In the same year, Gloag rephrased the same paragraph in another book. When *Good Design Good Business* came out, it was clear that he identified industrial design with industrial art:

Industrial design, which has sometimes been called industrial art, may be classified broadly under two main divisions, each subdivided into various sections, which are affected by its operation. The two main divisions may be headed:

1. INDUSTRIAL DESIGN
2. COMMERCIAL DESIGN.

(1947b: 4)

In spite of these alterations, both versions continue to present a slight problem, although this did not seem to annoy Gloag much. Yet, his taxonomy, hierarchy or ranking of terms is problematic. How could one of the subdivisions of industrial design be shown as industrial design itself? In other words, how could, let us say, A is equal to A plus B ($A=A+B$)? We can find other inconsistencies in his adjustments. For example, commercial art is now shown as to be commercial design. Is it the result of a purely logical deduction that 'industrial art' is substituted with 'industrial design' and that 'commercial art' should be replaced with 'commercial design'? Or does this simply demonstrate that the word design is becoming more popular, prestigious, definable and thereby an acceptable expression? I do not know the answer. However, what is clear to me is that the way in which the concept of industrial design, and design in general, have gradually gained recognition.

The difficult problem to elucidate is how these shifts in Gloag's idea occurred. It is useful to point out that Gloag's visit to the United States seems to have been very influential in the development of his ideas in the mid-forties. The foreword to the third, revised edition of *Industrial Art Explained* provides enough evidence for this assertion. He states: 'It [the first edition of *Industrial Art Explained*] was written before I had visited the United States and had acquired first-hand experience of the operation of industrial design in America. When I was invited to prepare a revised edition, I soon realised that the book demanded re-writing' (Gloag, 1946: 5).

So far, we have examined changes in John Gloag's vision of industrial design. The second issue that I would like to explore in his texts is the way he perceived the inception and the establishment of industrial design in the UK.

7.4 John Gloag: The acceptance of industrial design in the UK

Gloag makes a remark on the subject in *The English Tradition in Design* published in 1947.

> That industrial design was a subject demanding intelligent study and attention was an idea that gained acceptance only after an infinitude of misunderstandings; but in 1914 it had achieved official recognition, for in that year a joint scheme was framed and sponsored by the Board of Trade and the Board of Education for establishing a British Institute of Industrial Art, which was actually launched in 1920… Industrial design had certainly been discovered and identified by a few far-sighted and exceptional people at the end of the First World War.
>
> (Gloag, 1947c: 32)

After being revised, these sentences reappear as follows in the 1959 edition of *The English Tradition in Design*:

> The idea that industrial design was a subject demanding intelligent study and attention, slowly gained acceptance. By 1914 it had achieved official recognition, for in that year a scheme was framed and sponsored jointly by the Board of Trade and the Board of Education for establishing a British Institute of Industrial Art, which was actually launched in 1920.
>
> Industrial design had certainly been discovered though not clearly identified by a few far-sighted and exceptional people by the end of the First World War.
>
> (1959: 75)

The differences between these texts are subtle, but I do not think that the implications can be ignored. Gloag certainly changed his opinion and made cautious comments in later years. Although this amendment was featured in the 1959 edition, it had already been articulated in 1950 in an article entitled, 'Identity and Development of Industrial Design', printed in the journal *Eidos*.

> Industrial design in Britain has only been clearly identified as a technical subject during the second quarter of this century, before about 1925 it was difficult to classify and appraise its manifestations, which were still confused with the results, variously accomplished and desirable, of the handicraft revival that had been brought forth by William Morris in the eighteen sixties, and subsequently nourished by his disciples. This confusion prevented the industrial designer from being recognised as a technician.
>
> (1950: 34)

In the same article, after writing about the establishment in 1915 of the Design and Industries Association, Gloag continues: 'Nine years later, writers and critics were still failing to identify the industrial designer' (1950: 34). He tries to determine when industrial design gained its identity and why its emergence was delayed although Britain was the world's first industrialized country.

7.5 Characteristics of the method

It is probably time to end my survey and discuss the characteristics of the method used. Before proceeding, however, it is worth mentioning that I am not the only one employing this method and I do not think that it is entirely novel. Nevertheless, it is at least a systematic analysis.[2] While conducting my research and developing ideas, I encountered

---

[2] There are systematic methods of research based on a work of details and, in one sense, similar and inspirational to the one I employed here. For instance, historian Carlo Ginzburg illustrates a technique of investigating reality by a 'conjectural method' inspired by that of Giovanni Morelli's theory. Morelli, an Italian art historian, had claimed that studying the details and minor points in paintings reveals much about the techniques of painters so that, on the grounds of similarity in particular details, paintings can be identified or their authenticity checked. From studying details like hands, ear lobes, fingernails, toes and so on, he made new attributions, such as identifying Giorgione's painting in the Dresden Gallery, which for years had exhibited the work as 'a copy by Sassoferrato of a lost work by Titian' (Ginzburg, 1980: 7).

Ginzburg also builds his methods on clues and hints. He analyses texts meticulously and queries '"the favourite words and phrases" which "most people, whether talking or writing, make use of without meaning to and without noticing that they do so"' (1980: 24). In the light of Morelli's and Ginzburg's approach, a technique which I suggest for textual analysis in industrial design history is allied to them with regard to the basic principle of 'forensic evidence' although it is entirely new in its kind.

to my surprise a few years ago a similar approach applied to an article written by Robin Kinross (1988). Kinross had comparatively analysed the different editions of a 'cult book', *Art and Industry*, by Herbert Read. Kinross was interested in the history of the book to the extent that he considered all modifications, such as typefaces, graphics and pictures, as well as changes in content. Although he does not attempt to systematize this effort and propose it as a method, I would consider his article a good example of what I am trying to outline here.

I am sure that, for many people, John Gloag's changing ideas are incompatible. Again, for many scholars, he may not be an ideal source. Indeed, in spite of his extensive publications, few design works cite Gloag. I do not share this attitude, however, and feel the opposite to be true. Gloag has been a wonderful source for me to apprehend and come to grips with the spirit of his era. Not only what he said, but how he formulated and revised what he said, makes him an interesting reference. He does not provide us with a kind of text on which we can rely or to which we can surrender or subscribe to. He does however supply useful material to work with, which contains large amounts of information 'between the lines' and which requires a certain effort from the reader to pick, sort and compile.

When the attributes of this method are considered, one can see that it has a potential that can be elaborated and used to pursue mentality shifts. Some of the territories where this method can be viable include determining how the opinions of institutions and people change, how concepts are formed, consensus set up, common beliefs shaped, and ideas, words and terms become popular or obsolete. Processes are important, not dates or the minutiae of events. Transformations, mutations, permutations, changes, conversions, modifications, variations, alterations, amendments and substitutions are domains that need to be focused on. Careful generalization and accuracy must be not expected. The aim of this method is not to uncover the unknown but to map mentality changes, shifts in understanding and the destination of thoughts. Polarization is essential in tracing the direction of inclinations. What we learn from this inquiry into John Gloag's work is how and to what ends his observations were gradually channelled. If we want to know more about how these occurred, we need to consult other works to grasp how the other developments of the era are explored.

The main controversy here is the unconventional way of developing a method that mainly relies on dissimilarity and contradiction. Therefore, we need to inspect closely the proposition of inconsistency, which is crucial to the argument. It is perhaps time now to pose some questions. Is this search for consistency still valid, and should it still be valid today in every field of research? Is there not an understanding of history that leaves room for a method that dares to inscribe inconsistencies while not attributing a central importance to documented facts representing the 'truth', whatever the truth means? Is it really impossible for researchers to benefit from texts or ideas considered to be at variance? The answers are found in contemporary literature. To address the first question, I refer to Hans Magnus Enzensberger.

7.6 Inconsistency: Rising status

Enzensberger is one of the writers who cast a shadow on the concept of consistency as a logical category. He shows how consistency can lead to fatal consequences: 'Consistency as a logical category, is empty' (1990: 5). One can be a consistent thief, a smoker, a racist, a rapist or stalker. 'It is therefore not quite clear how consistency could ever lay claim to the status of a moral postulate,' says Enzensberger. Attributing prestige and value to inconsistency is not to defend it nor to attack rational thinking.[3] Rather, it is a phenomenon whose presence cannot be denied. Hence, we have to accept it and find ways to benefit from its existence. Enzensberger expresses this plainly: 'Inconsistency is not the answer to our predicament, but it has its attractions. It cannot be preached. It increases our freedom of thought and our freedom of movement' (1990: 13). I believe this statement encapsulates the theoretical essence of the method and defines the key elements of its premise.

People, politicians, theorists, philosophers, writers and ourselves occasionally redefine our position as opposed to what we previously believed, wrote or stated. To me, this has nothing to do with inconsistency or negation of the past; on the contrary, it is to review the situation, to rectify views not valid anymore or to keep pace with the times, and, finally, to bring ideas up to date.[4]

7.7 Inconsistency: A room in historiography

The second question is to seek a place for inconsistency in history writing. If a method is developed on the grounds of tracing the mentality change, could it have a chance of finding room in historiography? History, as one of the oldest disciplines, has been much

---

[3] There is a paradox here. On one hand, inconsistency cannot be defended with consistent terms; on the other, inconsistency cannot justify itself with inconsistent arguments. Furthermore, even an attempt at justification is itself a consistent action, a sign of acceptance of logic that is not attuned with the nature of inconsistency.

[4] History is full of examples. But I am satisfied with an excerpt from Baudrillard, who clearly presents a shift in his theoretical stance and introduces his new interpretation of media analysis:

> In reality, even if I did not share the technological optimism of McLuhan, I always recognised and considered as a gain the true revolution which he brought about in media analysis (this has been mostly ignored in France). On the other hand, though I also did not share the dialectical hopes of Enzensberger, I was not truly pessimistic, since I believed in a possible subversion of the code of the media and the possibility of an alternate speech and a radical reciprocity of symbolic exchange.
>
> Today all that has changed. I would no longer interpret in the same way the forced silence of the masses in the mass media. I would no longer see in it a sign of passivity and of alienation, but to the contrary an original strategy, an original response in the form of a challenge; and on the basis of this reversal I suggest to you a vision of things which is no longer optimistic or pessimistic, but ironic and antagonistic.
>
> (Baudrillard, 1988: 208)

discussed in the last three centuries, not only by historians but also by many people with interests in a wide spectrum, from philosophy to politics.[5]

Examining orthodox history shows that the principle of historiography relies on 'historical fact' and requires concrete evidence without any self-contradiction. Therefore, I believe inconsistencies and their merits are not well studied. Any challenge concerning the merit of 'inconsistency' is conceived to have a responsive attitude towards the concept of facts. Among other aspects of historiography, facts and their proof, evidence and documents, have always been hotly contested issues, much discussed by historians.[6] Their meaning, use, effects and importance, as well as the criteria for the choice of documents, were the main basis of debate. However, Foucault reveals the ultimate stance of history regarding this subject: 'history has altered its position in relation to the document: it has taken as its primary task, not the interpretation of the document, nor the attempt to decide whether it is telling the truth or what is its expressive value, but to work on it from within and to develop it' (1974: 6). In this explanation we witness a broader approach to history which has no problem of accommodating methods like one we discuss.

7.8 Inconsistency: The author and his/her work, the emergence of conflict

There are inexplicable relations and sometimes tensions between authors and their work, which may embody the seeds of future conflicts that lead to a paradox in some way or another. Here I would like to argue that inconsistency inevitably derives from a current position that may seem to nullify the previous stance. To some extent, it is possible to trace how authors move away from a point they held in earlier works. The author and his/her work are the two elements that determine the orbit of change. While the former represents actions and growth, the latter identifies and hardens external references. Regarding the question of the author versus work relationship, French literary critic Roland Barthes offers this insight:

> As institution, the author is dead: his civil status, his biographical person have disappeared, dispossessed, they no longer exercise over his work the formidable paternity whose account literary history, teaching, and public opinion had the responsibility of establishing and renewing, but in the text, in a way, I desire the

---

[5] For a brief history of historiography, see Arthur Marwick (1976).
[6] In this respect, opposing views are well-represented by two British historians, E. H. Carr and G. R. Elton in their books *What is History?* and *The Practice of History*. While Carr argues that historical facts cannot be found easily, documented objectively, narrated truly and so on (1964), Elton takes a straightforward professional line, criticizes Carr as a relativist and says that 'I may well be taken to believe that facts about the past are simple, discrete, knowable entities which need only be collected in order that a structure called history may emerge' (1984: 78).

author: I need his figure (which is neither his representation nor his projection), as he needs mine.

(Barthes, 1976: 27)

The author is a living entity, a person and a human being. In contrast to his/her work, the author is alive. His/her work is concrete, static, stagnant, rigid and frozen, which reflects the author's ideas at the moment it is produced. Once written, it comes into existence and acquires life. The text's life is then independent of its author. Once written, the ways of the author and his/her work become separate. They have different life spans, different standards of living. Nevertheless, they may have a very close relationship to each other, whether dynamic, reciprocal or dialectical.

Until the text is published, this relationship is under the absolute intimate sovereignty and total possession of the author as s/he may do anything, whether to change, rewrite, add, extract, edit and so on. It is a one-directional conversation, a monologue. The author is always active; the text is always passive. When the work is completed, however, its body comes into existence. When it is published, its life begins. When it is released, it gains its freedom. The author can no longer change it or touch it as it belongs to the public. It exists there as long as its propositions, axioms, theses, suggestions and narrations are valid and useful.

In the meantime, of course, there are positive and negative reactions. The text cannot respond beyond its content and, since it cannot change, it is invariable. The author is the one who responds, who is not static, who changes. The separation between the author and his/her work is due to the antagonistic nature of the two bodies. The body of the text is frozen and not subject to transformation whereas the body of the author is alive, hence open to change, as the French philosopher, Michel Foucault eloquently puts it at the beginning of this essay. When the author moves from one theoretical stance to another, his/her position alters in relation to the work.[7] The text represents its writer as long as the author agrees with the text. Whenever disagreement occurs, their ways diverge.

The value of the text has no relation to the author's current ideas and is independent of him. The one-to-one correspondence between the ideas presented in the text and the author's ideas are only present at the exact time the text was written. The author may

---

[7] Fernand Braudel delineates his personal experience very genuinely in the preface to his book *On History*:

> Like everyone else, I cannot recognise my own voice when I hear it recorded. Nor I am sure whether I can immediately recognise, in any real sense of the word, my thoughts of yesterday on reading them. Are such thoughts fed on so many echoes, so many memories, in which voices once heard come spontaneously to life again, really my thoughts? Yes and no. So many things have happened since then, so many things beset me today. Since I am not a man for polemic, being concerned only with my own path, my own particular path, and since polemic and dialogue are a double and unavoidable necessity, here I am holding dialogues and engaging in polemic with myself, in a natural process of detachment from texts for which I obviously remain responsible.

(1980: vii)

ignore, object and even reject his early work, whether partially or totally. However, this should not threaten our respect for either text or author. Nor does this exclusion by the author cast a shadow on the work's value. However, the work has no choice. It is faithful,[8] and never rejects or denies its author.

7.9 Inconsistency: A function within research

It is a widespread practice that a work found inconsistent is ignored or rarely mentioned. They are 'forgotten works' and politely referred to as 'out of date'. The reason is that discrepancy is simply not acceptable in common practice. Taking into account variations in attitudes towards the theory of history, cases of 'negated texts' may be discussed as a subject for scrutiny. We have recourse to so-called inconsistencies and could benefit immensely from their potential and latent serendipity. Especially in pursuing changes to concepts, it seems essential to pursue variations in texts, records, documents, films and so on. It would be useless, for instance, to seek the transformation of abstract and dynamic notions within a given single text. The dynamic analysis of a text can only be achieved by a series of comparisons with their revised editions. Bringing, let us say, all different editions of a book together and then discovering and comparing dissimilarities, determining the direction of differences and trying to date and explain them are preliminary steps towards more comprehensive research. Distinctions and modifications in documents are signs of dynamism. Alterations, transformations or displacements of ideas are no longer disputed as they used to be, probably as a result of increasing social tolerance. The modifications may then offer suitable material for research. The project described above is, in one sense, to reinstate and restore the prestige of works damaged by neglect. Since inconsistency is still widely used as the basis for repudiation, I venture to call my reparative proposal 'the reaffirmation of the negated'.

7.10 Conclusion

There are a few points I would like to make in summary. Mentality change in a particular society, the shift of ideas within institutions or individuals and the transformation of concepts all require an analysis of the periods within which they occur. Inconsistencies are one of the main sources of information about these processes. As such, they should be appreciated. This method can be more effective if it is used within the context of, and in relation to, other phenomena of the era, but not in isolation. The article by Robin Kinross is a good example of this. The method definitely requires a clear set of aims and

---

[8]Faithfulness has connotations of stagnancy, conservatism and resistance to change. Furthermore, it sounds like 'consistency', does it not?

objectives. No doubt, among others, it would need further experimentation, detailing, elaboration and refinement. It may not lead to generalizations but would be instrumental in mapping minds. I will end by taking refuge in a quotation by Carlo Ginzburg, who puts the case elegantly: 'Certainly, there is no need to exaggerate when we talk about distortions. The fact that a source is not "objective" … does not mean that it is useless' ([1976] 1980: xvii).

CHAPTER 8
OBSERVATIONS ON THE RISE OF DESIGN HISTORIOGRAPHY BY THE END OF THE TWENTIETH CENTURY IN THE UK
A VIEW FROM 'OUTSIDE IN' WITH A TOUCH OF GLOBALIZATION

The first version of this chapter was presented as a paper at the First International Conference on Design History, Barcelona, 26–28 April 1999. Later it was published in its proceedings, see: Calvera A. and Mallol, M. eds. (2001) Historiar desde la periferia: historia e historias del diseño / Design history seen from abroad: History and Histories of Design*, 117–139, Barcelona: University of Barcelona Publication.*

8.1 Introduction

Years ago, when I had an opportunity to look closely into the rise of design history in the UK as a 'foreigner', it surprised me to see the impact of several factors, especially art and architectural history, and the way in which they took precedence. While the documentation and literature for manufactured objects are impressive, design history, in its early years, appears to have struggled considerably with defining its subject matter as well as suffering from the lack of an original way of dealing with it. Designing, mass production, marketing, dissemination, use, recycling, disposal and the life span of objects require a different understanding and concept of history, which is not something that is easily built. Nevertheless, the British experience of writing design history offers immense potential for those sharpening their pencils to undertake a similar task.

This chapter recounts my observations on the emergence of design historiography in the UK and the problems it confronted. It is neither a short history of design historiography nor a critical review but maps out the important historical studies in the twentieth century. The purpose is to shed light on the pathways of history writing to learn some lessons that might help those working on their own local design history. The proliferation of literature is clearly encouraging and parallels the increase in design awareness and history consciousness worldwide. Although nation-based approaches to design history provide us with invaluable material and insights, they are rare while a framework in the context of globalization is yet to be established that situates local, national and cultural identities. To this end, the observations presented here may be useful to comprehend the journey of the historiography of design in the UK. I will conduct this journey with certain assumptions and try to explain the reasons behind them.

First, many factors caused the emergence of strong design historiography in the UK. The main hypothesis of this paper is that the conditions leading to design history have matured gradually since the beginning of the nineteenth century, although institutionalization commenced in the 1960s. It can be assumed for the sake of a sketchy illustration that the academic debate on design history that led to its institutionalization began in the 1960s while early works appeared in the 1970s, developed in the 1980s and flourished in the 1990s. During the last decade of the twentieth century, this discussion has been carried out on international platforms. Therefore, within the scope of this chapter, I will limit my observations to what I call the early years while leaving aside the 1990s for another investigation. Before going into detail, it would be useful to identify two important determinants paving the way for the ascent of design history in the UK: the historical conditions that matured in the 1960s and the government policy of supporting design in general.

8.2 Historical conditions

A reliable ground for the emergence of design historiography has surfaced in the UK, basically by means of institutionalization of design and expansion design practices amongst other things.

8.2.1 The institutionalization of design as practice and profession has been achieved

It is fair to underline that the UK was well situated to foster the rise of design history, for two obvious reasons among many others:

a) the emergence of the so-called 'industrial revolution', which opened an avenue for mass production of objects, and

b) the steady design debate that commenced by questioning the 'machine aesthetic' and the establishment of art and design schools in the nineteenth century, which continued to explore the concept of design in great depth.

Under normal circumstances, the history of a discipline appears as and within one of the final phases of institutionalization. Practice and theory might well be the first indicators of a new area. However, without substantial information flow, a discipline cannot exist. A growing practice may gradually turn into a profession through organizations, laws, rules, regulations, regulatory and professional bodies, associations and councils. The emergence of written, visual or other types of documents creates a basis for a prospective history. The presence of literature and archival material on the subject is crucial for historiography and also a kind of assurance of its establishment.

As soon as a community of professionals is formed, it is normal to expect that information flow will lead to the emergence of leaflets, brochures, posters, journals, magazines, books, broadcasting and moving or still imagery. Occasions bringing people together for the advancement of the practice, such as workshops, seminars, conferences, symposia and exhibitions, are particularly useful for completing the institutionalization of a particular subject. Education and research are the other aspects of institutionalization. Probably at this late stage, history comes to the fore to complete the scenario and provide people with a vision of the past, an interpretation of today and speculative powers for predicting the future.

What happened in the UK regarding design provides us with this simple looking but in fact rather arduous scenario. A few examples include the establishment of design education (Normal School of Design, 1837), the publication of design journals (*Journal of Design and Manufactures*, 1849), magazines and books, the establishment of associations (Design and Industry Association, 1915), radio broadcasts on the issue (1930s), exhibitions (1851, and so on) and the formation of professional bodies (Society of Industrial Artists, 1930). This list, which can easily be extended, is sufficient to convince us that the well-documented 'past' of design in the UK was mature enough to be investigated by historians in the second half of the twentieth century.[1]

It is not easy to identify when design history began. Some early writings, texts and books definitely included historical material and research, and showed understanding. For instance, *The Wheelwright's Shop* by George Sturt, 1923, is highly acknowledged.[2] There are, no doubt, a few more works bearing traces of historical research and perspectives encompassing Pevsner, Read, Bertram, Banham, Gloag and so on. Nevertheless, what is of concern here is not individual efforts but the formation of continuing debate leading to the rise of a design history consciousness and its institutionalization. In that sense, the position of design as a concept plays a determining role.

8.2.2 Design has risen as a dominant term and concept among other related nomenclature

Many researchers would agree that a clear definition of design would be of the greatest help to design historians. A short review of the history of nomenclature indisputably shows that there have been many terms since the beginning of the nineteenth century to name the activities covered by what we today call 'design'.[3] By the 1930s, industrial art and applied art were competing expressions. Pevsner, for instance, preferred *Industrial Art* as his book's title whereas Herbert Read used *Art and Industry*. Ironically, although he included industrial design as a subtitle, it is never referred to in the text.[4] The term industrial design, which became unequivocally recognized in the UK in the 1930s,

---

[1] Knowing that this part of history and literature is well studied by writers such as C. Dilnot, A. Forty, T. Fry, J. Heskett, V. Margolin, P. Sparke and J. Woodham, I will omit further details.
[2] My gratuities go to Frank Height and John Heskett, who separately had drawn my attention to this work in the late 1980s and told me that they regard George Sturt's book as one of the pioneering works in design history.
[3] For the transformation of the design concept and the battles of expressions, see Chapter 6 in Section Two.
[4] To my reading, he employs the term only once and in brackets.

first appeared as a proper book title (Holme, 1934) and was accepted in the 1940s (Read 1947, Gloag, 1946, 1947a, b, c, 1950). Since then, it has become ubiquitous in Britain.[5]

The formation of the Council of Industrial Design and subsequent events and activities expanded the employment of the expression. Industrial design was apparently beginning to acquire a strong voice in professional and educational institutions. In the early 1960s, after its introduction to higher education curricula as a new subject in degree courses, design became a powerful umbrella term, gradually covering more than the others. Although the popularity of industrial design was not at stake, areas that arose independently, such as product design, furniture design, transport design and vehicle design, fell under the aegis of design in general, although these relatively new fields often used to operate under industrial design.[6]

Interestingly, these changes were even reflected in official language. In retrospect, we immediately notice how the names of the design committees, exhibitions and councils varied and were subjected to alterations. The following list partially taken from the works of MacCharty (1979) illustrates this fluctuation of terms. Industrial art was replaced by industrial design, which was later substituted by design only[7] (books and publications are in italics while the relevant phrases are underlined):

8.2.3 The term design and its rise in official and formal titles

- 1915 Design and Industries Association founded
- 1919 *Art and Industry* pamphlet issued by the Ministry of Reconstruction
- 1920 British Institute of Industrial Art founded
- 1923 Exhibition of 'Industrial Art Today'
- 1927 The periodical *Commercial Art & Industry* was published
- 1929 British Institute of Industrial Art exhibition, 'Industrial Art for the Slender Purse'
- 1930 Society of Industrial Artists founded (SIA)

---

[5] At the beginning of the twentieth century, the term industrial design was in use for some time in Britain although not very frequently. As I mentioned in a footnote in Chapter 6 in Section Two, the first written evidence goes back to 1894, when Frank G. Jackson, employed the expression (only once) in *Theory and Practice of Design* (1894: 3) where he associates industrial design with decorative objects. (At this point it is worth developing a critical view questioning the argument and Raymond Loewy's claim that industrial design was born in America with Loewy as the first industrial designer.)

[6] This point should be made clear to avoid misunderstanding: on the one hand, the content of design history was subject to reduction due to the exclusion of certain design disciplines, such as architecture and city planning; on the other, design's content was extended thanks to the inclusion of industrial design and its specialist fields.

[7] Many items in this list are taken from Fiona MacCarthy's book, *A History of British Design 1830–1970*, and checked with the list in *Twentieth Century Design* by Jonathan M. Woodham, who later made some comments on the list above for which I am very grateful.

- 1933 Council for Art and Industry set up by the Board of Trade (it is first met in 1934)
- 1934 *Industrial Design and the Future* by Geoffrey Holme
- 1934 *Art & Industry: The Principles of Industrial Design* by Herbert Read
- 1935 Report on Industrial Art submitted by the Nugent Committee
- 1936 National Register of Industrial Art Designers formed
- 1936 The periodical Commercial Art & Industry renamed Art & Industry
- 1937 '*An Enquiry into Industrial Art in England*' published by Nikolaus Pevsner
- 1937 The Council for Art and Industry published the *Design and Designer in Industry* Report
- 1939 Central Institute of Art and Design formed
- 1943 Report on 'Industrial Design and Art in Industry' completed but not published
- 1944 Proposals for a Central Design Council and Industrial Design Centre published by the Industrial Art Committee
- 1944 Council of Industrial Design formed
- 1959 The periodical *Art & Industry* renamed again as *Design for Industry*
- 1963 Society of Industrial Artists (SIA) renamed as Society of Industrial Artists and Designers
- 1972 Council of Industrial Design renamed as Design Council
- 1987 Society of Industrial Artists and Designers (SIA) renamed as Chartered Society of Designers (CSD)

Of the hints heralding the shift, an obvious one is the Council of Industrial Design (CoID), formed in 1944, which was renamed the Design Council in 1972. Another example is the Society of Industrial Artists (SIA). MacCarthy observes that 'by the 1960s the profession had begun to look quite different, a change of outlook marked, in 1963, by the SIA decision to rename itself Society of Industrial Artists and *Designers*' [the italics are mine] (MacCarthy, 1982: 149). The substitution of terms appears to signify a switch from a specific, limited context to a wider spectrum, if not a statement of the dominance of design. Although there are departments, articles, books and so on, bearing the title industrial design, it is nowadays very common to employ the term design and use it to enjoy the comfort of its vast and flexible content unless special emphasis is needed like graphic design, textile design, product design and so on.[8]

---

[8] When a new course opened at Goldsmiths' College in the early 1990s, it was called 'Total Design'. This title 'has been adopted as a convenient vehicle with which to define and to develop new boundaries of design practice in a changing world' (Wood, 1990: 2).

8.2.4 The introduction of design history in British higher education instigated the debate in the 1960s

In 1960, the National Advisory Council on Art Education (NACAE) published its first report. It stated that 'history of art should be obligatory' and that 'each student should learn the history of his own subject – fashion including the history of costume, furniture, the history of furniture, and so on' (Ashwin, 1978: 98). Although the history of design was not mentioned specifically, it does not require great effort to imagine the anticipation of design history studies.

In 1963, a Diploma in Art and Design (DipAD) was instituted in British higher education. Initially, it was 'not a degree but degree equivalent' (Renzio, 1977: 11). However, this was soon amended to make it a proper 'Honours Degree' (MacCarthy, 1982: 155). According to Toni del Renzio, a principal lecturer, 'when art and design education sought respectability and academic parity, a decision was made that the course needed some intellectual stiffening, as though there were grounds for doubts as the intellectual components of art and design' (1977: 11). Whatever the initial considerations were as implied above, design was on the curriculum of higher education, requiring delivery with appropriate content and rigour. There were many obstacles but tutors have sought a way to teach it.

Firstly, there were not enough competent and specialised staff members but people with different backgrounds and expertise. Later, from the early 1970s, these issues would be brought into the open and discussed. Tim Benton portrays the situation with broad brushstrokes:

> There are a few specialist design historians pursuing the study of clearly defined problems in the development of modern design. There are the collectors and connoisseurs, freelance or in museum, who are mainly interested in objects for their aesthetic and rarity value.
>
> There are the cultural historians who use design as an expression of popular culture or social hierarchies. There are the historians of art or architecture who drift into design studies in pursuance of favourite themes.
>
> (Benton, 1975: 7)

Secondly, sources were very scarce, and the available ones were far from satisfactory for the various demands of different design departments. Additionally, there were many irrelevant subjects in the books because they represented a vast range of interests rather than being specially written for design. Renzio criticized this situation:

> Nearly all the books that have the word 'design' in the title, like Pevsner's *Pioneers of Modern Design* and Banham's *Theory and Design in the First Machine Age* for all the immense value of these books, are marginal to the general history of design, and treat special or architectural aspects; others, like Anthony Bertram's admirable

Penguin special [*Design*] now a valuable document, or Herbert Read's *Art and Industry* with its conceptually equivocal rhetoric, are not history.⁹

(Renzio, 1977: 11)

Thirdly, the lack of a precedence for design history teaching was a problem that created future disputes in the subject. Ultimately, art history lecturers found themselves extending the scope of their courses to include new issues and preparing lectures on design. They mostly took on the burden of design. Having said this, the conclusion can easily be drawn that 'design history is in Britain being defined and developed as a component of design education in the schools, colleges and polytechnics' (Kinross, 1985: 12).¹⁰ The early engagement of art history with design history may be an exigency, a historical coincidence or even maybe an undesired marriage. Although it undoubtedly solved the immediate delivery problem in the classrooms, it raised question marks in the long run, especially concerning its negative influences – some of which probably stemmed from its nexus with art history.

8.3 Government's policy: A market-oriented strategy supporting design generously

The overwhelming popularity of design fostered by the British government under Margaret Thatcher in the 1980s left no room for an alternative but the prosperity of design.¹¹ Given this policy of raising the quality of design and boosting exports, the government strongly supported design circles, consultancies and businesses. From 1982 to 1985, the Department of Trade and Industry and the Design Council implemented a programme called the 'Funded Consultancy Scheme' (FCS). This was followed by

---

⁹Of course, eleven years after this statement, Kinross' article 'Herbert Read's Art and Industry: a History' would tell us a different story (see Kinross, 1988).

¹⁰Alongside the determining role of higher education institutions, there have always been other circles interested in design. In this respect, the contributions of museum and gallery curators, and collectors and connoisseurs to the development of design history should not be forgotten.

¹¹Paul Reilly, who was the director of the Council of Industrial Design (1960–1973) and then the Design Council (1973–1977), describes in his autobiography how he introduced the subject to Margaret Thatcher while she was Secretary of State for Education.

> Of course, as Prime Minister she did more for design which she called 'a key factor in ensuring the economic health of the nation.' She encouraged the Department of Trade and Industry to finance what she called the Funded Consultancy Service, which provided first three million pounds, then ten and yet again ten to finance the employment of designers in industry.
>
> (Reilly, 1987: 82).

John Walker gives another figure: after a meeting at 10 Downing Street in 1982, he says, 'Government spending on the promotion of design was subsequently increased from £4 million to £12 million' (Walker 1989: xi). The employment figures illustrate this effect: '29 000 people were working in design consultancy business of which yearly capacity was over £1 billion' (Walker, 1989: XI).

another, the 'Support for Design' (SFD) scheme. A survey conducted with about 2,000 and 3,000 companies participating in the SFD and FCS schemes, respectively, reveals the success of the investment in design:

> This study shows that the Government's programme of subsidised design consultants has encouraged a proportion of small and medium sized UK manufacturers to make use of professional design, many of whom would not have done so without help. Although at the time of the subsidised design project over half of the firms employed full-time, qualified in-house RD&D staff, in nearly a third design/development was undertaken mainly by individuals with main jobs other than RD&D, and in most cases this was the first time the firms had used a design consultant or drawn on specialist expertise in areas such as industrial design.
> The study shows that, even in typical small and medium sized firms such as these, the development of new and improved products, components, packaging, etc. using professional design expertise can be an excellent commercial investment. Two-thirds of the projects were implemented and 60% were financially successful.
>
> (Design Innovation Group, 1990: 15)

Overall, this policy greatly popularized design and created a substantial market, both for new products and publications, including a proliferation of design literature and history books. Meanwhile, the establishment of the Design Research Society in 1967 and the Design History Society in 1977 created a considerable impetus for progress in the subject via their journals and annual conferences. In a well-planned coincidence, the inauguration of the Design Museum in 1989 and its subsequent exhibitions and other activities provided further stimulation to raise design history awareness. The money poured into the sector bore fruit.

8.4 The problems of design historiography in the 1960s

Design history encountered a few problems in its early days as the influence of art history was strongly felt even if it did not always leave a detectable imprint. Metaphorically speaking, the fallacy of art history legacy is discernible:
First, art history courses neglected many subjects that are a substantial part of design. It was, of course, not very easy to include design issues as much and as quickly as needed since no profound research had been conducted. In addition, the dearth of appropriate knowledge meant that art history could not be aware of crucial design subjects and set the agenda appropriate for another discipline. Indeed, it was not even considered a discipline at that time anyway.
Second, the special perspective of the theoretical analysis of design, without which the subject cannot be grasped thoroughly, was neglected. As Ashwin argues, the approach adopted disregarded the 'economic, technological or sociological mode of analysis which plays no part in conventional courses in the history of art' (Ashwin, 1978: 99).

Third, a distorted understanding of art history infected design with a long-lasting 'illness': as the pioneers, heroes and protagonists were epoch-making figures, they should be the main axis of history, within which their stories must prevail. This view reduced some studies of history to texts of the collected works of various well-known designers at the expense of the principal elements of historiography. Again, Ashwin makes it explicit: 'The history of design conceived as the history of "pioneers" is, it is claimed, particularly attractive to the art historian because it allows him to account for the evolution of design in terms of the unique personal insights of individual designers, rather than in the more complex terms of technological change and socio-economic transformations' (Ashwin, 1978: 100).

Fourth, the emphasis that art history put on design objects was either inadequate or ignored the prominent features. Superficial aesthetic concerns that dominate the descriptive approaches of some conventional art history were applied to the realm of objects where an artefact was concerned. Meanwhile, its most important element, its function, was ignored. This attitude caused another misinterpretation.

Fifth, since the objects were often reviewed in terms of their aesthetic merits, it became all too easy to categorise them with respect to the styles attributed to them. Ultimately, design history began featuring the same stylistic periodization as art history, that is, Arts and Crafts, Art Nouveau, Futurism and so on. In certain incidences, products came to be treated as if they were artistic pieces and classified accordingly. This account of the detrimental influences of the art history background can be prolonged as easily as the number of complaints expressed by commentators pointing out this fact: 'The problem of defining the object of study and finding an appropriate historiography have been fraught by design history's art attitudes and precedents. In attempting to assert itself, design history has sought to establish its distinctness from art history by defining its object of study as the useful and functional instead of the merely beautiful' (Attfield, 1985: 26).

8.5 Identity formation

What design history is, what it consists of, its subject matter, aims, methodologies and so on. have been major questions asked since the mid-1970s. Within this context, the identity of design history has surfaced as an essential problem. The exigency of forming an identity was discovered and discussed by scholars in the 1970s and 1980s. *Design History: Fad or Function?* is essential evidence while *Block*, an important journal of the time, devoted a few issues to the subject that included key articles.[12] However, at the end of the 1980s, John Walker insisted that 'There is now no shortage of books on design but the subject is still in its formative stages and hence suffers periodic identity crisis' (Walker, 1989: 18).

---

[12]See Hannah & Putnam (1980), Fry (1981) and Teymur (1981).

Walker was not alone in his criticism as Tibor Kalman, an American émigré graphic designer, strongly criticized contemporary design history simply for having no vision: 'We seem to be locked into a self-fulfilling prophecy: designers don't read, so design writers don't write. They write captions. Sometimes they write really long captions, thousands of words that do nothing but describe the pictures. Books of design history that are packaged for a supposedly illiterate audience only engender further illiteracy' (Kalman, 1991: 50). Kalman suggests that the method of transcending this difficulty is to perceive design history as 'a way of filtering the past, a way of selecting what should be remembered' (1991: 50). The phrase, 'filtering the past' brings up the issue of theory; the 'filter' is actually nothing but a 'theoretical framework' by which historians operate, well, at least some of them. In this respect, one could say that the subject matter, the content of design, the aims and objectives, and the theoretical frameworks, moulded the backbone of the initial debate that led towards the discipline's identity formation.[13] The following sub-sections look into each of these issues in turn.

8.5.1 Subject matter

As many critics have indicated, neither design history nor industrial design history has a subject matter agreed on by the majority of historians. Judy Attfield's remark quoted above is an example. Clive Dilnot, in an important article on the subject,[14] considers this issue as the first crucial problem 'in the movement toward creating a discipline of the history of design' (Dilnot, 1984b: 3). He holds that 'design historians as a whole have at best an incomplete grasp of their would-be subject matter' (Dilnot, 1984b: 3). John Walker seems totally in agreement with this statement. After discussing the object and scope of design history he concludes, 'unless the object of design history is precisely defined the sheer magnitude of its possible subject matter will reduce the researcher to impotence' (Walker, 1989: 36). This is not a kind of view that historians were willing to share easily in the 1990s. Adrian Forty has a clear vision and is convinced that 'the discipline of (design) history[15] as it has developed over the last century or so already provides a perfectly satisfactory definition of the "field"' (Forty, 1993: 132). The debate between Victor Margolin and Adrian Forty reflects the unsettled territories where the legitimization crisis of design history and design study is depicted (see *Design Issues*, Spring 1995).

The reason why the subject matter of design history has been a problem is the same old story: the lack of consensus on what constitutes design. Without defining the area covered by design, one cannot define the subject matter of design history. So far, it

---

[13]Whether design and design history is a 'discipline' or not is another arena of dispute, apparently especially in the United States (Margolin, 1999).
[14]At the Ohio conference in 1998, Dilnot presented a paper discussing the concept of knowledge and the epistemological dimensions of the object within the context of design (1999a).
[15]My edition. Although Forty did not use 'design history' in this sentence, regarding the context of his response, I assume this is what he meant.

seems that the definition of design itself is highly dependent on the scope of historical studies. If I were allowed to make a critical comment here, I would raise the question of why design has always been subject to 'static' definitions. The dynamic content and the uninterrupted transformation of design may well form a different interpretation of history, which is transformed as its object changes. The neglect of this dialectic relationship between the designed object and its history may also explain why we need a historiography specifically for design and its sub-fields.

8.5.2 Content of design

There was, is and will be an ongoing endeavour to define the content of design. Again, this is a definition-related problem. One of the reasons for the impediment derives from an attempt to narrow the content of design for practical purposes. Certain design-related disciplines or design-oriented activities employ this term to describe their particular area of action, product and production processes. However, they consciously or unconsciously, but no doubt unilaterally, disregard and exclude other fields of design.

When the so-called 'design literature' is examined, it appears that some disciplines and their professional practices, which are highly involved with design processes, are not mentioned at all, such as engineering design, landscape design, urban design and regional design. Architecture and craft are victims as well. However, one may venture to call them the relatively fortunate ones since, despite their elimination, their 'dismissal' is always felt in the same way and expressed 'regrettably'. *Design History: A Student's Handbook* edited by Hazel Conway is an example. As the editor, Conway, on behalf of the other contributors, openly presents their understanding of design history and the purpose of the book. She agrees that its scope is very wide: 'Although many historical examples are included in this introduction to design history, it is not intended to be a concise history of the subject' (Conway, 1987: 4). Design history was to comprise many areas of specialization, each of which requires separate study and some of which already have 'their particular professional institutions and publications' (Conway, 1987: 5). Among these are those mentioned above, that is, architecture, town planning, landscape and civil engineering. Conway prefers to bring them together under the title of 'environmental design' rather than reserving a chapter for each subject. In his review of this book, John Walker does not hesitate to draw our attention to this point: 'Architecture as a distinct topic is also excluded, although it crops up, of course, under interior and environmental design. Although some scholars feel that architectural history is an independent discipline, in my view it ought to have been given separate consideration because it has been so vital to the origins of design history' (1988: 80). In fact, it is not unusual or unknown for architecture to have a place in design histories. Independent of whether successful or not, Ann Ferebee shows in *A History of Design from the Victorian Era to the Present* how architecture is inserted into other design subjects. A survey of the literature gives us more detailed information about the shifting axis and changing content of design history. Nicolaus Pevsner's *Pioneers of Modern Design*[16] and Reyner Banham's *Theory and Design in the First Machine Age* (1989) are works where the relationship of 'design and architecture' or 'design in architecture' is not exposed. This literature corresponds to the years before the fragmentation and departmentalization of design. In contrast, sources from the 1970s and 1980s provide us with a new scenario in which specialized design books were published even more frequently. With them, themes like articulation, integration, harmony and unity with different design practices fade from the agenda. Parallel to this, there are fewer comprehensive and global design histories. Design history in general is being fragmented. New, smaller isles of sovereignty of various design histories proceed from this proliferation. As noted elsewhere, fragmentation leaves its traces firmly and stamps the era instantly.[17] Regarding fragmentation, the situation had become clear by the late 1980s, at least in posing the following questions: 'Does design include architecture? Is architecture part of the object of design history or art history or is architectural an independent discipline in its own right? Similar uncertainties arise in respect of the crafts, the minor or decorative arts and the mass media' (Walker, 1989: 22).

Although not direct, this statement is explanatory, especially when we read between the lines. Firstly, it appears that the area where design exercises its power is subjected to restrictions. There should be no doubt that design is a *sine qua non* that is integrant of architecture as well as intrinsic. With this interpretation, it is understood that architecture is to be stripped of its prime constituent, design, which is reduced to a negligible level. Such a perspective may help people who wish to limit the content of design in order to appropriate, possess and reserve the term, and thereby legitimize its use for particular disciplines, such as those dealing with mass-produced images, artefacts and everyday objects.

Secondly, it queries the position of 'others' that are obviously involved with design like engineering design, landscape design, urban design and so on. These others are treated by design history as if they do not exist. Their names are hardly mentioned in the literature if at all. For instance, Walker, who complains about the omitting of architecture and craft in the last quotation, does not speak of urban or regional design and their elimination. His interest in these 'others' remains limited to architecture and craft. Is there any room, then, for 'others' in design history? Probably, it is time to review the idea of global design history incorporating all fields concerning design. Colossal books, such as *History of the World or World Architecture*, might be extremely useful as a general reference and for educational purposes, but this is not what all historians repeatedly produce. Rather, a history of an object (Barcelona Chair), an institution (Bauhaus), a period (Twentieth Century Limited) or a country (Spanish Design), successfully completes the mosaic

---

[16]In the first edition, in 1936, the title was slightly different: *Pioneers of Modern Movement*.
[17]If we remember that fragmentation is one of the phenomena of postmodernism, we realize immediately that this is not a simple coincidence. In other words, the years of fragmentation in design correspond to the years of postmodernist euphoria. What sort of substantial link could be established is, of course, a matter for further investigation, although I believe it is worth taking note of this juxtaposition.

towards a better understanding of the past. Therefore, the proliferation of independent design histories is more than welcome.

Design euphoria and desire for objects is a creation of economies based on consumerism. If we look at society with this in mind, it appears that there are two fundamental phenomena in addition to the rise of information technology, which characterizes the period we live in: reproductions of objects and reproductions of images. Both of them form the main axis of everyday life because they are consumed or used by all without exception. No doubt, design is an inevitable element of both. Apparently, the quality and quantity of objects and images are being increased with a latent assumption that objects are vehicles for people to express and identify themselves. This popular trend encourages people to search for authentic, original, exotic, unique, extravagant, pompous or luxuriously designed things, which furnish their owners with a special status, identity and pleasure.[18] The more objects are available, the greater the opportunity is for one to choose for the fulfilment of services, enjoyment of function and exposition of self, whenever desired.

Whether virtual, real or conceptual, design provides us with a variety of new objects far quicker than technology does. This is because technology is inextricably bound to new inventions and can bring out novel forms only after being justified by considerable research input and discovery. This is not an obstacle for design since it is not necessarily dependent on scientific and technological discoveries but may be content with new forms and minor alterations utilising existing possibilities. Furthermore, design is being publicly understood today as a quality and value-adding factor which of course never contradicts how it has been considered by most designers. However, this understanding of design has been notably misused by marketing strategies so that almost everything produced since the 1980s has been labelled with the magic word 'design' as a kind of guarantee of quality and taste.

As a result, the number of designed products remained far behind the number of times the word design was uttered. Both designed products and the word 'design', which was turned into a commodity itself, are marketed. This plethora of designed goods was directly reflected in the world of publication. Many books came out: furniture design, chair design, car design, lamp design and so forth. Within this panorama, it is most probably correct to conclude that the fragmentation of design is also linked to the boom of designed articles, retail, corporate identity, branding and digital imagery (Press, 2003).

---

[18]Ideal examples of the role of objects in our life are marvellously illustrated in the novel *Things* by George Perec (1990), who explores the meaning of the goods we are besieged with. It is highly recommended for anybody who is interested in the obsession with objects. Another novella drew the attention of design circles. *The Mezzanine* by Nicholson Baker (1990) was reviewed by Jeffrey Meikle, writer of *Twentieth Century Limited, Industrial Design in America, 1925–1939* (1979): 'I am especially keen on convincing anyone involved in design history or material culture studies that they can learn more from this slender fiction than from most academic works of history or criticism' (Meikle, 1992: 3). For me, it is also important that objects, particularly designed objects, are being examined and studied from various points of view as objects of film, art and literature. Such enquiries undoubtedly increase our sensibility towards our physical environment and contribute to our understanding of material culture.

8.5.3 Aims and objectives

Arguably, one of the most important factors defining the identity of a discipline is that of its aims and objectives. Without them, no research can be conducted, and no discipline can operate. Unfortunately, design history lacks a sufficiently discussed set of aims and objectives, particularly in relation to its object of research with the particular methods evolved for the purpose. Of course, this does not mean that individual works and studies have no target to achieve or objective to fulfil. The fact is that aims and objectives were, to my knowledge, never proposed systematically and thereby properly debated and improved. The suggestions made have sometimes remained valid only temporarily or are inadequate. As a result, they appear to be far from constituting a coherent set of objectives and operational parameters for historians. I will argue the case through several examples.

Bruce Archer, the promoter of design awareness (1974) and the scientification of design in the 1960s, claims that 'the identification of designed objects, with date, attribution, history of ownership and so on, is a crucially important contribution to design scholarship' (Archer, 1977: 5). No doubt, it is! But is this the sole purpose of the historian? He continues:

> The simple cataloguing of every sort of artefact is a task as daunting as that of the cataloguing of the stars. In every sub division of the design area, nevertheless, there is urgent need for such cataloguing and classification to be done. And since the development of design scholarship, not to mention the attainment of ordinary, practical understanding, depends upon the maturing of design history from the tasks of cataloguing and commentary to the tasks of explanation and generalisation, there is urgent need for increase in the depth as well as the range of historical enquiry.
>
> (Archer, 1977: 10)

Cataloguing and classification are, of course, important. But whose tasks are these? Archaeologists of artefacts, archivists of products or design historians? This understanding is probably reducing the role of design historian to that of object identification and description, and, eventually, to explanation and generalization.[19]

Another example demonstrating the weakness of the aims and objectives of design history is Dilnot's article. He, very rightly, asks a series of crucial questions. Yet, these questions, apart from giving an impression of how crucial they are, show how vulnerable design history is. I would like to use these questions to illustrate the confusion on design history. Dilnot indicates the

> major problem facing the discipline: defining what design history's roles should be and who its potential audiences are. And *who* should they be? Should design

---

[19] It is also not explicit what the function and nature of explanations and generalizations will be.

historians write for themselves or for professional designers? Or is their role principally in design education? If so, what, if any, is the relationship between historical study and studio education? Or should design history be considered as wholly academic discipline, or, perhaps, as a contribution to design studies – the historical dimension of design studies' attempts, so far profoundly ahistorical, to analytically and logically model the design process?

(Dilnot, 1984b: 8)

These questions reflect the belief in a holistic design history. This is not what the writer of the text intends to do. Undoubtedly, widening the philosophical, theoretical and historical horizons of the discipline in scholarly work is one thing; writing design history books for different audiences with different levels of interest in design is another. Usually, the latter uses the results and findings of the former and adapts them to its own specific objectives and the requirements of its target market. Therefore, it is probably right to call the former primary and the latter secondary sources, such as some textbooks written for educational purposes that are not derived from original research. However, this does not mean that a very special work addressing the demands of a limited group cannot be a scholarly written design history. Naturally, the quality of the work is independent of the limits of its audiences and readers. Yet, it is important to distinguish the scholarly activity required by the discipline from that of the history books demanded by designers, students, connoisseurs, the public and so on. Any confusion on this issue clearly stems from the inadequacy or ambiguity of aims and objectives. Unless these are precisely uttered and a consensus on them established, comprehensive design histories can hardly be written. Dilnot is, of course, well aware of this and holds that 'design history, in the sense of a single, organised discipline with defined aims and objects, does not exist' (Dilnot, 1984a: 11).

Dilnot's article was published in 1984. However, eight years after his statement, we witness gradually increasing efforts to build up the discipline of design. Philip Pacey, pronouncing that he has 'a longstanding interest in non-elitist approaches to art and design', questions the position and attitude of design history towards non-professional designers. His argument is that 'design history should not merely chronicle the separation of designing from making and the subsequent history of the design profession, but that it should place this in relation to a broader picture which encompasses the non-professional which preceded and has co-existed with professional design' (Pacey, 1992: 224). Whether one accepts his argument or not, one cannot deny that this is a suggestion concerning the content of design history as well as its aims and objectives. This is also evidence of the uninterrupted debate on the nature of design history. In other words, it shows that the aims and objectives of design and industrial design histories were never finalized. Tony Fry advocates that 'a history of design should, therefore, be a history of formations and process, as well as objects and form' (Fry, 1988:43). Suggestions were still being made in the early 1990s. In his debate with Margolin, Forty remarks on the aims: 'To suggest that the aims of design history should be to write good history and shed light on how people in the past have discriminated quality may not seem very radical ambitions. None the less, I do not believe that the possibilities they offer for research have yet been exhausted' (Forty, 1993: 132).

Research has continued to flourish since then. Regarding the writings of the 1990s, I would say that the discussion on design history reached a new level thanks to the emergence of the quality work produced, which deserves a substantial analysis.

8.5.4 Theoretical framework

The argument here is rather simple: although the value attributed to the role of theory in history writing varies from one scholar to another, I believe that theory cannot be excluded. Therefore, design historiography should present its own account. Tony Fry justifies this with no difficulty:

> the object of study of design history is always constituted by theory. Even calling up the object as material fact is totally dependent upon the reality constructed by empiricism. There is no pure object which travels through time with an encapsulated meaning, which can be unpacked as an historical record. Here meaning is a product of the social output of knowledge in tandem with interpretative activity.
>
> (1988: 53)

Theory in relation to general history has been one of the issues preoccupying both theorists and historians since the middle of the eighteenth century, especially since Marxist approaches. Briefly, the question is whether history follows a discernible pattern of development. If it does, there must be a theory laying bare the course of history that enables us to predict the future and perhaps to construct it. The extreme version of this idea even claims that the social structure of society in the future can be known and planned in advance. These ideas were discussed much, both within and outside of Marxist literature. It is not difficult to show that the role of theory in history has not, so far, been entirely resolved. Even Arthur Marwick, the author of *The Nature of History*, who does not believe in 'claiming for history a theoretical basis' (Marwick, 1989: 152), admits that there is room for theory in history.

> History is a systematic subject which calls for a fully conscious and fully articulated statement of assumptions and methods, which employs generalisations, concepts, and theories (plural), which as and when necessary can be tested by empirical methods, and a subject which has complex, definable, but always expanding ranges of sources and means of exploiting them.
>
> (1989: 152)

Given this argument, if one looks at design or industrial design history, one finds that there is no distinct theory of historiography, neither to be developed nor be subscribed to. Furthermore, no comprehensive discussion on this issue is being carried out, except for some limited attempts. The 'closeness' of design circles to theory is known. In a quotation given above, Kalman draws attention to 'a self-fulfilling prophecy: designers don't read, so design writers don't write' (Kalman, 1991: 50). Dilnot makes it clear: 'Design activity since 1945 can be explained by paying attention to the main motors of economic-industrial motivation in this period. However, resistance to 'theory' and to concepts brought in from other disciplines or areas is often rooted in the dislike of the idea that the imported concepts are merely background' (1984b: 10).

Regarding these observations and given that current design literature offers far fewer theories than expected, I believe that design history as a serious scholarly activity demands more effort to improve its theoretical framework. To this end, I would like to look at the relationship of design history with history in general.

8.6 Degree of historical consciousness

My first set of arguments concerns the specific stages in which the connection of two disciplines was initially neglected, later recognized and eventually studied. My second point is how design history conducted a direct dialogue with history. A glance at the subject indicates that there is much common ground.

8.6.1 Stage of negligence

According to the view outlined above, one of the important sins of omission of the industrial design literature is not being fully aware of the problems of the discipline of history. What that history is, is the question that never appears in the overwhelming majority of design books. This negligence is most likely due to the direct co-operation of art and architecture. Since design history mostly developed under the aegis of these two disciplines, it did not need further methods, techniques or theories to fulfil expectations in its early years of formation. What art and architecture offered was sufficient to solve most of the problems faced in lecture halls, design courses and limited textual works.

Naturally, the question of what history is would be absurd in a milieu where conditions are not mature enough to raise it. The development of a discipline is a process of many stages: initially, it is fated to be dependent, followed by a period of imitation as the adaptation of tested methods offers a safe way. In many cases, before creating its own methods, a discipline must apply existing ones to check where they work and where they do not. Eventually, the discipline reaches adolescence, when it is preoccupied with the search for its identity. Originality and an appraisal of the past are inevitable. This period of identity seeking is a time of total consciousness and perpetual inquiry, hence also a period of independence when critical questions are asked more often than ever. The structure of the area of research is mostly formed through these efforts. I am convinced that design history, which is arguably in its mature years of formation, has followed this pattern with similar phases.

8.6.2 Stage of recognition

I have noticed that more critical questions have appeared after the mid-1980s as the identity of design history has come under scrutiny. In this context, one of the matters preoccupying scholars is the relationship with other areas. Clive Dilnot, a distinguished spokesman on the subject, asks: 'What is the relationship between design history and other areas of study and inquiry? To use the most obvious example, what is its relationship to art history? Also, what is its relationship to history in general and to the specialist histories of technology, economy, and business that impinge on the subject?' (1984a: 4–5).

Scholars have raised these and similar questions again and again. However, it seems that the answers have been less fruitful and abundant than the questions. A few works have attempted to throw light on this issue, such as John Walker's *Design History and History of Design*: 'Since design history is a branch of the discipline history, design historians encounter in their practice the same basic methodological and theoretical problems, as do all historians' (Walker, 1989: 74). Starting from this premise, Walker draws a parallel with the problems of history and design history, such as facts, narration, synchrony and diachronic periodization. Analysis of design history's relations with history not only introduces the current debates taking place in and around history but also furnishes the researcher with the vast experience and many methods of an established discipline. Moreover, it enables design history to locate itself within various histories and form its own reference points accordingly.

8.6.3 Stage of study

It is worth pointing out from the outset that approaching history should be carefully orchestrated. Otherwise, it could easily replace the position of art and architecture, and might begin to influence design history as much as the others. Nor is it a matter of the balance of influence between these three disciplines. Rather, it is simply the reconstruction of a healthy relationship that has been neglected so far. It should aim to give an account of design history's emancipation from art and architectural influence, and the provision of the backbone of an authentic identity based on a reasonable relationship with history in general as well as with the other disciplines.

At this point, two questions come to mind: why is an account with history necessary? And how can design history benefit from it? To respond to the latter is not as easy as to respond to the former. While a short answer suffices for the first question, a longer investigation is necessary to formulate a detailed method of usage for the second.

Let us take the first question. Given that the discipline of history is very old, it is naturally very experienced in the study of the past. Therefore, any scientific work in any field of research concerning the past is expected to have recourse to history's vast accumulation of erudition. However, this is not to say that history provides a single holistic way of looking at the past. Rather, there are many methods of studying the past and many distinct approaches, all operating simultaneously and representing diverse philosophical and theoretical stances. Hence, digging up the past without consulting these sources is both an isolated and limited effort in which the conjectures and conclusions may well be superficial.

To benefit from the experience of history is neither evidence of subordination nor dependence. It is unlikely that interdisciplinary relations can be comprehended with these terms. Thus, when we closely examine the situation, it becomes more and more transparent that the real problem is not to determine and label the position of disciplines with respect to each other but to inquire into the nature of their relationship and the essence of their interaction.

In such an interaction, for example, the methodologies applied in the writing of history could be inspirational if not provide a direct contribution to design history. However, the objects of study in these disciplines are rather different. Given that the objects and, most likely, the objectives of histories vary substantially, the extent to which their methodologies might be shared, becomes a matter of discussion. Therefore, particular historical studies have to develop their own methodological tools to meet their own specifications and provide their own research techniques.

Expressed directly and frankly, the nature of design history obliges further ongoing inspection. Without this, the definition and legitimization of its identity is difficult to be clarified. However, this resurrects the question reiterated over millennia: the nature of history. This has been profoundly studied and may well provide the young scholars of design history with a source of inspiration and reasonable examples to follow and improve.[20]

8.7 Notes for a prospective historiography

In light of the arguments and observations I have presented, I would like to make a few constructive remarks as a corollary. The impression I have is that if industrial design history is defined without addressing the issues mentioned above, it is doomed to be prescriptive, descriptive, static and therefore limited. The major reason why a direct answer is not adequate ensues from the ambiguity and the ambiguity surrounding the discipline, which has to be uncovered, probably by developing theoretical frameworks with which to consolidate its structure. The absence of such an endeavour opens the way for a wide range of questions in search of an identity for design history. Clive Dilnot continues his inquiry into its position and later its nature:

---

[20]In this respect, many works can be cited, particularly classics like Marc Bloch's *The Historian's Craft*, Fernand Braudel's *On History*, R. G. Collingwood's *The Idea of History*.

is it better to think of design history as a part of history in general? But if so what kind of contribution should or could it make? Is it, or would it be, merely a minor, if useful, subsection of economic, social, and technological history? Or might it be a more significant contribution, a different way of reading or comprehending history? In its twentieth-century guise and its more theoretically informed aspects, does not design history potentially deserve to be linked with cultural studies and the sociology of media and culture, even with aspects of anthropology and archaeology? And, finally, as a history of 'things seen,' what might its relationship be to art and architectural history and to the histories of the decorative arts?

(1984a: 4–5)

A quick response to these straight inquiries may perhaps be given as follows. To start with, all questions anticipating interdisciplinary, multi and cross-cultural approaches to the subject are undeniably valid and more than welcome. As long as an article is produced within a culture or belongs to a culture, a profound analysis involving all related fields becomes inevitable. From anthropology to industrial archaeology, numerous scientific research areas have definitely something to offer concerning objects. Yet, (industrial/product) design history should not be confused with the history of objects, for example with George Kubler's suggestion of a 'History of Things', which includes almost everything. He uses the term as opposed to the 'bristling ugliness of "material culture"', which is, for him, preferred by

> anthropologists to distinguish ideas, or 'mental culture', from artefacts. But the 'history of things' is intended to reunite ideas and objects under the rubric of visual forms: the term includes both artefacts and works of art, both replicas and unique examples, both tools and expressions – in short all materials worked by human hands under the guidance of connected ideas developed in temporal sequence.
>
> (Kubler, 1978: 9)

The broadness of this approach obviously differentiates it from what we understand by industrial design history. His controversial remark on the concept of 'material culture', made in 1962, seems to have failed to discourage researchers, given the rising popularity of the term (for example, Daniel Miller's 1987 book, *Material Culture and Mass Consumption*, received positive responses in those years).

Beyond the special role proceeding from the nature of its object, design history has a mission identical to that of history. Therefore, its readers should not be radically different from those of any other historical study. Design historians do scholarly work to contribute to the discipline. Hence, they do not write for themselves but to serve the development of design history. However, this does not mean that all scholarly written history incorporates knowledge in the form and content required by professional designers, educators, students, managers and so on. Identifying the requirements that different audiences demand from history and composing the information as necessary may require a special emphasis on certain subjects, details and cases. While these special demands cannot challenge the course of historical studies, they can encourage specialism and expertise within the field. However, it is also true that history written especially for a limited and defined audience may well provide a scholarly work that contributes to the discipline: 'Even meagre, scattered, and obscure documentation can be put to good use,' says Carlo Ginzburg (1980: xvii).

What these observations can do for local design historiography is a good subject for further research. Globalization brings a new perspective to historiography, which should not be ignored.[21] Fry considers this a 'fundamental challenge to the nature and authority of the current Eurocentric models of history writing'. He thinks that local history[22] 'will not be based on the same agenda, object, rhetoric or concerns. He insists that "Design history on and in the margins … is a different history"' (1995: 217). Fry's argument provides another perspective within which historians of the 'margin' may seek another trajectory to locate their findings through which they can examine in depth the enigmatic relationship with the 'centre' and global concerns.

---

[21] For a short view on particular aspects of globalization in design see Chapter 3 in Section One.
[22] The vocabulary of global and local is my emphasis. Although Fry uses these expressions – especially in *Design History: Australia* – the binary model of centre and margin is utilized more frequently in his article published in *Design Issues* (see Fry, 1995).

CHAPTER 9
UNCHARTED TERRITORIES OF TRANSNATIONAL DESIGN HISTORY WITH PARTICULAR REFERENCE TO TURKEY

This chapter was presented at ICDHS 2016 Taipei conference, entitled: Building Trans/National Design History, The 10th International Conference on Design History and Studies, 26–28 October 2016. Taipei. It was published in the conference proceedings. W. S. Wong, Y. Kikuchi and T. S. Lin, eds. (2016), Building Trans/National Design History, *San Paolo: Blucher.*

9.1 Introduction

This chapter aims at revealing and discussing the particular characteristics of transnational design history that we have encountered in Turkey. In order to study the subject with a coherent approach, the understanding of transnational history and its interpretation for the field of design will be briefly revealed. This will help define a conceptual territory within which an undefined area will be looked into with an example from design history in Turkey.

9.2 Transnational history

The expression of transnational is not new. It goes back to 1862 when German philologist Georg Curtius discussed 'transnational' languages in Leipzig (Macdonald, 2013). It took six years for its first English appearance, in an article published in Princeton Review (Macdonald, 2013). Nevertheless, the term gained widespread use and enriched substance since 1990, which has opened avenues for serious discourse as well as offering new ways for history research (Yuko Kikuchi, 2014; Katarina Friberg, 2007; Macdonald, 2013). The rise of globalization debates and the issues of migration are among the leading factors bringing the term transnationalism to the agenda. Simon Macdonald gives a good account of the evolvement of the term and concludes that 'Akira Iriye's influential call in 1989 for new research "to search for historical themes and conceptions that are meaningful across national boundaries" accelerated the emergence of transnational histories' (Macdonald, 2013: 4).

The relationship, meaning and position of transnational histories with respect to comparative studies, global and world histories were much discussed (Bayly, 2006, Tyrrell 2007, 2009). It would not be right to draw a straightforward conclusion and give precise definitions of each one, but a few sentences formulating the framework of this paper would be useful for the arguments presented later. Comparative studies have their own aims and objectives and are restricted to nations and states. The critical writers underline that comparative studies could be strengthening the national version of history and may treat 'its cases as autonomous and ignores the link between them'. In defence of comparative studies, Frieberg, Hilson and Vall argue that 'comparative methods, practiced as a heuristic search for similarities and differences across space, may transcend national borders without reinforcing dominant national paradigms' (Friberg, 2007: 735). Referring to Miller's article, many commentators would agree that comparative and transnational histories are not mutually exclusive, but they are complementary although the scope of transnational studies is much wider and inclusive (Szélpál, 2009).

The differences between world and global histories are vague as the differences between transnational histories and comparative histories. Bayly has stated 'that the distinctions between world, global, and transnational history have never adequately been explained' (2006: 1442). His explanation is to highlight the minor distinctions: 'I get the sense that "trans-national history" stands in the same relationship to "international history" as "global history" does to "world history": that it is much the same thing, except that the term "transnational" gives a sense of movement and interpenetration' (Bayly, 2006). Ian Tryyell's observations are in the same direction: 'The new transnational history was related to, but not the same as globalization, world history, and comparative history' (2007: 1).

Kikuchi gave a good account of these debates and analysis of the concepts with special emphasis on their reflection on design history (2014). To focus on the subject of this paper, her description of transnational history will be utilized for it is pragmatic and instrumental: 'The transnational approach identifies the porousness of national borders and allows us to see different flows of human activities, including interactions of people, objects, ideas and art and design movements; otherwise the perspectives are delimited by national borders' (2014: 325). Actually, this is a definition accepted by many scholars, as Thelen writes: 'We wanted to explore how people and ideas and institutions and cultures moved above, below, through and around as well as within the nation-state' (1999: 967).

9.3 Two cases from Turkey: Bruno Taut and Balians

Taking these sentences as starting points, two hypotheses will be formulated based on specific cases concerning design history in Turkey. The purpose of these suppositions is to raise questions, touch upon uncharted territories and perhaps generate new perspectives for the further development of transnational design history. The first situation is Non-Reflective Transnational Dissemination of Impacts, which denotes a one-directional process where design ideas mostly run from the centre to the periphery but not vice versa in particular areas. An excellent example is Bruno Taut who was born in Konigsberg in 1880, studied architecture in Stuttgart, designed the legendary Glass Pavilion for the 1914 Deutscher Werkbund Exhibition, built many housing compounds in Berlin, moved to Japan in 1933 and finally relocated to Turkey in 1936, where he died and was buried in Istanbul, just after he designed the catafalque for Mustafa Kemal Atatürk. Taut was appointed as the first Head of Architecture Department at the Fine Art Academy in Istanbul. Although his life in Turkey was short and limited to his last two years, the amount of work he created and his influence on the constitution of modern Turkish architecture is considerable (Aslanoğlu, 1976). Taut had worked as a practicing architect for the Turkish State as much as he operated as a head of department. Among the many buildings he designed, the Faculty of Languages, History and Geography of Ankara University is particularly important for its scale, appearance, materials selected and details, which made it a manifest for modern architecture in the late 1930s of Turkey. Among his other works, he made another fascinating move: as a cultural agent and a restless soul, after his experience in Japan, Bruno Taut designed and built a 'pagoda' house for himself in Istanbul (Figure 1).

When Taut's life, experiences and successes in various countries are taken into account, his irrefutable role and undeniable value for international architecture become apparent. In this respect, we can assume and expect that his work is the subject of intensive research, leading to vast quantities of publications. Unfortunately, this is not the case. As an exception to this general trend, we may include the works of Manfred Speidel, a Bruno Taut expert, an early text by Aslanoğlu (1976), a book section by Bozdoğan (1997), an article by Erdim (2007) and the seminal book of Esra Akcan published in

Figure 1 Pagoda House designed by Bruno Taut, situated at the Bosphorus in Istanbul. Photo courtesy of Senanur Ceylan.

2012. Most of the researchers on Bruno Taut have often focused on his worldwide known 'Glass House' or his achievements in national scopes, for instance, his housing schemes in Berlin, his buildings and pedagogical role in Turkey or his endeavours in Japan.

Three issues surface here: (a) he is underrated and ignored by many historians in the West; (b) his works in countries far from the West, namely in Turkey and Japan, remain distant from current design discourses and have been missed out; and (c) national histories and comparative studies have failed to uncover his transnational significance. Reyner Banham's remark on Taut supports these observations. Referring to his 1914 Glass House, Banham writes: 'Quite apart from the possibility of its having been influenced by Paul Scheerbart's book, Glasarchitektur which came out in the same year, its rare qualities suggest that it was produced in a moment of genius that Taut was unable to repeat' (Banham, 1989: 81). Is 'unable to repeat' not a judgemental statement proposed without evaluating Taut's later work in Japan and Turkey?

İnci Aslanoğlu encounters another kind of reserved approach to Taut (1976: 35). Aslanoğlu, referring to Walter Segal's article (1972), notes that post-war architectural historians had focused sufficiently on the Bauhaus and many German émigré architects but they avoided Taut and his work for this is a very difficult subject matter that they did not know how to handle or classify. Thanks to a transnational approach, Esra Akcan has worked to overcome these difficulties forty years after those sentences were written (2012). Akcan prefers the word 'translation' instead of 'transnational' in her book. However, her definition of the former is not dissimilar to the definitions of 'transnational' that we use here, a 'term I particularly find accessible since it is a common experience, whether one has translated between two languages, mediums or places. ... a cultural flow from one place to another' 2012: 4).

Nevertheless, even Akcan's work serves to prevent further inquiries: Taut's house in Istanbul known as Japanese House, due to its pagoda-like appearance, offers a wonderful view of the Bosporus due to its architectural configurations (Akcan, 2000). But, why 'pagoda', a form used for temples in Japan, should be employed in Istanbul for a dwelling is not very clear. Akcan considers it a 'critical and innovative gesture' while Taut, in a letter to Walter Segal, stresses that his designs are samples of his architectural understanding (Akcan, 2012). Bozdogan underlines that this house 'stands out from the rest of his built work in Turkey as the symbol of his preoccupation with the lessons of vernacular in Japan and Turkey' (1997: 185–186). If we take the Turkish design concepts used in this building into account, one may conclude that Taut has created an amalgamation of transcultural design appropriate to geography and climate with innovative features reflecting a contemporary taste of his own.

What effect this house and Taut's other works in Turkey have made in architectural practice and education in Japan or in the West has not surfaced in this initial survey. Probably none. Is it because Istanbul and Taut were not part of cutting-edge design discourse in the West? Could we assume that this may be a Non-Reflective Transnational Dissemination of Impacts, a one-directional process where design ideas among others, flow from centre to periphery but not vice versa? Could the centre (or some countries of the centre) be more introverted and self-oriented and, thus, closed to the periphery at certain time periods?

This brings the second example to the fore for examination: the Balian family (Balyan in Turkish). Three generations of the Balian family, members such as Kirkor (1764–1831), his son Karabet (1800–1866), and his sons Nikogos (1826–1858), Sarkis (1835–1899) and Agop Balian (1830–1875), were the key figures of nineteenth-century Ottoman architecture (Goodwin, 1992). They were working for Ottoman Sultans and had erected the most important buildings, comprising Dolmabahçe, Çırağan and Beylerbeyi Palaces, Ortaköy and Valide Sultan Mosques, Beyazıt and Dolmabahçe Clock Towers, and houses at Akaretler in Istanbul to name but a few. Nikogos, Sarkis and Agop had studied at Sainte-Barbe College in Paris, where Alexandre Labrouste, brother of renowned French Architect Henri Labrouste, was the head. Goodwin wrote years ago about their attendance at Sainte-Barbe College and underlines how Henri Labrouste was influential on Nikogos (1992: 419).

What concerns us within the scope of this paper is how Balian's works are treated by national and transnational histories. The situation from the viewpoint of the former is not something that one can be proud of. Deliberating the great number of buildings they built more than a century ago, we discern that studies on their works are limited and publications are inadequate and are mostly comprised of articles, except for a few books on the subject. The main reason for the shortage of knowledge may derive from the 'little information concerning Balians themselves in the documentation of the Ottoman archives' (Wharton, 2010: 93). The list published in the book *Armenian Architects of Istanbul* portrays well the scenery and inevitably leads to the following critical observations:

First. In recent years the variety of commentators has increased and has been mostly and understandably researchers of Armenian origin who study the architecture of the Balian family. Benefiting from Armenian sources is obviously an advantage to getting further information at least for cross-checking.

Second. Up until a few decades ago, some historians kept a distance from Balian's designs and mentioned them in nothing more than a few superfluous sentences. When mentioned, Balian's architecture is neither praised nor acknowledged properly. A respected architectural historian, Abdullah Kuran, successfully describes several nineteenth-century Balian buildings without mentioning the originators' names in the text but in the footnotes only (Kuran, 2012). For art historian Oktay Aslanapa, Çırağan Palace is a hybrid example of a stupefaction period in which foreign constructions were destroying the portrait of the city where Italian architects were prevailing (Diez and Aslanapa, 1955). C. E. Arseven writes that Ottoman architecture was in total collapse in 1861 and adds, 'respected Rum and Italian architects of that time, used to make sort of weird buildings totally alien to Turkish Art' (Arseven, 1984: 180). (Rums are people who lived in East Roman Empire. As a Turkish expression, in common parlance, it refers to people of Greek origin who live in Ottoman territory as her citizen).

Third. The role of Armenian architects in Turkey is a minefield and an ideological battleground. For example, Aygül Ağır's assertion is that there is a lack of evidence to support that the Balian brothers officially studied in France (Ağır, 2005). Alyson Wharton, a researcher working on Armenian architects and architecture (Wharton, 2015) thinks the opposite and tries to prove it (Wharton, 2016). In a conference paper, Şerafettin Deniz claims that Nikogos Balian could not have built Ortaköy Mosque (Deniz, 2006). Selman Can takes the proclaims further: for him, Balians were not architects but constructors. Having said that, he then gives a list of architects as the designers of many buildings ascribed to Balians (Elmas, 2008). While nationalist history discourse attempts to ignore or discredit Balians or try to diminish their role in the design and construction of notable premises certified to them, their church designs are not even mentioned or not considered part of Ottoman architecture (Kuban, 2007).

Irvin Cemil Schick has very recently taken part in the writing of an edited book entitled *Türk Mimarisinde İz Bırakanlar* [Those Leaving Traces in Turkish Architecture]. The Ministry of Environment and Urban Planning has initiated an edited book project on Turkish architecture. Schick has been invited to become a member of the editorial board. He realizes that there is almost no foreign or non-Muslim architect on the list prepared. He insists that the list needs alterations and succeeds in getting some names included. His experience with the authorities and his narration of the publication process of the book illustrates clearly and ironically the current state of a prevailing nationalist attitude (Diler, 2016).

National histories do not grasp entirely the realities of fundamentally homogenous but at the same time multi-ethnic structure of Ottoman urban culture (Cerasi, 1988). Edhem Eldem articulates the situation eloquently: 'Nation-states are often incapable of understanding empires' (Eldem, 2010: 13). To this end, it becomes evident that transnational history finds another fecund soil within which to grow justification of its presence and effectiveness. Exactly here, the aforementioned question surfaces again: what impact has Balians' Baroque and Empire style architecture made on global or world history? Afife Batur and many other scholars accentuate that their work is not a copy of Western architecture but an original approach adopting and taking it further, which definitely requires a substantial investigation.

What can be said regarding Taut could also be reiterated in this point: Non-Reflective Transnational Dissemination of Impacts could also be valid for Balians. In other words, one would always like to know the influence and contribution of their architecture beyond the borders of the Ottoman Empire if there is any. Where does this stand in relation to conventional Baroque and Empire style and within the dominant discourse? How could transnational history draw a perspective within these niches of uncharted territories?

9.4 Conclusion

These questions are intended to indicate the necessity of new approaches as well as new directions needed in the design history of Turkey. However, the current nationalist streams also present gaps, voids and domains to be scrutinized. A nation-state born out of the ashes of a huge, cosmopolitan empire is substantially different than a nation-state based on one or two ethnic groups. In a sense, Turkey is to suffer from non-comprehension and non-embodiment of these diversities, which render the materialization of various religious and political fractions, societies and communities possible. This fragmentation causes and forces each group to search for and built its own identity. Historiography as well as design appears to be the victim of these affords, for they are being used and abused from time to time (Balcioglu and Emgin, 2014). Therefore, 'Trans-community Design Trends' drives from this multi-layered and, perhaps, as a positive remark, colourful mosaic but at the same time chaotic situation.

As a corollary, this paper draws the attention of design historians focusing on Turkey on two methodological concerns: Non-Reflective Transnational Dissemination of Impacts and Trans-community Design Trends. These two unexplored areas of transnational historiography, which definitely demand further study, may not be a Turkish-specific specificity but might be applicable in and for other countries as well. Therefore, historians have to be prepared to construct bridges over troubled waters.

CHAPTER 10
TURKISH GRAPHIC DESIGN
FROM THE AGE OF THE ALPHABET REVOLUTION TO
THE END OF THE TWENTIETH CENTURY

The first version of this paper was presented at the 4th European Academy of Design Conference, Aveiro, 10–12 April 2001, and published in its proceedings: R. Cooper and V. Branco, eds. (2001), d3 Desire, Designum, Design: 4th European Academy of Design Conference Proceedings, 476–481, Portugal: University of Aveiro.

10.1 Introduction

This chapter provides an overview of graphic design history during the Republican Era, from 1923 to 2000.[1] It is structured in three sections. The first one, 'a historical perspective' summarizes the political context of the period, which is closely related to graphic art as it was utilized for propaganda and advertising purposes. The second section, 'an analytic framework', proposes a classification and a theoretical approach to graphic design in Turkey, using examples of works produced by distinctive graphic designers. It is an attempt at a stylistic categorization of graphic works in terms of their design characteristics. It provides a general framework to study the history of graphic design in Turkey and refers to a group of selected works. Needless to say, there are many more well-established graphic designers in Turkey whose works deserve attention and take place in history books. It is unfortunate that this chapter cannot include more due to its limits. The final section presents the debate concerning the artistic value of graphic works.

10.2 A historical perspective

Research on Turkish graphic design is still in its infancy with only a handful of publications. Therefore, this chapter presents analytical observations on the development of graphic design in the Republic of Turkey based on the available material. This is not

---

[1] Please note that all Turkish words are transliterated and translations (in brackets) are by the author. The English translations are given without alteration as they appear in Turkish documents. Some world-famous books, plays, films and so on, were given new titles in Turkey; when such media are quoted here, their Turkish titles, rather than the original ones, will be used. If the original titles are known, they are indicated in brackets.

entirely a historical account; neither is it an attempt to uncover and name heroes or heroines. Rather, it is an endeavour to define a framework for further studies.

10.2.1 From 1923 to 1950

After being established in 1923, it was vital for the Turkish Republic to emerge fresh from the ashes of the old Ottoman Empire with a new identity. The caliphate was abolished and replaced by a secular and later democratic state. A Latin script alphabet (Sadık 1928, Sâdullah 1928) was introduced as part of Atatürk's reforms in 1928. The canonical legislation of Islam was replaced with laws mostly borrowed from the West; the fez was replaced with the hat; traditional garments with suits and ties. A poster by İhap Hulusi Görey (hereafter İhap Hulusi), the leading designer of the era, illustrates how traditional religious marriage was replaced with a modern one (Figure 2). Modernisation was associated with Westernization at a time when the West was embracing modernity. Therefore, the project of modernization imported into Turkey the ideas of modernity and Westernization without differentiating between them. Statism was adopted as an economic strategy of development with the bourgeoisie created through the state itself. The entire country was being rebuilt. State railroads, state banks, The Turkish State Maritime Lines and so on were being re-formed and established.

Figure 2 Propaganda postcard by İhap Hulusi Görey showing old and new marriage ceremonies. Image courtesy of Sinan Niyazioğlu.

On Design

Figure 3 Atatürk introducing the new Turkish Alphabet with Latin script in 1928. Photo courtesy of Sinan Niyazioğlu.

Regarding graphic design, the most drastic transformation was experienced in 1928, when the Arabic script was replaced with the Roman alphabet. As a result, graphic practice – however limited it was – changed irreversibly (Karamustafa, 1999). Atatürk, the founder of the Turkish Republic, introduced the new alphabet himself (Figure 3) and his image dominated the covers of the book 'Alphabet' for decades. The new alphabet (Figure 4) had the ironic mission of introducing itself as much as introducing the project of modernization within which German influences were prominent.[2] The well-known graphic designer – or, using the expression of the time, commercial artist – İhap Hulusi (1896–1986) was instrumental in the introduction of German graphic design. He was the most important name on the Turkish graphic design scene until the late 1950s. He had studied in Germany in the 1920s, having first trained as an artist and later as a poster and graphic designer (Maden, 1999). After returning to Istanbul in 1925, he worked as a freelance designer, mostly for state companies, banks and free enterprise. His famous triangular signature appeared on countless posters until he retired in 1975. During his long career, he also designed book covers, labels, logos and lottery tickets, among other things. Although he is now considered one of the pioneers of the profession, he hardly

---

[2] I recently did a Google search and found out that there are a number of new alphabets published in 1928. See Sadık (1928), and Sâdullah (1928).

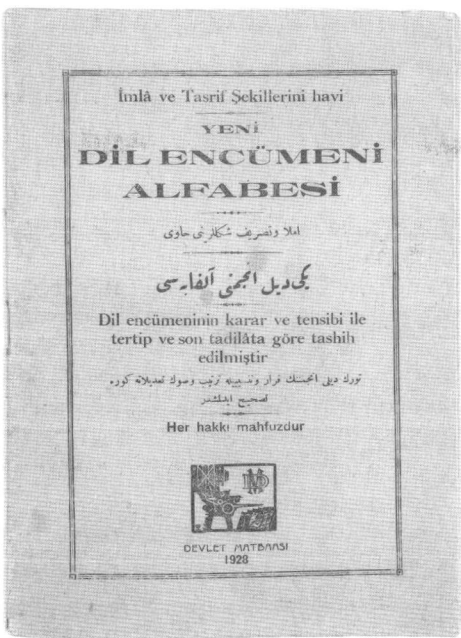

Figure 4 One of the first editions of the new Turkish Alphabet with Latin script by the Language Committee, 1928. Image courtesy of Sinan Niyazioğlu.

enjoyed this status in his lifetime. Instead, he was rediscovered in the late 1970s after graphic design had been recognized as an important commercial activity and the profile of the profession was elevated and gained wider status.

Although İhap Hulusi was the most important personality of this period, others also practised graphic design. Sait Maden (1989), a graphic designer and researcher, acknowledges Mithat Özer, Münif Fehim, Cevat Şakir and Ali Suavi among those practising in the 1930s, 1940s and 1950s (Maden, 1989). In an interview with the author, Yurdaer Altıntaş, the senior character in the field, remarked that he had not seen many works from the early period. He believed the great majority disappeared while people working in what we now call graphic design were not fully aware of the discipline as such. A few did graphic design among other occupations to earn their living but had no concern for the advancement of the profession.

Unfortunately, I had not come across substantial research to uncover and evaluate the works of these pioneers when this chapter was written in 2000. However, thanks to the recent revival of interest in design history, as attested in several design journals,[3]

---

[3]Mimar Sinan Fine Arts University, Centre of Graphic Design Research and Archive was recently established thanks to Prof. Dr. Sinan Niyazioğlu. Research projects are being conducted on key figures of Turkish graphic design (Erdem, 2003).

names like Latif Ariş whose work and life were the subject of a short article[4] are being reclaimed.

10.2.2 The 1950s: The Democrat Party

The years of the Second World War and those in its wake were not very fruitful for graphic design. After the war, Turkey abandoned the one-party system and entered the 1950s with a political election. During the 1950s, a new party, the Democrat Party, was elected with a large majority. Its adoption of a market economy and investment in industry changed the domestic political atmosphere drastically. Joining NATO and taking part in the Korean War helped open Turkey to world affairs. On the one hand, notions of independence, a multi-party system, social consciousness, workers, unions and democratic rights were entering the agenda; on the other, nationalists, religious fundamentalists and the extreme right were stepping in. From this perspective, the 1950s were interesting years of transformation, witnessing the birth of free capitalist enterprise and a new spirit in Turkish social and political life.

Sait Maden mentions the work of Kenan Temizan, who won third prize in the NATO poster competition of 1951 and who also opened an exhibition at the Fine Art Academy in 1953. In addition, he refers to a few new graduates, such as Mesut Manioğlu, Selçuk Önal and Fikret Akgün. He considers Manioğlu to be the greatest master of the 1950s, with his logos, posters and exhibition designs (Maden, 1999). No doubt, the graphic design of this period also needs further scrutiny.

10.2.3 The 1960s: The first coup d'état

Turkey experienced three coups d'état, in 1960, 1971 and 1980. Although each had its own social, political and economic consequences, it is widely accepted that the 1960 coup was a turning point for many developments, including graphic design. Sait Maden stresses that 'an intense and qualified application of graphic arts in every branch took place after the 1960s' (Maden, 1999). In the late 1950s, two designers who graduated from Istanbul State Academy of Fine Arts, and who would become two of the leading names, were already practising: Mengü Ertel and Yurdaer Altıntaş.

Graphic design education had been introduced at the Istanbul State Academy of Fine Arts in 1927. Later, in 1957, the State School of Applied Fine Arts was established. Both schools benefited from German expertise, which contributed considerably to Turkish higher education, design and architecture in the early years of the Republic (Karamustafa, 1999). Although design education was never adequate in those years,[5]

---

[4]See Umut Kart, *Art Decor*, September 2002. *Art Decor* is a Turkish journal publishing on art, design and decoration.
[5]In an interview in 1987, Yurdaer Altıntaş described his years at the Academy between 1952 and 1957: 'The first year was devoted to drawing busts, the whole time no life work or colour.... You were given seven or eight subjects a year; no briefs or tuition' (Erkmen, 1987: 40).

there were a few trained designers practising in the 1960s who were the major characters in introducing contemporary graphic design in Turkey. Mengü Ertel was the leading figure, who raised the stakes in the development of graphic design, while Yurdaer Altıntaş was the first graphic designer from Turkey whose work was published abroad. He was instrumental in establishing the Society of Graphic Artists, founded in 1968. He also organised the publication of Turkish designers' work in the German magazine *Gebrauchgraphic* in 1967. Other important contributors to the profession included Sait Maden (1985, 1989, 1999), Aydın Erkmen, Cemalettin Mutver and Erkal Yavi, mostly through their theatre posters, book covers and logo designs.

10.2.4 1971 and 1980: Two more coups d'état

The 1960 coup ushered in a liberal, democratic climate within which Marxist ideas flourished in line with the political events of 1968 internationally. By contrast, the 1971 coup brought restrictions and oppression, although the subsequent proliferation of political posters, leaflets and publications played a significant role in the rise of graphic design. During the 1970s, graphic practice in Turkey began to change. Another important factor in the rise of the profession was the establishment of the Higher School of Applied Industrial Arts with its policy of employing professional and practising graphic designers. In those years, despite political difficulties, there was an increase in democratic organizations and political awareness, improvements in industry and the market economy, and a growing number of advertising agencies, which became harbingers of a new era. Television, which had become part of daily life, colour press and offset printing, which were developing rapidly, and political activities, all required intensive communication while publicity was becoming more important. Hence, conditions were now ripe enough for graphic design to flourish. Among many new designers emerging and enhancing the profession, Bülent Erkmen and Sadık Karamustafa, with their strong graphic works, and Emin Barın, with his original typographic research, began to make statements in the field. Although calligraphy had been a widely explored art form during the Ottoman period, typography has never been the strongest point of graphic design in Turkey. Only after the 1980s has it become an area in design, with a few pioneers developing typefaces for logos and posters with limited use. While I assume that young, new-generation designers are working on the subject, I have not come across any Turkish fonts used in publishing, which makes Emin Barın's efforts invaluable and unique.

10.2.5 After the mid-1980s

The big leap in graphic design development took place after the mid-1980s. The 1983 elections brought Turgut Özal to power with his Thatcherite free market policies. After serving as Prime Minister, he later became president until his death in 1993. In the years of Turgut Özal, graphic practice in Turkey was affected by the way in which it was commercialised. An export-oriented open market policy, privatization of state-owned companies and the abolition of the state's monopoly on communication, including TV and radio, all boosted the private sector considerably. As a result, retailers, large sectors of industry, businesses, banks, publishers, press insurance companies and so on launched consumer-targeted promotion campaigns undertaken by advertising agencies as complete – and very expensive – packages. Partly to meet deadlines and maintain quality, and partly to increase profits, these agencies then invested in in-house production, developing as many services as possible from graphic design studios to publishing. Even filming and post-production facilities were incorporated. However, this left no room for individual freelance designers, who eventually found themselves seeking employment in advertising agencies. Small graphic studios could hardly survive on minor commissions. Even today, Turkey has only a few independent respected designers fighting against the mainstream.

Of course, under these circumstances and thanks to computer and digital technology, graphic design was radically transformed. The talent and experience once gained through designing educational, cultural and political posters, book covers, calendars and leaflets were now being 'consumed' through billboards, TV advertisements, filmmaking, corporate and promotional materials, website designs and so on. Commercialization and a culture of consumption prevailed, with no difference to the West, except in scale.

Today's graphic designers operate across a great range of fields, the number of designers and design schools has grown considerably, and the gender balance has also improved, with women designers working on the front lines with great success. Contemporary graphic design in Turkey is already part of global culture. Under the leadership of Yurdaer Altıntaş, the Society of Graphic Artists (Grafik Sanatçıları Derneği) was established in 1968 and it shaped the foundation of the Turkish Society of Graphic Designers (Grafik Tasarımcılar Meslek Kuruluşu, GMK) in 1978. GMK regularly organizes annual exhibitions, publishes catalogues and awards prizes for designs in categories such as posters, book covers, logos, promotional materials, letterheads and press campaigns (GMK, 1995, 1998, 1999, 2000). Turkish designers are exhibiting and getting published abroad and receiving overseas awards. Indeed, a lot of work produced in Turkey is world-class. The problem, however, is that we do not know to what extent they are close to the cutting edge, fostering new ideas and potential, just as we do not know to what extent they are doomed to disappear within the market after completing their missions successfully.

10.3 An analytic framework

During the research for this paper, it became apparent to me that certain periods and groups of works can be described and may even be categorized under specific headings. I name these Realistic/Representative, Symbolic/Illustrative, Abstract/Integrative and Conceptual/Referential. These are by no means either rigid or canonical but rather a set of open-ended descriptions to understand and place the work in context. However,

I believe their emergence is sequential and sometimes overlapping. Of course, other groupings can also be obtained from these four. For instance, some works may straddle Symbolic/Abstract graphics; others may be Abstract/Conceptual. Nevertheless, it appears to me that the majority of the works fall into the initial four categories, with which I feel confident to cover most of the design territory explored, especially in relation to the historical periods described. With this framework in mind, I would argue that the works produced in the early years of the Republican period can be classified as Realistic/Representative. To support this claim, I examine below the graphic works of İhap Hulusi, Münif Fehim and Latif Ariş as examples.

10.3.1 Realistic/representative

İhab Hulusi developed his strong drawing ability by drawing from life every day for two years at the Heimann Schule in Munich in the early 1920s (Erkmen, 1987). This makes his work very characteristic of the era in that it is directly informative, based on realistic representations and conveys a straightforward message. The visual image depicts what the text says. Take the poster for the Bank of Agriculture (Figure 5), it reads 'Whoever saves lives comfortably' while the image shows a money box – for savings of course – and a relaxed peasant resting on the ground enjoying his cigarette. Or take the poster of Beykoz Shoes (Figure 6): it reads 'Beykoz shoes are like seagulls, they are waterproof'

Figure 5 Advertisement for Bank of Agriculture, designed by İhap Hulusi, 1948. Image courtesy of Sinan Niyazioğlu.

On Design

Figure 6 Advertisement for Beykoz Shoes, designed by İhap Hulusi. Image courtesy of Ömer Durmaz.

and you see a pair of shoes, with flying seagulls and raindrops above, all realistically rendered. Removing the image changes nothing because the image is subordinated to the text; the text is explanatory, making a clear statement about the message. İhap Hulusi also resorted to photography to create images and figures. For example, used a photograph of himself to design a label for rakı, a popular Turkish alcoholic drink (Figures 7A and 7B). More than seventy years after his design, the label still represents the brand, Kulüp Rakısı [Club Raki]. He used the same technique to design the cover of the alphabet book published in 1932. He took a photograph of Atatürk, the founder of the Turkish Republic, teaching the new alphabet to his adopted daughter Ülkü (Figures 8A and 8B), and he modified it by replacing the person behind Atatürk with Ankara Castle and by slightly manipulating the posture of the girl.

A similar relationship between text and image can be observed in the works of Münif Fehim, who started designing book covers in the 1930s. The illustrations are again realistic, descriptive and with painterly qualities; they either represent a certain moment of fiction or refer to it. For instance, the cover of Edgar Allan Poe's *Incredible Stories* was derived from one of the stories, *The Golden Scarab* (Figure 9) (Gönenç, 1985). Others present an extraordinary moment of action, excitement and mystery. *Amok* (Figure 10) and *Bir Kadının 24 Saati* [24 Hours in The Life of a Woman] by Stefan Zweig, *Acıkan Taşlar* [The Hungry Stones] by Rabindranath Tagore are as if cut and taken from an action movie, making you wonder what happens next (Figure 11).

Figures 7A–B Photograph of İhap Hulusi drinking rakı (7A), and the label of Kulüp Rakısı (7B). Photo and image courtesy of Ömer Durmaz.

On Design

Figure 8A–B Photograph showing Atatürk teaching the new alphabet to his adopted daughter Ülkü (8A) and the new alphabet book cover derived from this photograph (8B), 1935. Photo courtesy of Ömer Durmaz, cover of the alphabet book courtesy of Sinan Niyazioğlu.

Figure 9 The cover of Edgar Allan Poe's book, *Incredible Stories*, designed by Münif Fehim, 1938. Image courtesy of Izmir National Library.

Figure 10 Münif Fehim's design: the cover of *Amok*, a book by Stefan Zweig, 1939. Image courtesy of Izmir National Library.

On Design

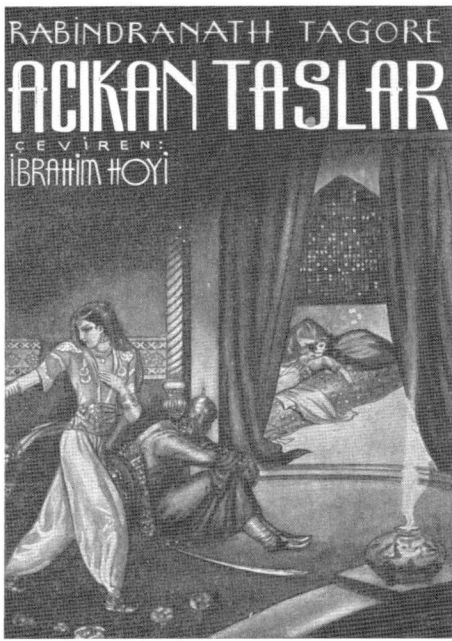

Figure 11 Münif Fehim's design: the cover of *The Hungry Stones* by Rabindranth Tagore. Image courtesy of Ömer Durmaz.

Thus, the attraction of the graphics lies not in the images themselves but in what they depict. The designer promises a good story behind the cover. In fact, what you see is not a cover but the inside of the book, so one may feel that any illustration inside the book could have been selected and turned into the cover with no difficulty. The cover is like a window looking inside the book, foreshadowing the stories, probably the most intriguing ones.

Latif Ariş, born in 1908, studied graphics at Galatasaray Academy in Istanbul and graduated in the late 1930s. He lived and worked in Adana, in southern Turkey, as a freelance graphic designer and as a teacher (Kart, 2002). His work ranged from package graphic design for a salt company, to posters for several state institutions. His ticket design for the national lottery looks like the German fifty-Pfennig coin regarding the structure of the layout: the use of borders, big letters, big images and so on. It appears that the fifty-Pfennig coin was designed in 1921 (Haller, 1998: 105), and I wonder whether it was used as a source of inspiration for the lottery ticket design.

10.3.2 Symbolic/illustrative

During the late 1950s and 1960s, a new era of graphic design emerged. One designer widely recognized and appreciated as responsible for this breakthrough is Mengü Ertel. The characteristics of this period marked a radical departure from earlier work. In particular, realistic rendering is no longer essential while images are mostly symbolic

Figure 12 Poster for the play *Amadeus*, designed by Mengü Ertel, 1983. Image courtesy of Murat Ertel.

representations that, in many cases, stand on their own merits independently of the text (Figure 12). Strong emphasis is put on representation while the text is either not important for the design, or secondary, as if it were an addition to the image (Figure 13). In many cases, the lettering has clearly been inserted afterward and placed in the appropriate part of the illustrations. Sometimes, the illustration is so powerful and the meaning so obvious that no text is needed (Ertel, 1999).

What one can also observe is that the main success of the work derives from the artistic and drawing abilities of the designers. That is why, perhaps rightly, they call themselves 'graphic artists'.[6] Since their training was heavily based on art education, it is no coincidence that the quality of the work stems from the artistic quality of the illustrations. Therefore, when a founding member of the Society of Graphic Artists, who later became Head of the School of Applied Industrial Arts, Yurdaer Altıntaş, says 'I love my profession but have occasionally wished I were a painter', we understand the feeling as well as the link established with art (Erkmen, 1987: 47). Sadık Karamustafa, who was elected Vice-President of ICOGRADA in 1995, has considerably contributed to the

---

[6]Expressions such as 'commercial artist', 'graphic artist' and 'graphic designer' mark the transformation of the profession in the twentieth century; their use in Turkey is more likely than not the reflection of closely following developments in the West.

On Design

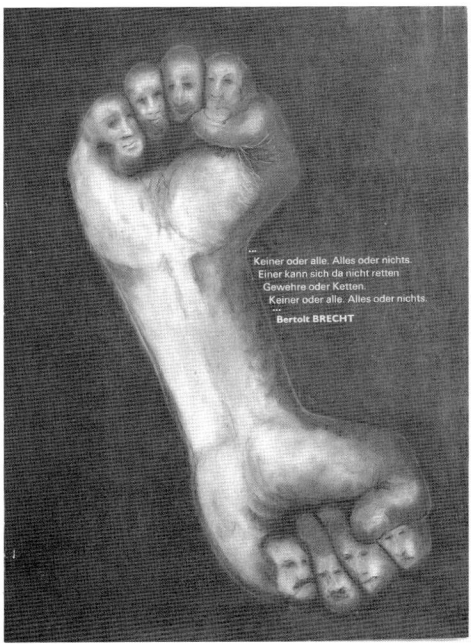

Figure 13 An illustration by Mengü Ertel. Image courtesy of Murat Ertel.

Figure 14 Poster for Istanbul Festival by Mengü Ertel, 1973. Image courtesy of Murat Ertel.

theory and practice of the profession (1999, 2002) calls the years between 1970 and 2000 a transition period from the stage of graphic art to graphic design (Erdem, 2003: 82).

These designers were undoubtedly aware of works being produced in the West and trying to keep up with world standards. They also made cultural references to traditional objects, archaeological findings and local attributes in Turkey from time to time. For example, Mengü Ertel's poster for the Istanbul Festival is made of mosaic-like images depicting the city itself as well as referencing famous Byzantine mosaics and the notion of festival (and even that of the city) as a mosaic of people representing

Figures 15A–C Logo designs by Mengü Ertel: Logo for a real estate company, 1984 (15A), the Social Democratic Party, 1984 (15B), and the Fair for Affordable Clothing, 1976 (15C). Logos courtesy of Murat Ertel.

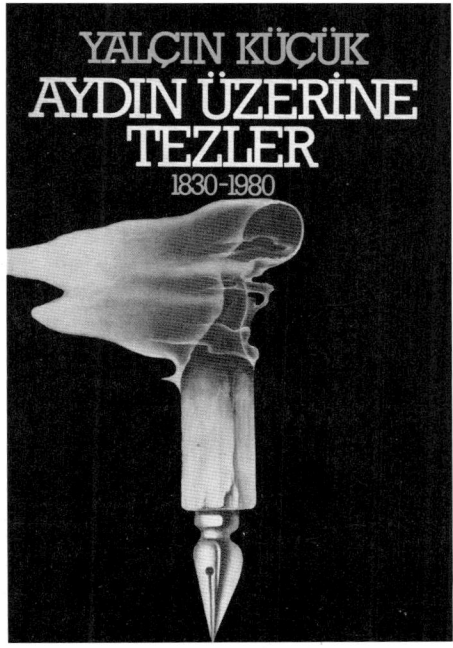

Figure 16 Erkal Yavi's book cover design for Tekin Publications, 1984. Illustration courtesy of Erkal Yavi.

the whole world with a wide variety of colour and texture (Figure 14). Some of Ertel's logo designs also incorporate strong elements of symbolism and illustration, as in those designed, variously, for a building company, the Social Democratic Party and the Fair for Affordable Clothing (Figures 15A, 15B and 15C).

Erkal Yavi's book cover design for Tekin Publications and poster design for Adam Publishers present powerful images loaded with political messages (Figure 16). One features a pen tip that appears to be one end of a burning match. Although it is open to various interpretations, I think it symbolizes the difficulty of writing under oppressive regimes, the risks that controversial writers are taking and the courage of touching upon hot issues. The poster for Adam Publisher is perhaps more optimistic showing beautiful daisies planted into an empty glass ink bottle (Figure 17). We do not see the ink bottle but we see its traces in its absence on the soil where daisies flourish. We immediately notice that to obtain this view, the ink bottle must have been broken and become useless. Does it mean writers were silenced and ink bottles ceased to function? Does it mean, even if it is not used for the purpose it is designed for, it is still capable of producing beauty and serves for peace and betterment of life? The image embodies lots of meanings and is open to further interpretations.

Other powerful visual expressions are produced by incorporating distorted images, cartoon-like characters, simplified silhouettes and outlines, which, together with signs like the dove and olive branch for peace, underline the symbolic nature of these works.

Figure 17 Erkal Yavi's poster design for Adam Publications, 1990. Illustration courtesy of Erkal Yavi.

Figure 18 Book cover for *The Iliad* by Homer. Designer: Sait Maden, 1967. Image courtesy of Ömer Durmaz.

Prominent designers such as Yurdaer Altıntaş, Sait Maden (Figure 18) and Aydın Erkmen, employed similar techniques to forcefully express their subjects.

10.3.3 Abstract/integrative

The major characteristic of this new generation of work is its emancipation from the illustration/typography duality, which had dominated the previous period. Designers began to use various techniques and media to convey the message, such as unfinished sketches, free-hand drawings, handwriting and doodling, as well as techniques such as silk-screen printing, photography, collage and air-brushing. Through this, they experimented with and explored the notion of graphic design further and further.

During this era, the overwhelming dominance of fonts like Helvetica, Times and Futura fades away while the unity between image, message and typography is highlighted. Early examples of these elements of integration include Mengü Ertel's poster for *Keşanlı Ali Destanı* [The Ballad of Ali of Keshan] (Figure 19) and for Ionesco's *Gergedan* [Rhinoceros] and Altıntaş's poster for Georges Feydeau's play *Bit Yeniği* [A Flea in Her Ear], which are not unlike a dialogue between image and typography. Later, there are some extreme instances of typography itself constituting the image. These include Karamustafa's posters for the Istanbul Film Festival (Figure 20), a play by Philip King entitled *Papaz Kaçtı* [How They Run] (Figure 21)) and the Third International

On Design

Figure 19 Mengü Ertel's poster design for *Keşanlı Ali Destanı* [The Ballad of Ali of Keshan], a play by Haldun Taner, 1984. Image courtesy of Murat Ertel.

Figure 20 Sadık Karamustafa's poster design for the Eight Istanbul Film Festival, 1989. Photo courtesy of Sadık Karamustafa.

Turkish Graphic Design

Figure 21 Poster for a play by Philip King, entitled *Papaz Kaçtı* [How They Run], designer: Sadık Karamustafa, 1987. Photo courtesy of Sadık Karamustafa.

Conference on Design History and Design Studies (Figure 22), B. Erkmen's designs for Garbarek, and exhibition and dance performance posters (Figure 23) and Yurdaer Altıntaş's Hitchcock poster (Figure 24). Although they represent different approaches, they all enjoy the hidden pleasures of letters that themselves create visual images, illustrations or maybe even paintings.

10.3.4 Conceptual/referential

During this era, a few designers resisted the visual pollution created by the tabloid press, mass media and the dominance of advertising agencies. The following examples reflect their conceptual search, which I believe also includes a strong element of referential quality. References to history, ideas and movements are probably part of multiple readings, pluralist attributes, post-modern metaphors or irony. However, even an experimental exercise, a journey into the wilderness or a passage into the unknown requires a known referent. Here I critically analyse a few example works.

The first is Bülent Erkmen's poster for International Prison Watch (Figure 25). It is a minimalist piece of vertical parallel lines with two words, 'outside' and 'inside', written in white on black. The former is behind the lines whereas the latter is in front. Within this simplicity lies an enormous depth. You feel the three-dimensionality immediately while the vertical lines turn into metal bars. You notice that the word 'outside' is in fact

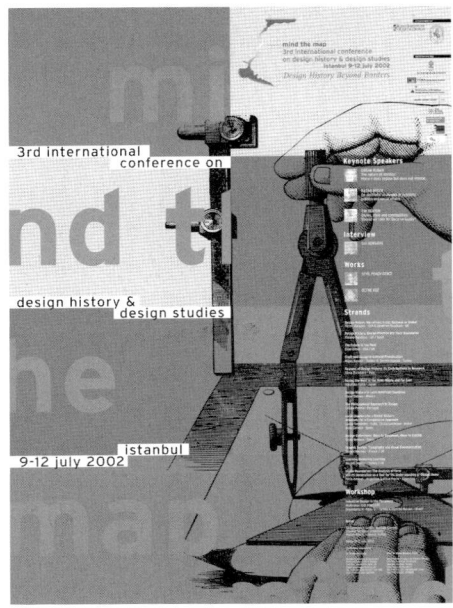

Figure 22 Sadık Karamustafa's poster for the Mind the Map, the Third International Conference on Design History and Design Studies, ICDHS, Istanbul, 2002. Photo courtesy of Sadık Karamustafa.

Figure 23 Bülent Erkmen's design for Jan Garbarek's jazz concert, Istanbul, 1998. Photo courtesy of Bülent Erkmen.

Figure 24 Yurdaer Altıntaş's Hitchcock poster for Eighteenth Istanbul Film Festival, 1999. Image courtesy of Ömer Durmaz.

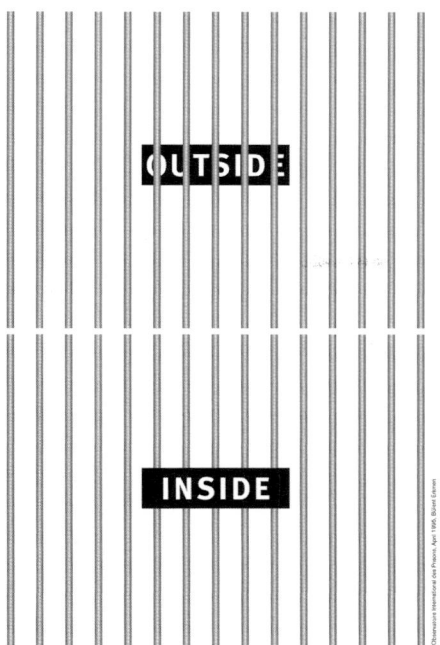

Figure 25 Poster for International Prison Watch, designed by Bülent Erkmen, 1995. Image courtesy of Bülent Erkmen.

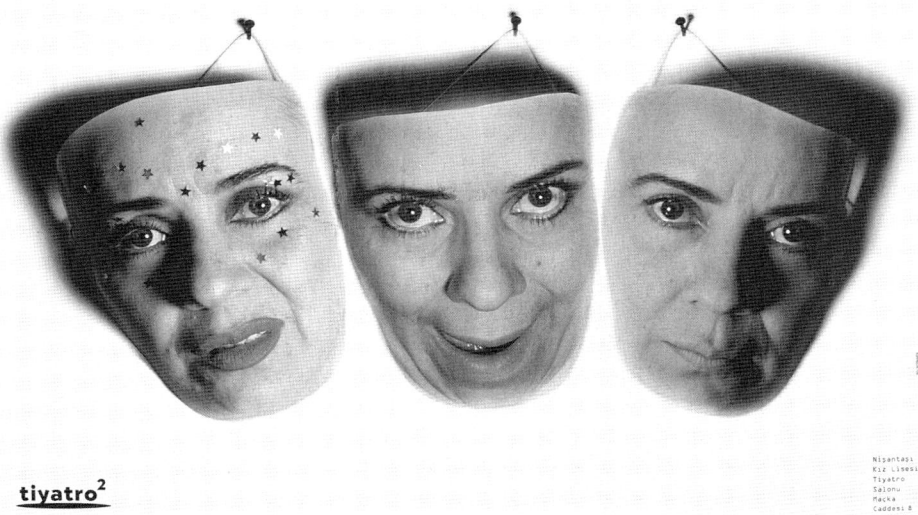

Figure 26 Bülent Erkmen's poster for the play *Cadılar Zamanı* [The Pope and the Witch] written by Dario Fo and Franca Rame. Image courtesy of Bülent Erkmen.

on the other side of the bars. Hence, you as a viewer/reader are inside, and the word 'inside' is shouting at you that you are 'inside'. Inside of what? A prison? A cell? Or within yourself? Are these my own bars that I set against myself? Against others? Am I protected because I am inside? Or are they being protected from me because I am inside? What is the difference between inside and outside? They look the same, both pretty grim. Then you realize that the entire audience watching the poster is inside, together with you – we are all inside. We are all insiders! And maybe no one is out there! We are all surrounded by bars.

The dramatic reading may continue since the poster is like a text that you can read, and read again. The occasion, the title and the rationale for the poster, that is, 'prison watch', fades in significance and becomes secondary. The range of potential meanings goes beyond the brief. The poster stands on its own with its sophisticated and unfolding content that exists as much as – and as long as – we interpret it.

Bülent Erkmen, who publishes his design works each year in a book format (1992, 1994, 1997 a, b, c, 1999, 2000, 2001), works with themes to create a series with which he makes his mark with a strong design identity. In particular, he widely uses objects, faces, masks and masked faces to expose layers of meanings, metaphors and ironies that leave the door open to post-modern interpretations (Figures 26 and 27).

Sadık Karamustafa's cover design for Dudu Akpınar's book blends black humour with irony (Figure 28). The title reads: 'The Only Thing I Ever Wished was to Write

Figure 27 Bülent Erkmen's poster design for the film *Arabesk* [Arabesque]. Photo courtesy of Bülent Erkmen.

a Book'. The front cover is in the form of a blank ruled notebook page. You know that you buy a book, yet you buy a book that looks like a notebook. At the same time, you wonder whether it is a notebook given to the author whose wish had always been to write a book. If so, you know that the book has yet to be written, in which case you might not be surprised if, when you open the book, all its pages were blank. Yet, you do not know this until you do open it. The visual reading of the cover already initiates a dialogue with you. You begin to read the book before you even open it. The image, of a blindfolded girl, adds to the suspense. Is she the author? Is 'writing a book' her last wish before the death squad? You will never know unless you read the book. But before you do, by placing the inside sleeves side by side, the girl reveals a little more of herself, and from closer (Figure 29).

The third example is by Esen Karol, a female, freelance Turkish book and graphic designer (Karol, 2001). Her theatre poster for *Macbeth* has a depth requiring closer examination (Figure 30). The stage photography instantly indicates that this is a play, even if you do not know what *Macbeth* is. The silhouetted figures, occupying the stage in groups or on their own, reveal that they are soldiers. Figures with rifles and long coats remind you of the First or Second World War, signalling a modern adaptation of the play. Their irregular distribution on stage is offset by, and weighed against, the title of the play, spelled in rigidly geometric and equally spaced letters, which contrasts with

Figure 28 The sleeve and cover for the book entitled *Benim Tek İstediğim Bir Kitap Yazmaktı* [The Only Thing I Ever Wished was to Write a Book] designed by Sadık Karamustafa. The image, *Vadedilmiş Topraklar 3* [Promised Lands 3] by Gülsüm Karamustafa, Istanbul, 1999. Photo courtesy of Sadık Karamustafa.

the lower half of the poster. The letters seem to be hanging from above like destiny or the Sword of Damocles hanging over the soldiers' heads. The uncompromising visual effect is further enhanced by Karol's use of colour, with a deep shade of red almost tangibly evoking spilled blood. Meanwhile, the other words float all around like scattered soldiers. They are in harmony with the rest, but neither their colour nor their size can challenge 'Macbeth'. That is, the strength, dimension and placement of the letters spelling 'Macbeth' exert real supremacy over the others; an ongoing and unfinished struggle is there on the surface. Observers feel the tension, blood and destiny. Esen Karol explores a similar approach in a poster for an art photography exhibition called *Sokaklardan* [From the Streets] by Şakir Eczacıbaşı (Figure 31). She presents the title as if it were graffiti scrawled on a large wall. In doing so, she shows her appreciation for one of the photographs in the exhibition, which she uses for the poster, yet she is not shy about making her own statement as a graphic designer.

Gülizar Çepoğlu explores the potential of the intersection between typography, meaning and depth of graphic communication. The exhibition poster that she designed for İpek Aksüğür Duben shows the transparency of floating letters forming layers above each other while the negated dialogue of overlapping images speaks in their dignified silence, each of which has its own orientation (Figure 32). Çepoğlu's newspaper designs

Turkish Graphic Design

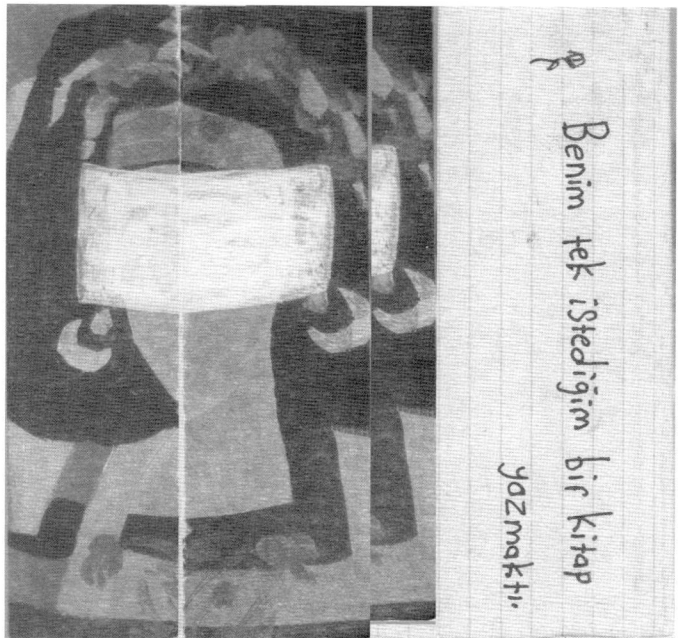

Figure 29 Image showing the folded front and back sleeves of the book entitled *Benim Tek İstediğim Bir Kitap Yazmaktı* [The Only Thing I Ever Wished was to Write a Book] designed by Sadık Karamustafa. The image, *Vadedilmiş Topraklar 3* [Promised Lands 3] by Gülsüm Karamustafa, Istanbul, 1999. Photo courtesy of Sadık Karamustafa.

from the late 1980s (Figure 33) are highly advanced and rather bold in their free-floating positioning of images and texts, which somehow expose a concealed three-dimensionality.[7]

10.4 Conclusion

The artistic value of a graphic work is a matter of discussion, which could go on indefinitely perhaps. My readings of the works presented here may well be at variance with the intentions of their respective designers, who may or may not agree with me. However, what makes these works significant is that their conceptual core allows various interpretations, which deserves inquiry and bridges the gap with works of art.

---

[7]Another successful publication in this respect is the *Tasarım Gazetesi* [Design Newspaper] a weekly supplement to *Radikal*, a daily newspaper published at the beginning of this century. Emre Senan, who is responsible for its design, bestowed a dynamic contemporary look perfectly matching its content. His mastery is obvious when one considers that 'designing for design' is probably one of the hardest things to do especially considering that the audience members are mostly designers who know what good design is and are keen to criticise any weakness they notice. (Footnote added in 2023.)

Figure 30 Esen Karol's poster design for *Macbeth* by William Shakespeare, Istanbul, 1999. Photo courtesy of Esen Karol.

Figure 31 Esen Karol's poster design for an art photography exhibition called *Sokaklardan* [From the Streets] by Şakir Eczacıbaşı, Istanbul, 1996. Photo courtesy of Esen Karol.

Figure 32 Gülizar Çepoğlu's poster for the exhibition *Manuscript*, Istanbul, 1994. Photo courtesy of Gülizar Çepoğlu.

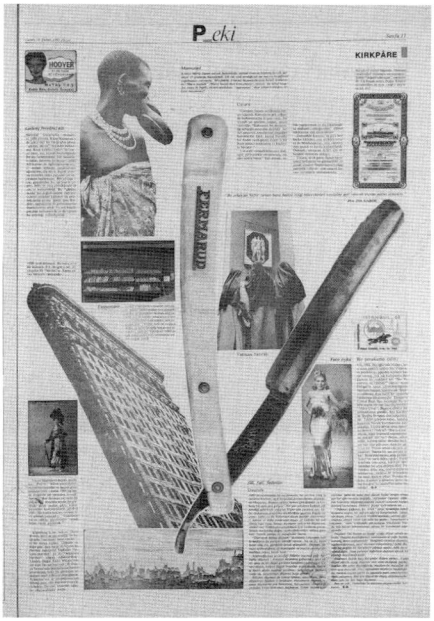

Figure 33 Sunday Supplement of Güneş Newspaper, designed by Gülizar Çepoğlu, Istanbul, 1990. Photo courtesy of Gülizar Çepoğlu.

Some designers disagree with the idea that a graphic work can be an artwork in itself. They argue that the mission of a graphic work is to serve the product or its subject matter, rather than impose itself. What should cause the product to sell are the qualities of the product represented appropriately, not the quality of the graphics attracting consumers or telling more than what they are supposed to tell.

This modernist view of respect for the product or the subject matter, which reduces the graphics to a mere conveyor, is currently being questioned in Turkey. In fact, what some designers challenge is the temporality of a graphic and its message in comparison to works of art, which envisages a wider audience (as opposed to just consumers) and longevity[8] (as opposed to effectiveness).

Longevity in a given graphic work can be achieved through added value, which entirely depends on the designer's creativity. If this added value has the power to survive longer than the actual subject matter itself, then the work lives longer. The ephemeral nature of advertising and the message can be reversed by an idea, which could be another layer of reading and meaning because ideas arguably live longer than products. The conceptual approach is a font of possibilities for designers who are pushing boundaries in a relentless creative search. Luckily, the contemporary Turkish graphic scene is not without such designers, as I hope this chapter has shown. Granted, they are not many but they are keen and committed to exploring depths of meaning, thus keeping company with dedicated researchers.

10.5 Acknowledgements

I would like to thank Bülent Erkmen, Sadık Karamustafa, Esen Karol, Gülizar Çepoğlu and Yurdaer Altıntaş, Yeşim Demir, Tevfik Barın, Ayşe Karamustafa, Sinan Niyazioğlu, Emre Senan, Ömer Durmaz and Erkal Yavi who kindly gave time for interviews and/or provided me with valuable printed and/or digital materials. Behiç Ak and Yılmaz Aysan offered their ideas and comments on many occasions during informal discussions on the subject. Finally, I would like to express my gratitude to Manuela Antoniu for editing the first version of this text presented as a conference paper at the Aveiro Conference in 2001.

---

[8] With some exceptions, of course, such as self-destructive artworks, performances, installations and so on.

CHAPTER 11
4T DESIGN AND DESIGN HISTORY SOCIETY
A CRITICAL ANALYSIS

The first version of this chapter was presented at Istanbul Graphic Design Days, Mimar Sinan Fine Arts University, 3 May 2017, and later published in Grafist *21, (2017).*

11.1 Introduction

Based on my observations, I believe a trend began in 2016 that called into question the functions, objectives and benefits of design associations, institutions and organizations. Inside the design circles I am familiar with, this issue was first pronounced during the 2016 Taipei Conference between 26 and 28 October 2016, organized by the International Committee for Design History & Design Studies (ICDHS), which was founded in 1999. During this tenth international conference, the committee's board of directors felt the need to come up with an evaluation, published a book (Calvera, Woodham and Barbosa, 2016) and debated the issue in a panel discussion at the end of the conference. A few days later, in early November, Brighton University's Internationalising Design History Research Cluster posted a call for papers for a conference on 9 and 10 November 2017 (Cluster, 2016) with the theme International Design Organizations: Histories, Legacies, Values. In the meantime, I was invited to deliver a speech in a conference in Istanbul. Seeing Grafist 21 in the title, I thought of a graphic design article I had written many years previously and assumed that the invitation is related to it. However, Prof. Dr. Ayşegül İzer clearly defined the following framework:

1. Observations of and experiences with foreign design organizations
2. Foundation, development and maturation phases of 4T[1] (including accounts of interactions with institutions and individuals in neighbouring countries such as Greece and Bulgaria as well as other West Europeans and Far Eastern nations)
3. In comparison with these countries, regional and institutional diversifications in terms of design historiography

---

[1] '4T' stands for Türkiye Tasarım Tarihi Topluluğu/Design History Society, Turkey. It is the early name of the group which was founded in 2006. Later, as explained in this chapter, the name changed in the course of time, and the society was established as a formal body under the name of 4T: Tasarım ve Tasarım Tarihi Topluluğu/ 4T: Design and Design History Society in 2014.

4. The role and significance of the developing discipline of Turkish design historiography within the broader framework of international design history

Thus, this topical issue of the evaluative study of design associations appeared again. In offering a critical analysis, this chapter inevitably touches on the personal role of the author as well as conveys a historical perspective of developments to analyse the status of 4T within the context of similar relevant institutions. Undoubtedly, a thorough study is needed to provide a global list of significant organizations, associations, councils and institutions operating in architecture, interior decoration, graphic design, furniture design, industrial design and so on, and to define their boundaries. Only then can we begin to scrutinize 4T in light of these findings.[2] Some organizations in Turkey, such as the Industrial Design Association (Turan, 2006), the Industrial Designers' Society of Turkey (Hasdogan, 2009) and the Association of Industrial Designers, fall outside the limited scope of this chapter, which considers previously unrecorded events and phenomena to outline a critical yet integrated network of progress and relations.

11.2 Observations of and experiences with foreign design organizations: The accumulation behind the foundation of 4T

Regarding the foundation and progress of 4T, two significant factors can be highlighted: my experience of living in London and observing first-hand the working principles of similar organizations in Europe – a slowly growing web of international relations woven with mutual trust and respect. Other contributing factors are obviously good fortune by being in the right place at the right time. The following section elaborates on these points by first looking at organizations that are similar to 4T.

11.2.1 Design organizations similar to 4T

Looking into similar organizations, we immediately encounter two reputable names based in the UK and renowned for the quality of the design conferences they organize: the Design Research Society (1966) and the Design History Society (1977). In fact, both originated from conferences. The first was established after heated debates following the conference on design methods in 1962 (Design Research Society, 2015). The foundation of the Design History Society also resulted from a series of writings, discussions and conferences. From the 1960s, British universities and polytechnics began to include

---

[2] The guilds (of artisans and/or merchants) in the Middle Ages were transformed into professional associations. This process accelerated in the early nineteenth century, driven by a momentum experienced in design, especially architecture. Pioneering bodies that played key roles in the history of design institutions and organizations include the British Institute of Architects (1834), the New York Institute of American Architects (1857), Deutscher Werkbund, led by Hermann Muthesius in Germany (1907) and the British Design and Industries Association (1915).

design history in their curriculum. However, since design historian was hardly a recognized profession at the time, art historians were responsible for these courses. By the 1970s, several discussions and conferences had considered the nature of design history and its role in education. Out of these, the one with the greatest impact was Design History: Fad or Function? (Design Council, 1978). The conference proceedings were published with the same title, and the Design Research Society was established within the year.

Conferences obviously assemble people of similar interests. As they became annual, the assemblage gradually transformed into a society and continued its presence in a new format. It was a generative model followed by many other similar future formations. However, by the mid-1990s, there was increasing criticism of institutional bodies. The standard format of societies naturally demanded adherence to certain procedures, such as membership fees and subscriptions, which led to the renting of office space, hiring of various administrative staff, forming of executive boards, general assemblies, meetings, written communications and so on. These bodies inevitably turned into formal structures in which bureaucratic functions – mostly disliked by academics – became rather overbearing.

One organization that successfully avoided this pitfall was the European Academy of Design (EAD), established in the UK in 1994. With a biannual conference and operating in as many overseas locations as possible, EAD played an important role in the field. Prof. Rachel Cooper (who can be considered the founder) is a pioneer in the area of design management.

A few years ago, she received the Order of the British Empire for her services to the field. While Cooper began her work with a conference focusing mainly on design management, the European Academy of Design (EAD, 2017) gradually extended its scope. For example, the twelfth EAD Conference in 2017 was titled 'Design for Next'.[3]

EAD has never organized itself formally. Rachel Cooper and later Paul Atkinson did not become the chairperson through a written or officially voted decision by EAD's board of directors. Instead, these decisions were based on mutual understanding and general consensus. In 1995, on the last day of EAD's first conference, held in Salford and themed Design Interfaces,[4] a forum was held to discuss future possibilities. Dr. Elizabeth Svengren of Stockholm University announced that she would organize the 1997 conference and invited participants. University members who attended both conferences ended up forming EAD's Executive Committee. Even today, it is university members rather than private individuals that provide EAD's structure.[5]

The Executive Committee meets once every two years before the conference to determine the next venue and the people in charge. The board comprises people who previously organized EAD conferences and/or university representatives. However, since not every member can attend this biennial meeting, the Executive Committee is always

---

[3]See https://ead.yasar.edu.tr/conferences/ead-12-italy-2017/.
[4]See https://ead.yasar.edu.tr/conferences/ead-01-uk-1995/.
[5]See https://ead.yasar.edu.tr/committee/.

enriched by a dynamic flow of new faces. EAD's small budget relies on a little income from the *Design Journal*, published since 1997. The conferences are hosted by universities and funded through attendance fees. EAD's Executive Committee supervises the process to ensure the smooth running of all operations. This flexible structure has survived thanks to the sustainable system developed by academics working in the same field, as well as a sense of mutual trust and inexhaustible enthusiasm shared by the older and younger generations.

Another example is the International Committee of Design History and Studies (ICDHS), which aims to promote design history in developing countries. Its foundation was motivated by university lecturers led by Prof. Dr. Anna Calvera who gathered for a conference in Barcelona in 1999. At a conference in Havana in 2000, it was decided that meetings would be biennial. The Istanbul conference of 2002 ensured the future of ICDHS. As distinct from EAD, ICDHS chooses a different international location for each conference and takes responsibility for motivating and encouraging the local design community, including researchers, thinkers and historians, to actively participate on the global platform.

ICHDS has developed a clear management model. The core team, the Executive Committee, keeps expanding with the addition of conference organizers who rejuvenate it with their experiences of such events. The leading positions were taken by senior historians from various continents, such as Anna Calvera, Jonathan Woodham, Victor Margolin, Pekka Korvenmaa and Oscar Salinas. This seems to have endowed ICDHS with a distinctive mission and perspective (ICDHS, 2008). A critical eye cannot easily ignore EAD's and ICDHS's scientific contributions. They have provided many young researchers and future lecturers with ample opportunities to construct a perfect web of experience and communication. Through their democratic structures, which allow space for the maturation of sophisticated discussions, they have managed to create a globally effective and reputable heritage.

Their main weakness is a lack of concern and adequate instruments for self-promotion, which could otherwise enhance their visibility, consolidate their prestige and increase their membership. Their prestige has been limited by the consistent ability to organize biennial conferences. Naturally, their success has always been linked to the success of these events. It is a problem encountered not just by ICDHS and EAD but all similar institutions without a formal structure. One could avoid problematizing the situation and choose to honour this success attained through minimal effort. One could also ignore post-conference concerns about the location of the next venue, which hang over the board members' heads like the Sword of Damocles. Yet, it is also true that this ignites a perpetual search for young teams to run the next conference, which creates an exhilarating momentum.

11.2.2 Web of relations

Earlier, I defined the second most influential factor driving the formation of 4T as the gradually evolving web of relations. This network was formed partly through chance encounters but mostly through diligent efforts to build and maintain solid friendships.

In 1987, Michael Preston, the Exhibitions Director of the London Science Museum, was collaborating with Teoman Aktüre to establish a Science Museum in Ankara, Turkey. With the incentive of Michael Preston, I was granted a two-month research scholarship at the London Science Museum. During this time, I became acquainted with several prominent British designers. As a result, Sir David Carter, who was contacted through Michael Preston, Prof. Frank Height and Prof. John Heskett, the author of the first serious book on industrial design history, gave conference presentations for the Industrial Design Department of Middle East Technical University, Turkey, during the academic year of 1987–88. Having kept in contact with Heskett, I invited him to take part in the Somerset House conference that I organized in 1995 at the Courtauld Institute of Art, which I discuss in more detail below. One of the most important focal points of the web of relations is the Royal College of Art (RCA). The time I spent at the RCA during 1988–90 created opportunities to meet many designers, historians and thinkers. One such figure is Prof. Manzini, who later spoke at the Somerset House conference.

To sum up, connections made at the Science Museum and RCA, and relationships that developed during EAD and ICDHS conferences exemplify the formation of 4T and later proved very helpful in securing its international visibility. Regarding my initial experiences before EAD and ICDHS emerged, a localized initiative in London is worth noting. The following section examines in more detail the nature of this undertaking, The Inter-Cultural Forum For the Arts, which has not taken its place in the written historical record yet.

11.2.3 Beginning of the story: ICFA

As emphasized above, personal experiences and relations played a significant role in the emergence of 4T. To observe how these ties developed over the years, one needs to revisit London before the 1990s. Back then, following the lead of three people resident in the UK, a series of meetings were held with a gradually growing number of participants. This wave led to the emergence of an informal group in February 1993 called the Inter-Cultural Forum for the Arts (ICFA).

The three initiators were İsmail Ertürk, a senior lecturer at the University of Manchester, Dr. Sedat Aybar, a member of SOAS at the time (now a member of Istanbul Bahçeşehir University) and Dr. Saliha Paker, a professor of translation studies at Bosphorus University, Istanbul. ICFA's vision and objectives were to encourage interest in modern Turkish arts, literature and culture, engage in promotional activities based on a thorough understanding of global trends while enabling the exchange of ideas and the flow of information through an intercultural perspective and take an extensive approach towards the study of connections and relations. Although ICFA was dominated by Turkish citizens, its members made a point of creating an international environment for different cultures to meet. A document from 12 September 1996 lists Musa Farhi as ICFA chairperson, James Christie as vice-chair, Nilgün Canver as treasurer, Miranda Griffin as secretary, and Tevfik Balcıoğlu, Adem Özer and Selma Göker as board members. Activities included a concert by Cihat Aşkın, literature talks by Vedat Türkali and Murat Belge, memoirs by Maureen Freely, a seminar on Mediterranean cuisine by Claudia Roden, and design presentations by Necdet Teymur, Marco Susani and Defne Koz. Other well-known attendees of ICFA meetings included Bernard Lewis, Cem Mansur and Orhan Suda. After organizing its last event, a jazz concert by the Ahmet Gülbay Trio presented by Füsun Levet on 9 March 1997, this venture disappeared into the unrecorded annals of history.

ICFA is an interesting case in terms of its organizational model. Despite lacking any official registration whatsoever, it still functioned as an association. There were membership application forms, a logo designed by myself, a board of directors ready to serve with a chairperson, vice-chair and treasurer in place, and regular meetings with carefully prepared agendas and minutes.[6] Relying on nominal entrance fees to run the events, ICFA operated on the basis of good intentions, solidarity, mutual trust and respect.

Another important experience is relevant here. In 1995, it was decided that an Industrial Design Pathway would be established within the Department of Three-Dimensional Design affiliated with Kent Institute of Art and Design[7] in Rochester, UK. As the course leader, I asserted the need to develop an educational strategy based on the latest developments in design. I convinced the institute's administration that an international conference would be absolutely indispensable towards this end. The conference title was quite ambitious: 'The Role of Product Design in Post-Industrial Society'. The conference proceedings were later published under the same name (Balcioglu, 1998).

Based on my experience with ICFA, the invited speakers were Prof. Ezio Manzini of Milano Polytechnic (Italy), Dieter Rams, a designer at Braun Company (Germany), Victor Margolin, a professor of design history at the University of Chicago (United States), John Heskett, a professor of design history (UK), James Woudhuysen[8] of Henley Centre for Forecasting and Prof Jeremy Myerson[9] of Royal College of Art (RCA).

Strong connections and fortuity both played a role in gathering reputable people from varied fields and countries. Heskett and Manzini's confirmations encouraged Margolin and others to participate. It is important to note here that the event was hosted by the Courtauld Institute of Art, located inside the Somerset House building in central London. Somerset House is a grand building that housed the Government School of Design, the very first design school, founded in 1837. Thus, the location was significant in terms of design history and an attraction in itself, which helped ensure the success of the conference.

---

[6] I would like to extend my thanks to Selma Göker Wilson, who sent me an electronic copy of the ICFA archive.
[7] In 2005, Kent Institute of Art and Design merged with Surrey Institute of Art and Design and became part of the University of Creative Arts in 2008.
[8] Woudhuysen later served as Professor of Estimation and Innovation at De Montfort University.
[9] Myerson is the founding editor of *Design Week* magazine (1986). In 1999, he co-founded the Design Center with Helen Hamlyn at the RCA and has been the director of this center.

11.3 The foundation, development and maturation phases of 4T

The foundation stones of 4T were set in place during the meeting led by Prof. Haruhiko Fujita at Izmir University of Economics (IUE), Turkey. I was then the Dean of the Faculty of Fine Arts and Design and knew Fujita through some work I did for the ICDHS Executive Committee. While working at Kent Institute of Art and Design, I co-organized with ITU (Istanbul Technical University) ICDHS's 2002 conference, titled 'Mind the Map'. The success of this conference strengthened ICDHS's influence and contributed to promoting design history studies. Possibly driven by this momentum, Fujita had been travelling abroad to gather international support for an online publication, *Design Discourse*,[10] published by the Design History Forum founded in Japan in 1998. He also wished to motivate and support the formation of similar institutions in other countries. Our meeting took place on Wednesday, 9 August 2004, attended by academic staff from IUE, Izmir Institute of Technology and Dokuz Eylül University. The discussion following Fujita's presentation resulted in a decision to schedule a conference in 2006.

This first conference of invited speakers took place on 12 May 2006 with the theme of Design History and Discourse in Turkey. The second conference was held on 11 May 2007 with the same format and the theme of Design and Daily Life in History. The next conference on 12–13 May 2008 had the theme of Designing Identities. The fourth conference (14–15 May 2009), Other Design Histories, included both invited guests and commissioned papers. This tradition, started by Prof. Jonathan Woodham, still continues today. In 2010, a peer review system was introduced using Turkish academicians. That year, when English-language papers were first accepted, the theme was Deciphering the Object, while in 2011 it was Design, Technology and Experience. Until 2012, Turkish papers were accompanied by a brief summary in English and vice versa. While many 4T contributors have come and gone, some names have remained within the core team.[11] One of the key figures behind the theoretical framework of the conferences and symposium organization is Prof. Gülsüm Baydar. For example, thanks to her personal connections, Hilde Heynen participated in 2013 as a guest speaker.

4T changed its name when some of the founding members transferred from IUE to Yaşar University. The Dean of the Faculty of Architecture insisted on drawing a distinction. Consequently, 4T continued the conferences as 5T (Türkiye Tasarım Tarihi Topluluğu Toplantıları/Turkish Society of Design History Meetings between 2012 and 2014, for three year only). The graphics and format of the conference publication also changed. After the 4T society was founded on 4 June 2014, the official terminology of TÜBİTAK (Scientific and Technological Research Council of Turkey) was accepted,

---

[10]Design discourse was one of the most popular concepts of the 1990s. The concept of discourse developed by the famous French philosopher Michel Foucault was also applied to design. In this context, it is worthwhile to mention Necdet Teymur's Environmental Discourse (1982) and Victor Margolin's Design Discourse (1989). We can assume that what happened in Japan was partly influenced by this atmosphere.

[11]I would like to extend my gratitude to all fellow academicians, assistants and students for their selfless efforts.

and the word symposium was used instead of the word conference for annual meetings. Many foreign experts were invited to act as referees while all papers, presentations and books were published in English after 2013. Between 2010 and 2013, the organization's books were published by Yaşar University. 5T's most recent publications include *New Relationship: Design History and Virtual Design Museum* (2012) and *Gender Perspectives in Design: Turkish and Global Contexts* (2013).

We can now return to the question posed at the beginning of this chapter regarding meetings with institutions and colleagues in Western and Eastern Europe, the Far East and Turkey's neighbours such as Greece and Bulgaria. Experiences of several Western European bodies contributed indirectly to the foundation of 4T, including RCA, ICFA (based in the UK), EAD and ICDHS (based in Barcelona), while the Japan Design History Forum was an encouraging example from the Far East. For some reason, however, Eastern Europe has never been an influence for either EAD or ICDHS. The only connection was established with Tallinn, Estonia, thanks to Prof. Pekka Korvenmaa. This inertia was probably because Eastern European organizations lacked centres and financial resources to send people abroad to build communication bridges for this particular field of design.

In any event, the absence of a formal structure hardly allows the management the freedom to use their initiative for creating other projects. Another objective that motivated 4T as a society was to develop its capacity and influence in the design world. Regarding ties with Turkey's neighbours, Greece provides the only example. Although there have been no official contact with its design institutions, Dr Artemis Yagou and Dr Kalliopi Amygdalou, two dedicated academic experts, have maintained their relationship with 4T and other design institutions and universities in Turkey.

11.4 Regional and institutional diversification in terms of design historiography

Although a serious analysis of this topic requires extensive, a limited evaluation and personal observations may contribute towards future studies. Instead of making deductions about other countries, this chapter focuses on a number of interesting qualities, strengths and weaknesses observed in Turkey. Comparisons can be drawn from three areas: research methods, writing style and the selected themes.

11.4.1 Research methods

I believe that we have enough knowledge of methods of research. However, despite the significant growth in first-hand studies, archives and field studies in recent years, which have increased the visibility of a few competent academicians, it is still a far from well-established and widespread practice. Therefore, while not ignoring second-hand resources, returning to the archives and the field, conducting studies in oral history and carrying out documentation work to illuminate the recent past will noticeably increase the quantity and the quality of research.

Here, I'd like to highlight some important points that require the attention of critics, writers, historians and theoreticians. These include claiming and illuminating our own history, performing an archaeology of knowledge, recording and spreading findings while accentuating certain characteristics that are unique to us and building our critical framework with our own resources. One of the greatest obstacles preventing the institutionalization of design in Turkey is the lack of strong intellectual design thinking and debate platforms. This is the main reason why we have developed a seemingly natural habit of depending on foreign resources. An interesting anecdote can illustrate this issue. One day, I was asked – with all good intentions – to review an article. It was an original work that I appreciated and commented on positively. I then asked the author: 'You are Turkish and you work at a university in Turkey. Your research is based on Turkey and it concerns an authentic product of this country. Your article is in English, which is fine, but why are all the references in the bibliography foreign? Why are there no Turkish references?' The author replied: 'You are right. I never realized.' It may well be that there are no Turkish publications on some subjects, so the intention to publish abroad may encourage the use of foreign resources while attaining a doctorate degree abroad may direct one's focus to resources accumulated overseas. Although this is all understandable, it still cannot justify our neglect of creating our intellectual framework in design. I believe that this is the current topic that must be brought into sharp focus in Turkish design writing.

Towards this end, we would be well advised to take the following steps. We need to identify the unnoticed heroes (educators, designers, producers and so on) of our design history, shed new light on their work, and, through this effort, create a legacy that will help us build the future. These steps are sure to elevate us to a higher level.

11.4.2 *The style of writing*

This is an area in need of much improvement. Diligent attempts at scientific writing are known to produce extremely technical, boring and monotonous narratives, so it would be a benefit to liberate design writing from the confines of engineering jargon. A writing style that relies heavily on descriptions and chronological linear narratives, and is neither critical nor challenging, is no longer acceptable. A flowing, striking, humorous style that is generous with references and proofs is a lot stronger and more convincing. The same aspiration towards scientific writing is also apparent in the titles of papers that can be extremely long, trying desperately to pinpoint issues and end up alienating the reader. Instead, titles must be short, simple and striking.[12]

Another error often encountered in our writing style is frequent and abundant referencing of the writer's own work, as may be detected in the bibliographies of some papers. Except for pioneers and leaders of certain fields, extreme self-referencing is hardly persuasive. On the contrary, indicates a vicious circle. It seems as though such writers have limited themselves

---

[12] I would like the readers to know that I don't hold myself exempt from these criticisms. I must confess that I suffer from the same ailments. Ultimately, we all grew up within this culture. I would therefore like to warn the youth and encourage them to think about developing a different, original writing style.

to their own thoughts and findings, writing and reading what they have written, and rewritten it. Such self-referential writing indicates conceit and is extremely unattractive.

Multi-authorship also needs our attention. In a speech given a few years ago in Izmir, a top executive at Elsevier said that multi-authorship was the new trend in writing with scientific studies encouraged along this path. It is indeed a trend that is highly compatible with our current research culture. However, here too, we need to avoid some of our traditional mistakes in Turkey. For example, dissertation students are known to put the names of their tutors – sometimes out of respect – on their papers, regardless of whether the tutors have made any meaningful contribution. If it is truly a collaborative work produced by student and tutor, then there is no problem. However, the academic code of conduct should not allow giving credit out of kindness.

11.4.3 Topics

The drive to be topical is an irreplaceable passion that must always be pursued as a primary objective. At the 2016 ICDHS Taipei conference, Dr. Sarah Teasley, who is the department head of design history at the RCA, told me in conversation about what differentiates 4T from similar formations: 'Your study of history is based on the hottest contemporary issues reflecting today's problematiques. That's why you're special.' For me, this was the most precious compliment of 4T yet and provided a more accurate definition than any we had come up with before.

The search for a design identity is a rather prevalent trend, not just in Turkey but in many other countries. Historical research initiatives are launched to facilitate this quest. To give an example, I have witnessed first-hand many Japanese academicians studying relationships with the West, the influence of Western design education and modernism. The identity issue is always on the agenda for us, too. Just as it is with teacups or coffee machines, social research based on design – whereby traditions and historical forms are questioned both practically and institutionally – is a prevalent practice. This approach reconstructs contemporary utility objects to harmonize with the current requirements of technology, fashion and aesthetics. While doing so, it also generates material for historical and theoretical studies.

On the other hand, given Turkey's challenging geopolitical position, we can appreciate that continuing societal tribulations and the current economic situation directly influence local design practice. This is why the number of research projects focused on material culture and politics is popular in Turkey.

11.5 The role and significance of the developing discipline of Turkish design historiography within the broader framework of international design history

The response to this issue can help us determine our roadmap on a number of levels. Here is the critical point: when will a Turkish design historian ever write about world design history or design history in the West? In other words, in our handling of topics, we need to break away from the dichotomy of 'us and them', 'local and global' and 'local and universal', and try to put a more holistic approach into practice. If the practice of transnational design historiography finds a breeding ground in Turkey, then the writing of design history will be sure to evolve to a higher plane (Akcan, 2012).

Just as mentioned at the 2017 ICDHS Taipei Conference, Turkey is one of the countries where we observe a steady growth of design history studies, the quality of its research projects, the number of researchers and their participation in meetings. Nevertheless, these appreciative comments can hardly mask the lack of a single well-prepared and comprehensive design history book in Turkey (with the exception of architecture, which was a very early developer within design).

Having said that, the increasing presence of original and high-quality work in interior architecture, industrial design, graphics and other related disciplines, and of culturally and politically advanced publications in comparison to other countries, shows that Turkey is progressing confidently. The efforts of academicians based abroad have contributed significantly to this success in the international arena. The global platform offered by 4T and its role as a facilitator will continue to encourage design practices and the writing of history. But how far does 4T's support extend?

11.6 The ultimate tipping point: Does 4T have a future or not?

Inevitably, both EAD and ICDHS have concerns about their own sustainability. In meetings held after each conference, determining the next venue and organizers is not as easy as expected, and there is often anxiety about the future. 4T faces similar problems. Moving ahead as a society is much more difficult than being organized under the wings of a university. Having come out of this protective shield in 2016, 4T held its first symposium in a neutral setting, at the Izmir Center of Architecture, which proved its ability to stand alone. This venue was used again in 2017, with over sixty papers submitted and forty chosen. For the first time, the referees included both symposium members and renowned and published foreign academicians.[13]

Since 2009, the invited speakers have always been visitors from abroad the exception of the film director Cem Kaya in 2016. As mentioned above, all symposia since 2013 have been conducted in English. However, there is still plenty of room for improvement. The website, for example, needs urgent attention while some books covering recent works are still due to be published although they should be printed as soon as each symposium ends.

Obviously, 4T must also organize other kinds of events, support members' projects, plan activities and be more active generally. To meet these expectations to a certain extent,

---

[13]See http://cargocollective.com/4T2017/Scientific-Committee.

meetings called 'one in four' have been held at the end of every month on the forth day of the forth week, since 23 February 2017, when a roadmap and a twenty-five-item to-do list were drawn up. These meetings were carried out for a while, however, the number of people who took on the tasks was rather disappointing. Unfortunately, political tension and a prevailing mood of pessimism affected both university staff, who see no hope for the future, and 4T members. Although the society is an institutional body, its lack of regular income makes it dependent on the contributions of a few dedicated individuals, which arouses concerns for the future. The society has strong international relationships, but they are mostly built on a personal basis. Transferring these connections to younger generations requires much attention and diligent care. Our wish is for 4T to grow with contributions and, as a sustainable international design platform, offer academicians opportunities to make global connections, come up with new ideas, create grounds for discussion, realize their projects and build their careers.

SECTION THREE
EDUCATION AND PRACTICE

The chapters in this section fall into two groups: the first four are related to education in general while the following two concern design practice in Turkey specifically. The first chapter of this section, Chapter 12, presents the integrated design approach (IDeA), which formed the foundations of a new fine arts and design faculty established by the author at Izmir University of Economics. IDeA is a philosophy requiring all departments to work together closely, introducing common courses for all students, encouraging joint projects and without allocating space to specific departments except for specialized workshops. Instead, staff members teach wherever their expertise is needed throughout the faculty, sharing offices with colleagues from other departments and all research assistants located in a large open space. In other words, integration is achieved on all fronts, wherever possible, from top to bottom, from curricula with common elements to the use of offices, studios, workshops and so on.

After the fashion design department opened in 2004, four more departments were added by 2010, together with a research centre and two MA programmes. Staff members also designed the new faculty building in accordance with the IDeA philosophy of being a purpose-built premises. It was officially inaugurated on October 20, 2010, at 20.10. The faculty somewhat resembles Bauhaus with its five departments, namely fashion design, architecture, industrial design, visual communication, interior architecture, and environmental design, and its integrated curricula and new building. Although the advantages and disadvantages of the common curricula and the performance of the overarching philosophy have not yet been scientifically analysed, this experiment was implemented successfully during the author's deanship, and its graduates have proved themselves in professional life, according to the feedback from the industry.

The following three chapters consider PhD and doctoral studies, which were a focus of debates in the UK during the late 1990s. Briefly, professionals, artists and designers argued that existing PhD programmes were inappropriate for their postgraduate education which is based on theoretical works only. Instead, they argued, postgraduate students could only progress through practical work accompanied by a supportive theoretical thesis. This instigated a debate in which the curricula, titles and positions of practice-based programmes and the quality of their results were discussed at a series of conferences organized by universities and the UK Council for Graduate Education.

These three chapters of section three are closely linked and complement each other. However, there are other chapters in this book touching upon the same subject. The fourth and fifth chapters of the first section, entitled respectively 'The essential elements: The unity of work and transferability of knowledge' and 'Research, knowledge and doctorate programmes: Toward the third domain', explore similar issues with reference to postgraduate studies but from a different and theoretical viewpoint. I, therefore, considered that they are more suitable for the theory rather than the education section. The connections are so obvious that the reader may well notice that they sometimes raise comparable ideas, albeit with different arguments and references.

Chapter 13, 'PhD, DFA or both', argues that we need both because they are at the same academic level despite being different in terms of their nature. Chapter 14 looks into the characteristics of professional doctorates, while Chapter 15 examines the balance and relationship of practice and theory in postgraduate studies. This debate primarily focused on the nature of doctoral studies in art and design, and the identification of the right title for these studies.

Nowadays, the heated debate seems to be over, and it appears that universities have developed practice-based programmes and adopted new titles. Thanks to the UK Council for Graduate Education's annual conferences, the results are being presented while examples of works are discussed in academic papers. In addition, there were two major international conferences in Ohio, United States, in 1998, and La Clusaz, France, in 2000 (Buchanan, 1999; Durling, 2000). My main argument was to keep the title 'PhD' for scientific research and use a different title for practice-based studies and consider both to have an equal academic level. It appears that universities preferred to keep the title of 'PhD' and added a few words to differentiate it from 'classic' PhDs, hence Practice-based PhD, PhD in Art, PhD by Design and so on. Regarding higher education systems, practices vary widely in many countries concerning doctorate studies.

For example, the Council of Higher Education (which is 'Yüksek Öğretim Kurulu: YÖK' in Turkish), responsible for all higher education institutions in Turkey, resolved the issue long before the UK debate in late the 1990s without mentioning the word PhD. Instead, the degree is called 'Proficiency in Art' and includes all kinds of practice-based subjects like fine art, music and design. In academic terms, this degree is equivalent to a PhD, and those who have it can apply for a professorship in due course. Unlike UK practice, professors in Turkey shorten their titles to 'Prof. Dr.' if they hold a PhD degree while those who have a Proficiency in Art use the abbreviation 'Prof.' without 'Dr.' attached.

In this respect, my argument in these chapters includes different and sometimes controversial views. However, I find this useful since the main rationale in compiling these essays concerns their validity and the possibility that they may be beneficial and inspirational for those who have not yet launched practice-based postgraduate programmes.

Chapter 16 deals with a specific aspect of design practice and seeks a new agenda for Turkish industrial design, which fluctuates in relation to Turkey's political and economic situation. It was originally established in 1998 to determine a design route for Turkey. This chapter was recently extended, updated and rewritten with Aren Kurtgözü for this book in light of the current position of Turkish industrial design. A substantial revision was needed because the content was referring to the design agenda that has changed drastically since the delivery of the original paper. The chapter proposes a draft action plan and an agenda that may interest both the Turkish audience and those in other countries at a similar stage of development. Based on my experience and observations, I offer several new practical suggestions for Turkish design in penultimate and final chapter of this book.

Actually, each field of design requires a separate analysis and strategy for its advancement. For instance, wedding dress manufacturing is an important element of Turkey's fashion design industry. Its products are exported to more than forty countries, which requires special attention and appropriate policies to make the sector more effective worldwide. The proposed agenda is nothing more than a provocative statement, urgently demanding a state policy for design, carefully crafted for each sector, which demonstrates specific patterns of progress that are perhaps unique to Turkey. For example, there has been an attempt in Turkish product design practice to redesign traditional everyday artefacts with new approaches, shapes, forms, meanings and symbols. Accordingly, the final chapter investigates why cult objects are targeted and redesigned, and tries to unearth the hidden expectations in these motivations. Strangely enough, many well-established designers have been involved in this process and created new forms and products for traditional objects, such as tea glasses and coffee cups.

The chapters presented here only touch on certain features of design practices in Turkey, which are of course, very limited. However, I believe they highlight rather interesting areas. The evaluation of general design practices in Turkey and the results are beyond the scope of this book. Instead, the chapters explore certain characteristics of design theory, history, education and practice and present new insights on these subjects.

CHAPTER 12
INTEGRATED DESIGN APPROACH (IDeA)
REFLECTIONS ON A NEW SCHOOL OF DESIGN BUILDING

The first version of this paper was presented as a keynote speech at the 9th European Academy of Design Conference, Aveiro, 4–7 May 2011.

12.1 Introduction

Originally derived from a notion, the Integrated Design Approach (IDeA) has gradually turned into a method formulated at a theoretical level. The main principle of IDeA comes from the argument that the fundamental principles of all design disciplines are the same and that design education must include as many interdisciplinary projects and group work as possible. From this, a structure emerges whereby the walls separating design disciplines are perforated and cooperation platforms are widened. The key features of IDeA are transparency and permeability between design disciplines, more internal communication within the faculty, more common projects and lessons, employment of instructors capable of lecturing in different departments and the provision of integrated studios, workshops and studio spaces. IDeA emphasizes an inquisitional, critical, analytical, creative, innovative and research-based approach.

This process occurred as the Faculty of Fine Arts and Design (FFAD) at Izmir University of Economics (IEU) developed under the founding deanship of the author. Therefore, we are not discussing a predetermined and applied education model. On the contrary, we are discussing a design education practice that gradually took shape within a faculty from scratch. Before proceeding further, some brief background information is needed about Izmir University of Economics and the Faculty of Fine Arts and Design.

12.2 Brief information: Izmir University of Economics (IUE) and Faculty of Fine Arts and Design (FFAD)

The Izmir University of Economics was founded by the Izmir Chamber of Commerce on 14 April 2001, as the first foundation university in Turkey's Aegean Region. There are six faculties, including a recently established Faculty of Law, three graduate schools, two institutions and eight application and research centres. Twenty-seven different undergraduate departments, eighteen master's and three PhD programmes are currently on offer in these academic units. The language of education is English while a second foreign language is obligatory during the four-year undergraduate programme. Having opened with just 304 students in 2001, IUE had 6,150 students in 2011.

FFAD, which was established in 2003, benefited from the pre-existing Higher School of Fashion and Couture course, which it incorporated under a new name and curriculum to launch FFAD's first department: the Department of Fashion Design. The first cohort of students graduated in 2005. In 2004, four new departments were launched: Industrial Design, Communication Design, Interior Architecture and Environmental Design. These were followed by the Department of Architecture in 2005, the Design Studies graduate programme in 2006 and the Architecture graduate programme in 2010. Student numbers grew from 142 in 2003 to 1,168 in 2011, including those in the preparatory school of languages.

12.3 The FFAD'S general education strategy

Undergraduate university education lasts four years in Turkey. Each year has a different level and purpose within FFAD. There is a hierarchical structure that begins with more general and universal issues and ends with each student choosing a specialism and developing an individual design identity.

12.3.1 The first year

Here, students learn what it is to be a university student and also what it means to be a design student in a design faculty. The first-year curriculum includes various core university courses, such as Introduction to Computer and Information Technologies, Principles of Social Sciences and Academic Skills in English. During the first year, students are introduced to general concepts through courses that broaden their perspectives and construct a common foundation of art and design. All design students share a first-year studio in which they work together on a common ground to understand the meaning of design using a common vocabulary. This structure helps students to develop a better understanding of each design discipline, which in turn enables them to transfer between departments in later years within the regulations. Significantly, students begin to understand the integrated design approach not by discussing or reading about it but through first-hand experience. In studios, design education is executed using project work.

12.3.2 The second year

In the second year, students enter departments. They progress to their own disciplines and learn the foundations of their specific professional fields, through theoretical and applied classes, and studio projects. During this year, students are first exposed to the introductory concepts and issues of their prospective profession and learn its fundamentals together with other support courses. During this year, students begin to feel clearly that they belong to a department.

12.3.3 The third year

If second-year students belong to their department, then third-year students begin to belong to a specialization. The third year can also be described as a year of options. In the departments of Fashion Design, Industrial Design and Visual Communication Design, students choose a specialization, such as Fashion Design or Fashion Business, Product Design or Design Management, and Graphic Design or Multimedia Design. Each specialization is studied in the departments of Architecture and Interior Architecture through third- and fourth-year elective courses. IUE has also recently reviewed all its academic programmes in line with the Bologna Process to enable students to obtain double or minor degrees through electives

12.3.4 The fourth year

This year is the year of the student, when students write a thesis on a chosen subject and present their chosen project. This allows each student to form their own design personality and identity. In principle, faculty never impose a design style, trend or approach. Instead, they introduce as many as possible and encourage students to form their own design identity. Given that they are largely preoccupied with a graduation project and thesis, and preparing a portfolio, fourth-year students gradually formulate their own design thinking, preferably in terms of the needs of the country and with a social consciousness within a global context. The graduation exhibition and fashion show provide both closure for the students' formal design education and mark the beginning of their professional careers.

12.3.5 Reflections on the Integrated Design Approach

The structure outlined above is intertwined with a series of common courses to give students a broad sense of design and a wider vision of current social responsibilities. FFAD achieves unity for both students and staff through commonalities created at various levels and fields

12.3.5.1 Architecture within the framework of design
Although there are independent architecture faculties in Turkey, historically architecture departments have generally been established within faculties of engineering. Consequently, 'design' is a relatively new and recently popularized word as part of the

titles of faculties. Traditionally, architecture has occupied its own realm in Turkey outside the domain of design. Thus, FFAD in IUE enjoys the unique position of assembling many design fields under one roof. For the first time in a faculty, architecture sits with the other design disciplines, cooperating and working closely with other departments. This is achieved thanks to the commitment of the architecture staff members to FFAD's integrated design approach (IDeA).

12.3.5.2 The common first-year studio

As outlined above, the common first-year schedule is an ideal component of IDeA. From the students' point of view, the first semester helps them to locate and position themselves in the university, understand the visible and invisible rules and codes of conduct of this new study environment and encounter the essentials of basic design and art studies. Students get to know each other and the way that the university and the faculty operate. In the second semester of the first year, a rearrangement of studios enables students to make new friends from other design departments. As a result, starting from the first year, students become familiar with various design disciplines, increase interdepartmental communication and can instigate collaborative projects – in addition to and independent of what the curriculum offers. In the second semester, there are several discipline-specific courses that are not common to all, whereby students attend for the first time a course delivered by their own department, such as Introduction to Architecture or Pattern Making & Sewing Skills.

The Art and Design Studio is the keystone of the first year. A group of fifteen to eighteen lecturers conducts studio teaching under the supervision of a coordinator. Each department has several representatives among the first-year staff members and contributes to forming the first-year curriculum and design projects. Communication is essential and is established both among students and the whole group of lecturers from these different departments.

12.3.5.3 Common courses

During the four-year programme, two courses are common across every FFAD department: Drawing and Representation, and Computer-Aided Technical Drawing. Some common courses are delivered with different course codes and slightly altered content depending on the needs of each department. Model Making, Advanced Design Presentation, and Furniture Design courses are taught in the Interior Architecture and Environmental Design (IAED) and Industrial Design (ID) Departments. Computer-Aided Architectural Graphics, and Architectural Environmental Control Systems are common to Interior Architecture and Environmental Design and Architecture. Multimedia Applications in Design are given to both Fashion Design (FD) and Visual Communication Design (VCD) students. Branding in the Design Industry is given in both the Fashion Design and Industrial Design Departments. Design Semiotics is common for both Visual Communication Design and Industrial Design. In the third and fourth years, students may select courses from other

FFAD departments or even other faculties. The level of integration within FFAD can easily be understood from the following list of common courses:

Common to all five departments:

FFD101 & FFD102: Art and Design Studio 1 & 2

FFD121 & FFD122: History of Art and Design 1 & 2

Common to three departments (Architecture, IAED, ID):

FFD111: Drawing and Representation

FFD104: Computer-Aided Technical Drawing

Common to two departments (IAED, ID):

FFD142: Model Making

FFD202: Advanced Design Presentation

FFD301: Furniture Design

Common to two departments (Architecture, IAED):

FFD201: Computer-Aided Architectural Graphics

FFD203: Environmental Control Systems

Common to two departments (Fashion, VCD):

FFD204: Multimedia Applications in Design

Common to two departments (Fashion, ID):

FFD304: Branding in the Design Industry

Common to two departments (VCD, ID):

FFD401: Design Semiology

This list does not include the joint projects and electives in which students from various departments can mix. Clearly, the degree of commonality cannot be easily illustrated. However, it is assumed that the students mix in their classrooms, work on assignments and projects in mixed teams, and are able to understand each other and each other's design language more and more. This collaboration can only happen if the lecturers and tutors of these courses thoroughly embrace the idea of common courses, improve the course content accordingly and thereby achieve the desired integration. To be fair and critical, one must confess that this is not always the case. In fact, some instructors of common courses do not embrace the idea. Instead, they attempt to offer different content to students from different departments registered for the same course. However, this contradicts the very nature of the concept of common courses.

No doubt, each lecturer and tutor has tried to deliver the common courses to the best of their ability. Nevertheless, their concern has been focused on the content needed for each department rather than creating common content for these mixed groups. When this perspective is not embodied, appropriated and embraced, it is very difficult to achieve unity within the classroom. Instead, it becomes relatively easy to divide the groups according to their departments and teach specialized subjects in their own fields.

I understand that there may be pressure on staff members from students who know nothing about IDeA and hence force the curriculum towards what they want (for example, fashion design students want more fashion design content, architecture students want more architecture and so on). Nevertheless, our aim should not solely be to feed the students with what they want but to apply a coherent education policy that is contemporary, self-critical and self-evaluative, endowed with universal values and in line with the vision and mission of our university. All said, one has to accept that this is the weakest link in the chain of IDeA.

12.3.5.4 Academic staff employment policy

In January 2004, the faculty comprised two assistant professors, three research assistants and one technician. In 2011, there were four professors, two associate professors, eighteen assistant professors, twenty-four lecturers, eighteen research assistants, seven technicians and two secretaries. These include fifteen foreign academics from nine different countries. The faculty was effectively created from scratch. The connection between the employment of new staff members and the integrated design approach is understandable: whenever a new academic post became available, we looked for lecturers with a background and ability to instruct in several departments. From the beginning, staff are acquainted and make friends with each other across FFAD. For some courses, the heads of departments decide in consultation with other heads about who should teach which course. This strengthens the idea of being under the same roof within FFAD rather than the feeling of belonging to a separate department.

Even today, when we consider an application, we do not limit ourselves to the curriculum of any one department. Instead, we look more widely across the faculty to identify courses in other departments that a candidate could teach. We do this because qualified academics are usually specialized in one or two areas and also because there may not be enough courses in one department to offer someone a full-time position. For example, although art and design history is a first-year course in all five FFAD departments, each department cannot afford to employ a full-time art or design historian because there are only two courses related to art history throughout the year, which does not justify full-time employment. Clearly, therefore, we must share staff members across departments based on their expertise and specialism.

12.3.5.5 Research assistant employment policy

Each FFAD department has research assistants who are either master's or PhD students. Posts for assistantships are advertised regularly and open to students registered in such programmes from any university in Turkey. Research assistants are salaried, given an office, work on their research and help the department by attending certain courses and assisting tutors. On completing their master's or PhD, the assistants leave the university and are replaced by a new cohort. Depending on their academic achievements, some are offered a teaching post during their study or soon after. This system is designed to support young researchers, especially those who are bright and display potential as academicians.

In theory, each department aims to employ master's or PhD students with a background education directly related to its design specialism. In reality, this is not always the case. While this conflicts with IDeA policy, the lack of applicants in an FFAD department's required field can necessitate employing research assistants from other fields. For example, a research assistant registered in a city planning PhD programme is currently working in the Department of Industrial Design while one research assistant in Visual Communication Design is an architect and another has a BA in philosophy. Indeed, in a sense, this diversity is a very beneficial outcome that supports IDeA.

12.3.5.6 Gradual and controlled growth

As previously explained, FFAD started with the Fashion Design Department. The employment strategy and the arrival of new staff members each year have caused a gradual expansion in faculty numbers. As new departments opened and postgraduate programmes were introduced, steady growth was achieved with new courses joining the existing structure as a natural integration. Unsurprisingly, this situation had begun to change by 2011, with five departments and 1,168 students. Inevitably perhaps, each department felt that it must emphasize its own identity once it has produced graduates, when its final projects and degree shows have demonstrated the results and quality of student work. With more staff, interdepartmental teaching has decreased, although it still continues.

12.3.5.7 Common activities

One of the main factors sustaining FFAD as a whole is common activities. Since its inception, there have been monthly wine and cheese parties for tutors, lecturers and research assistants to present their academic work to colleagues. Other academic and social activities to bring faculty together include an Architecture Talks programme for which the Department of Architecture invites famous designers, the 4T: Design History Society, Turkey – (4T: Türkiye Tasarım Tarihi Topluluğu) symposia, fashion shows and graduation exhibitions.

12.3.5.8 Shared offices

Another factor that has supported bonding within the faculty is the mixed office experience. Although this was not planned, each new staff member was given an office space wherever it was available and suitable to their rank, but never according to their department. As a result, staff members from the same department rarely share offices while single rooms are allocated for professors and assistant professors according to university policy. Other academic staff share double or triple offices depending on their academic ranking. Because there is no office allocation for specific departments, two or three staff members from different departments share offices and sit together. This naturally-developed policy of mixed offices has further added to FFAD's unity and increased internal dialogue, cross-departmental communication and friendship.

12.3.5.9 The awareness of being different

Situated within a university focused on economics, our staff members had a sense of being different from the very beginning. We hold glamorous fashion shows with an annual budget of approximately 50,000 USD. We have degree shows, degree catalogues, exhibitions and so on. Thus, we consider ourselves as different from the rest of the university – like an elaborate façade. This helps us gain publicity, recognition and respect. Soon after its establishment, FFAD became the public face of IUE, which occupies a large building complex of several linked premises. Therefore, when it came to building IUE's first separate faculty building, the opportunity was given to FFAD. This was either because of our success or because we are different – whatever it means to be different for designers situated among engineers, economists, mathematicians and so on.

12.3.5.10 The idea of being a team

On almost every occasion since FFAD's very early days, the idea of being a team has been adopted and reiterated as a unifying factor. The faculty was like a steadily growing club. Each year about ten people joined, which enabled people to get to know each other reasonably well. However, recently, once all the year programmes were running fully, a sort of competition emerged between FFAD departments, which brought the identity of each department to the fore. Therefore, the sense of being a member of a team is probably shifting from the faculty to the departments.

12.4 The emergence of IDeA

The issue of the identity of the individual departments within FFAD arose from the specific demands of each department's academic programme. Along with Fashion Design, which requires handcraft and technical skills to educate better qualified, competent and experienced students, the Department of Architecture, which requires technical proficiency, insisted that only the first semester of the first year should have a common curriculum. Thus, in 2009–1010, a debate was opened.

I started this debate with a short paper entitled 'At the Crossroads: Let's not Throw out the Baby with the Bath Water. Or: In Search of a Faculty Philosophy'. The paper, which was circulated in March 2010 within FFAD, reviewed the current situation, analysed FFAD's structure of the faculty and coined the term **I**ntegrated **De**sign Approach**: IDeA.**

It has since been discovered that this concept already exists in that The Design School in New York has a programme called Integrated Design Curriculum based on the same or similar ideas. Both part-time and full-time staff members joined the dialogue by e-mail. Over time, the discussion turned into a comprehensive document. However, while FFAD was debating its own academic programme, the university had already decided to review and restructure all its academic programmes in line with the Bologna Process, commencing in the 2010–2011 academic year.

Consequently, FFAD was simultaneously conducting an internal debate on IDeA during 2009–2010 while also revising academic programmes and designing a new faculty building to move into by October 2010. Miraculously, the five-floor, 13,000 m^2 'béton brut' [raw concrete] building was completed in just eight months. All preparations were made to move into the purpose-built new building assuming that construction would be completed by the new academic year in September 2010. A risk was taken since the faculty moved out of the present premises and prayed that it would be ready on time before the new academic year commenced. During this waiting period, we had no idea whether it was going to be an 'annus horribilis' or 'annus mirabilis'. It turned out to be the latter. The building was officially opened at 20.10 on 20 October 2010 (Figure 34).

Figure 34 Faculty of Fine Arts and Design, the building at the opening night, 20 October 2010. Photo: author's archive.

12.5 Reflections of IDeA on the new FFAD building

In July 2009, İzmir Metropolitan Municipality gave the university permission to build on a 20,000 m² site within the campus. IUE's administrators decided to build a new faculty building for FFAD designed by faculty members. It would be approximately 13,000 m² and built on the university's covered car park, which had been constructed three years before with this possibility in mind. The architect designing the parking building had incorporated a strong structural system. The brief was short: a faculty building to create a difference that could be designed to go out to tender and be built in thirteen to fourteen months. The story behind the building and its architectural criticism is interesting, but another issue. This chapter does not discuss the building's sustainability, environmental factors, circulation patterns or accessibility. Instead, I would like to focus on how the building was planned according to the above criteria of IDeA.

The building consists of two blocks (one with three floors; the other with five), connected by three bridges placed on top of each other (Figure 35). The five-floor structure can be considered the main building. The third and fourth floors of the main building are two stories in height. The Dean's office, administrative offices and instructor's offices are on the top floor (Figure 36). From the fourth floor to the first, the studios are the dominant features of the main building (Figure 37).

Figure 35 Faculty of Fine Arts and Design building, bridges connecting blocks. A view from the courtyard. Photo: author's archive.

Integrated Design Approach (IDeA)

Figure 36 Interior of a typical staff room. Photo: author's archive.

12.5.1 Studio locations: Not according to departments but year groups

Each floor is allocated to a specific year group. The fourth floor belongs to first-year students, the third is for second years, the second floor is for third years and the first floor belongs to the graduating students. As somebody said, 'first-year students are on top because they need to broaden their horizons and the fourth-year students are on the ground floor to graduate and walk out quickly'. However, the main purpose is to enhance visual communication in building circulation. Generally, in design education, senior students do not normally visit the studios of junior classes as the learning curve is the other way around: junior students are expected to follow the work of senior students. Therefore, buildings are designed to enable the younger year groups to watch and learn from the elder students, which is why studios are located from top to ground in a hierarchical order. On the other hand, placing students from different departments but the same year on the same floor encourages cooperation between students of various disciplines.

12.5.2 Studios expanding to corridors and open areas for critiques

The building has vast areas of indoor open space and large corridors (Figure 38). These open, wide hallways situated around the studios are used for exhibitions of studio work and reviews of student projects. This ensures that project critiques take place in

Figure 37 Common design studios. Photo: author's archive.

open spaces within the building so that everybody can observe and participate in the activities.

12.5.3 Collateral, transparent and open

The essence of the building's design is transparency. Many locations, including studios and offices, are separated by only glass walls. Clarity, visual communication and transparency increase and encourage democratic participation. Of course, there are untouchable departments and 'ivory towers' in some universities here and there. Metaphorically speaking, we can see that the many walls between the departments in our school are removed, perforated or made permeable. Some of the walls were replaced with glass while the identity of each department is carefully protected and respected. From FFAD's experience, I would say that the balance between transparency and privacy is a sensitive issue that must be adjusted gently.

12.5.4 Numerous and wide range of common areas

Shared spaces were thought to be another element connecting the faculty. Consequently, the ground floor includes a wide courtyard area developed as a street concept, multi-purpose hall, open-air amphitheatre, meeting place, open classroom, designated smoking area, canteen and exhibition area. The wide corridors on each floor provide additional shared spaces. The open bridges connecting the two parts of the building provide vista points and enrich the potential for common area usage.

Figure 38 One of the vast areas of indoor open space and large corridors. Photo: author's archive.

12.5.5 Zones separated by functions not departments

Departments do not have special areas allocated for them. In line with this policy, the spaces in the building belonging to departments are reduced to a minimum. Naturally, the sewing workshops belong to the Department of Fashion Design; however, the press workshop, wooden, ceramic, metal and model workshops are in common use. Each area has a designated technician or a person responsible. Each academic year, a studio is allocated to a group, and a table, chair and locker are assigned to each student. There are no specific zones belonging to departments; rather, there are functional zones. The classrooms are grouped on the third floor; likewise, the computer laboratories, studios and offices are grouped together in particular areas.

1. Offices

    Offices can be separated into three categories.

    a) Fifth-floor offices

    The offices on the fifth floor are reserved for the department heads and the senior faculty members. The Dean's office and secretaries are also on this floor in a separate wing of the building.

    b) Open offices

    Open offices are workspaces located in the middle of the fifth floor surrounded by the offices for heads of departments and other faculty

Figure 39 An open office and work area for research assistants. Photo: author's archive.

members. Two meeting rooms and a common informal coffee/staff room are also located here, mostly serving those working in the open offices. Research assistants use an open office where they have their personal work area (Figure 39). The remaining desks and drawers in the open office are reserved for the part-time academic staff, who utilize them for studying, preparation before or after a lesson, or as a meeting place for student consultations.

c) Offices on the mezzanine floors

The third and fourth floors of the building are two storeys high. Two studios on these floors have a mezzanine with offices overlooking the studios below. Academic staff mixed from various departments occupy these offices, although priority is given to academicians and tutors responsible for studio teaching below. Visual contact helps to facilitate communication with the student body. However, some tutors are not very happy with this arrangement and would probably prefer to have more isolated offices.

The main aim of allocating rooms and desks is to consolidate unity within the faculty. Conventional procedure is avoided by seating staff from different departments together. The placement strategy also includes placing local with foreign staff, male with female staff, and experienced members with new recruits to maintain further balance and harmony within the school.

12.5.6 From the specific to the common

From another perspective, the building's spatial distribution reflects an interesting quality. It was previously mentioned how the top floor is reserved for academic and administrative staff whereas the ground floor is reserved for common use and the workshops are located in the basement. In other words, the level of communality intensifies from the top floor to the ground. In general, upper floors have more specific usage while lower floors have more common areas sheltering various activities and services

12.6 Conclusion

It is not often that a design faculty is offered the opportunity to design its own school building in line with its own pedagogical philosophy. Even when such permission is granted, the work is normally undertaken in a project office under the supervision of a few people. Thus, FFAD was both lucky and unlucky: lucky for being afforded the opportunity to conduct its own project; unlucky due to the vast amount of hard work involved and the very limited period of time to relocate. The intention was to include as many designers and students from the school as possible. It is by no coincidence that the project started with an open meeting and a poster with the slogan 'Have your finger in the pie.' It would be impossible to name all those who have contributed to this project, but three main groups must be thanked: first, Michael Edward Young and Özlem Akın from the Department of Architecture, who along with five students designed the first concept and the first project within EKOTAM (the University of Economics Design Research Centre); second, Erguvan Ünal, a part-time instructor from the department and her husband Mahir Ünal, who considered the needs of all departments and developed the project, and prepared the application details and the bidding documents; third, the team that implemented the project, particularly architect Hüsnü Alpan, the university's Project and Construction Manager, and Kuryap Construction under the supervision of Pelin Doğan, who had graduated from IUE's Department of Architecture in 2010. The furniture was supplied by two Turkish brands, Koleksiyon and Yenkur, while the studio furnishing, including tables, chairs and lockers, was designed and produced specially for our new school.

It is not an easy task to design a school of design where almost everybody is a designer. Perhaps the most difficult thing is to meet the demands of all these designers as well as those of the top management. We should highlight that many designs fell through the cracks while the final result is pleasing for the majority rather than everyone. Of course, the FFAD building will be criticized but the critical point is to what extent it fits the purpose and reflects the philosophy of the faculty. Would it work as presupposed and planned? Would it embody and represent IDeA? Would the staff embrace and adopt IDeA and apply it systemically despite all the challenges summarized in this chapter? We don't know yet. We will find both the answer and its proof in time.

CHAPTER 13
PHD, DFA OR BOTH
THE PROTECTION OF IDENTITY, NATURE AND THE POTENTIAL POWER OF DIFFERENCES

This chapter was presented as a paper at 'Exchange 1999: Facilitating Art & Design Research', a one-day conference, Wednesday, 3 February 1999, University of the West of England, Bristol.

Since September 1998, this has been the fourth conference I attended on the subject of research. Many of the presentations and papers during that period focused on a key element of PhD definition, namely to 'contribute to knowledge'. The main argument, developed mostly by practising artists, designers and their supporters, frequently emphasized that research as an instrument of advancing knowledge is intrinsic to practice, which should form a substantial part of the PhD. Thus, it is crucial to explore the concept of contributing to knowledge. In this chapter, I unpack the phrase in relation to PhDs and professional doctorates, with particular emphasis on the differences between them.

I am concerned with two attributes of the phrase: the way we contribute to knowledge and the nature of knowledge. While this chapter focuses on the former, I would like to make a few remarks and highlight the significance of developing an understanding of knowledge for art and design. The second part concerns epistemology by raising the question: what is knowledge? This is a legitimate question since we cannot contribute to knowledge if we do not know what it is. This is also a daunting question for it drags us into a theoretical debate in a foreign territory of epistemology while attributing immense importance to the definition of knowledge in art and design. From reading various papers, I understood that the issue of knowledge dominated the Ohio Conference,[1] which took place a few months before the conference where this chapter was presented as a paper.

Klauss Krippendorff (1999) makes an alarming observation: 'Too often, *design is seen as a service to industry*, as having no right to claim a separate body of knowledge … having no right to claim a separate body of knowledge.' However, I do not believe this is the case in the UK because, if it were, the notion of a PhD in Design could be abandoned. Victor Margolin explains the solutions proposed: 'There have been continuous efforts, particularly among design educators, to rigorously ground design in a body of domain knowledge that they believe will insure its social acceptance as a serious endeavour' (1999: 197).

---

[1] The Ohio Conference is titled 'The 1st Conference On Doctoral Education', and was organized by R. Buchanan, D.P. Doordan, L. Justice and V. Margolin in 1988.

Rather than being 'preoccupied with justifying a separate sphere of domain knowledge as the primary subject of investigation', Margolin prefers an open conception of design, such as 'Design Studies' as opposed to 'Design Science' (Margolin, 1999). Challenging this problematic from an epistemological viewpoint, Clive Dilnot tries to secure an independent zone of knowledge for design. He refers to 'a third way of knowing' and develops arguments for it as explained in Chapter 5 of the theory section. His argument is that if science generates knowledge mostly numerically and humanities narratively, then design does so artefactually. Considering that the main preoccupation of design is artefacts, Dilnot's proposal has a basis and requires an enquiry into the nature of knowledge embedded in artefacts.

Having indicated the significance of epistemology, I will pose some questions regarding other aspects of knowledge, especially those related to the concept of contribution:

1. How should we identify a certain field of knowledge that is to be contributed to?
2. Why should that particular knowledge be prioritized over others?
3. Why does that particular knowledge need to be contributed to at that particular time?
4. How should the contribution be defined, and its importance, quality and quantity evaluated?

These questions could be answered easily if we art and design educators were operating in an academic milieu with an established research agenda and appropriate specialisms. Many disciplines operate with set agendas. In medicine, for instance, there are ongoing research areas, such as heart disease, cancer or AIDS. In addition to ongoing research, new research subjects are proposed and money invested accordingly. Certain research fields come to the fore, enjoy popularity and huge financial support, dominate others and set the research programmes of the day.[2] Of course, universities as institutions have enormous power and an undeniable role in constituting research programmes within their fields of expertise. This is one of the major challenging missions of universities: to generate new ideas and contribute to the advancement of disciplines through research.

In his seminal book *The Structure of Scientific Revolutions*, Thomas Kuhn explained clearly how researchers and their communities work: 'Aristotle's *Physica*, Ptolemy's *Almagest*, Newton's *Principia* and *Opticks*, Franklin's *Electricity*, Lavoisier's *Chemistry*, and Lyell's *Geology* – these and many other works served for a time implicitly to define the legitimate problems and methods of a research field for succeeding generation of practitioners' (Kuhn, (1970: 10). Kuhn identifies two characteristics about the achievements of these works: 'An enduring group of adherents' and being open-ended, thereby leaving many possibilities to be explored by practitioners. Regarding these two

---

[2] Elon Musk's space programme, metaverse, artificial intelligence and digital technologies are among those that tend to lead today's agenda. (Footnote added in 2023)

characteristics, Kuhn refers to them as paradigms: 'some accepted examples of actual scientific practice'. As he describes it, paradigm reminds us somehow of movements and styles in art and design. Although it would require further study to make a direct correlation, there are similarities between the active members of research communities, whether within a movement, style or paradigm. To illustrate this, I will quote Kuhn again. However, I will substitute the word *science* with *art*, and the word *paradigm* with *style*:

> *The study of styles (my words)* ... is what mainly prepares the student for membership in the particular artistic community with which he will later practice. Because he there joins men who learned the bases of their field from the same concrete models, his subsequent practice will seldom evoke overt disagreement over fundamentals. Men whose research is based on shared styles are committed to the same rules and standards for artistic practice. That commitment and the apparent consensus it reproduces are prerequisites for normal art, i.e., for the genesis and continuation of a particular research tradition.
>
> (Kuhn, (1970: 11)

Given that it reads well and is not contradictory at all, can we talk about a dominant art or design paradigm today? Since postmodernist and deconstructivist discourses faded, there is to my knowledge no single strong debate currently prevailing but there are a few. In order to portray the situation we can look at universities.

In art and design, the characteristics of certain influential colleges are easily distinguishable. However, I find it impossible to claim that certain schools determine the debate on current issues, let alone set the agenda. Of course, successful graduates represent their institutions perfectly well as alumni once they become practising artists and designers. However, this does not necessarily mean that their activities can be considered organized research. On the contrary, working as individual artists and designers, they pursue their own business and personal objectives.

Theoretically and ideally, academic institutions comprise a community of scholars who influence the agenda regarding current issues, create and participate in a discussion platform, and undertake research to advance knowledge, particularly in their subject specialisms. Therefore, by entering into the research culture through increased publication and the proliferation of conferences, art and design colleges have a new responsibility of creating and sustaining research programmes and projects. This inevitably leads to the establishment of a research agenda. Without strong academic dispute and a dominant discourse in art and design, someone like Charles Saatchi[3] feels sufficiently confident to behave as an institution, launch a new movement – the so-called Neurotic Realism – and set the agenda on his own. Well, at least for a couple of weeks!

---

[3]The Saatchi Gallery exhibits the works of emerging artists, and, as stated on its website, 'the Gallery acquired a strong reputation for introducing artists who would later gain worldwide recognition.'

If we go back to my earlier questions regarding the contribution to knowledge and acceptability of research subjects, we can see how an established schema can help. First, we can assume that academic staff members will be working on current research issues and research proposals outside their interests will not be appropriate and acceptable to them. Second, the knowledge to be contributed will probably be defined in terms of current issues or the unresolved problematics of the prevalent paradigms that scholars deal with. Many PhD subjects will be derived from the needs of this agenda.

To this end, we encounter the necessity and potential power differences between PhDs and professional doctorates. We need both due to the functions they fulfil. Institutions need PhD students and theoretical research at that level to advance the discipline and actively produce its knowledge. Let's accept that the advancement of a discipline cannot be left to fortuitous individual activities only. Rather, this is the essential mission of universities and research institutions. The PhD is a means both to contribute to knowledge and educate prospective expert researchers.

Professional doctorates, such as DFA, D.Des or D.Art, are new eighth-level degrees that are different in nature. The necessities for these degrees are various and perfectly justify their presence. Unlike PhDs, their main concern is and should be the advancement of knowledge in a practice and the development of highly evolved professional skills and research ability as required by industry. No doubt, their contribution to knowledge may not be restricted to practice-related issues. However, their main potential is to explore the nexus between practice and theory, and thus contribute to knowledge from a very fruitful point of view.

Another undeniable opportunity given to candidates wishing to pursue a professional doctorate is the choice of subject. The subject matter of research in professional doctorates may stem from personal aspirations, whereas PhDs are somehow expected to be associated with a current discourse. This greater freedom to define the subject encourages creativity and the creation of exceptional works beyond the borders of mainstream and conventional PhD research schemes.

While PhDs prioritize improving philosophical, theoretical, historical and methodological aspects of a given discipline, advanced professional degrees, such as Doctor of Design (D.Des), Doctor of Art, (D.Art) or Doctor of Fine Art (DFA), enable students to develop and apply projects and research techniques, and explore their relationships with theory and practice within the context of personal work. In light of these arguments, I would venture the following short definitions of both categories: a PhD is an advanced theoretical research degree mostly for those who wish to pursue academic and research careers and contribute to knowledge, especially within a theory. A professional doctorate is an advanced practice-based research degree for those who wish to improve subject specialism and research skills, pursue an educational and professional career, and contribute to knowledge, especially within a practice.

In short, PhDs and professional doctorates fulfil different missions, with neither less important than the other. Rather, they complete each other by covering areas not covered by the other. Hence, I argue that PhD and D.Des, D.Art., DFA and so on are equal degrees with different purposes, emphases and outcomes. Therefore, we need both.

CHAPTER 14
TOWARDS AN UNDERSTANDING OF PROFESSIONAL DOCTORATES

This chapter was first presented as a paper at the International Conference, 'Matrix 4: Research in Fine Art & Design', Central Saint Martins College of Art & Design, 5–7 July 1999, London.

14.1 Introduction

The previous chapter discusses the necessity of both PhD and professional degrees. This chapter takes the subject further and looks into professional doctorates within the same context. As mentioned before, the debate regarding research degrees in art and design has exposed an interesting shift towards a refined exploration of the theory–practice relationship. This appears even in the proliferation of nomenclature. For example, the term 'studio-based PhD' has been replaced by 'practice-based PhD' to express its wider perspective while, a sensitive final touch, political correctness, has offered a more promising and appealing suggestion: Practice-led PhD. However, is it really justifiable to seek a niche within the established concept of the PhD for the sake of creating room for art and design research degrees in which practice plays a key role and the work produced has its own nature and capacity? While the 'traditional' PhD is available to art and design graduates, is it not more enhancing to open another avenue where the full potential of theory and practice, and their relationship are rigorously examined by integrating theoretical and practical work? This paper explores some aspects of the hidden or ignored potentials of professional doctorates. To this end, I will look into

1. PhDs and professional doctorates
2. The academic level of professional doctorates
3. Practice and research
4. The advantages of professional doctorates
5. Factors in assessing work
6. The separation of art and design

14.2 PhDs and professional doctorates

Sir Ron Dearing's report allocates level 8 for doctorates although it does not define qualifications offered at this level (Dearing, 1997: 18). In reality, excluding honorary titles, there are two schemes: PhDs and professional doctorates. In recent years, the concept of the PhD and the concept of knowledge more generally have been severely scrutinized. As a result, a new set of nomenclature has emerged. Although expressions like art-practice-based research, studio-based PhD, practice-based PhD and practice-led PhD are helpful to create a constructive discourse towards transparent definitions, I believe they damage and cast a shadow on the concept of the PhD unless it is redefined and accepted by the majority with consensus. An article in *Connoisseur*, titled 'PhD in Pastry', exemplifies how concepts are consumed in common parlance and exhausted carelessly for the sake of an esoteric cover (Kimmer, 1989).

We all know that the way in which we acquire, develop and use knowledge, and the way in which we contribute to knowledge are changing, which is in fact manufacturing the pressure that we face and the force dragging us towards new programmes. One of the ways to deal with this is to question the status quo of the exiting PhD structure and reform it as necessary. It is no coincidence that Professor Tim O'Shea (1998) of Birkbeck College titled his article 'How New Technology is Changing the Nature of the PhD' at the Annual Summer Conference of the UK Council for Graduate Education in 1998. The way that I prefer is to identify the causes, address the issues encountered and constitute programmes accordingly. I believe the need for programmes that combine practice and theory is so high that there is no need for distorting, extending or reshaping the established concept of a PhD. An architect with a PhD degree is not necessarily a better architect than one who has not – likewise for artists. A PhD is not a licence for better practice or better practical work but an advanced study for research and scholarly activity.

What we are actually doing is restructuring the highest level of education in the wake of current developments. Therefore, if there are reasons, causes and needs to create programmes to improve the quality of practical work, we should not hesitate to propose them. I think professional doctorates are well situated for these purposes. A higher education programme composed of PhD and professional doctorates is not new at all. For example, Harvard University has a system in which a Doctor of Design is considered advanced professional research. They describe the scheme with clarity:

> The program leading to the degree Doctor of Design (DDes) offers advanced study and research in the design disciplines of the built and natural environments. It is intended for persons who have already mastered professional skills and who seek to make original contributions to their fields. At the same level of academic standards as the PhD program, the DDes program focuses on applied research and emphasizes the advance of knowledge in the design disciplines.
>
> (GSD, 1999: 39)

I think the distinction between the PhD and the professional doctorate should be drawn as follows. A PhD is basically an advanced theoretical research degree, designed mostly for those who wish to pursue academic and research careers. Therefore, its essential contribution to knowledge is often achieved at a theoretical level and mostly by means of theory, although this may vary from one discipline to another. Although the knowledge produced is generic, it is not unusual to witness the advancement of a particular discipline, especially regarding theoretical and philosophical matters. Within this perspective, the professional doctorate is also an advanced degree based on research that combines practice and theory, and is mostly for those who wish to improve their subject specialism and research skills, and pursue educational and professional careers. Here again, the contribution to knowledge is essential and achieved often within a practice and by means of practice and its theorization and contextualization. As opposed to PhDs, the knowledge produced is discipline and, in some cases, profession specific. Hence, it is fair to say that the advancement is accomplished for a particular profession and/or discipline, especially for knowledge concerning practice and practical matters. This by no means rules out the possibility of producing generic knowledge through professional doctorates. On the contrary, it is highly possible that the proactive and interrelated process of theory and practice relationship may yield results in both areas rather than one.

14.3 Academic level of professional doctorates

I suggest that the level of professional doctorates is doubted for two main reasons. Firstly, many people are cautious about professional doctorates because of prejudice regarding their status. A booklet by the UK Council for Graduate Education addresses this explicitly: it reads: 'There is … debate as to whether they (that is, professional doctorates) are superior or inferior to the PhD depending on the subject, institution and recipient' (UKCGE, 1997: 25). This idea that professional doctorates cannot be considered equal to PhDs understandably makes artists and designers reluctant to register for these programmes. A consultation paper circulated by the Quality Assurance Agency makes the following statement about allocating doctoral titles for works not containing original research: 'Awards at doctoral level for work other than original research (or an artefact or other form of work accompanied by a written explanation that is examined) should use doctoral titles other than PhD (for example, DMus)' (QAA, 1998: 8). Whether covertly or overtly, this supports the impression that because professional doctorates may not be as original as PhDs or not include original research, they are not at the same level. I believe that a work at level 8 must contain original research and contribute to knowledge, whether as a doctorate or PhD. The difference between the two is not and should not be a question of the originality of the research but the way in which the knowledge is generated. What makes professional doctorates different to PhDs is the way they build and contribute to knowledge. This is the real merit and the value of professional doctorates that makes them both distinctive and justifiable. By the same token, the incentives rendering professional doctorates desirable emerge from the characteristics of a research process that incorporates a dialectical and reciprocal relationship between theoretical and practical components.

The second reason stems from the novelty of the scheme. No one knows yet what a professional doctorate will mean in the art and design world. Therefore, it appears rather comfortable for many applicants to take refuge in and benefit from the established status of PhDs rather than struggle to raise the status of the new research degree. I think these two points, that is, the position of professional doctorates with reference to PhDs and the endeavour of building a status from scratch, should not be deterrents for those aiming at long-term benefits. The real danger is to jeopardize the concept of the PhD for the sake of expanding its scope to accommodate work, which is different in nature.

14.4 Practice and research

Although the following chapter is to concentre on the relationship between practice and research, I would like to touch upon a few key aspects here. The connection between research and practice is often confused. Practice that intrinsically incorporates research encourages the idea that doctorates can be achieved by practice only. This has already been ruled out, as Nigel Cross observes: 'I do not see how normal works of practice can be regarded as works of research. The whole point of doing research is to extract reliable knowledge from either the natural or artificial world, and to make that knowledge available to others in re-usable form' (Cross, 1998: Editorial). Clive Dilnot agrees: 'Design practice per se is not research since its practice is not oriented, in the first instance, to knowledge. But this does not mean that practice cannot become knowledge (1999b: 86). Here, intention is the key factor that determines the outcome. Therefore, one of the aspects of professional doctorates consolidating the distinctive position of this degree is to develop methods to acquire and build knowledge derived from practice, which may not be within the framework of PhDs.

14.5 Advantages of professional doctorates

The possibility of advanced research in art and design has already motivated both industry and education. A few indicators of anxiety, interest and enthusiasm regarding this are the rising quality of theoretical debate, the increased number of conferences, and national and international enquiries for MPhil/PhD programmes. In the longer run, art and design will have their share and be influenced distinctly. Optimists such as myself unreservedly expect a sudden rise in quality and a surprising diversity of practical work and theory in the near future. Some advantages of professional doctorates are the following:

1. Stronger links, cooperation and collaboration with industry and education.
2. Development of practice and professional work.
3. Sustainable exploration of the relationship between theory, practice and communication.

4. Emergence of a new category of educators belonging to neither history and theory nor the studio team of the traditional academic duality, but operating in between and possibly bridging the gap.
5. Steady advancement of knowledge of/on/in/for practice.
6. Unique and distinct contribution to theoretical knowledge by means of and through practice.
7. Encouragement of new research, works and products as well as their discourse.

14.6 A few points to consider regarding the assessment of work

The final submission in professional doctorates normally contains two major elements, written and practical work, so assessment should inevitably focus on this duality. During the assessment, responses will probably cover the following areas, either in a written format as part of the dissertation and report or in the viva voce.

1. Justification of the practical work or research taking place in an academic institution.
2. Explanation of the relationship between theoretical and practical elements, which could be:
   i. Complimentary
   ii. Exploration of the theory
   iii. Application of the theory
   iv. Theorization of the practical work
3. Documentation of the process as a component of practical work.
4. Contextualization of the practical work.
5. Identification of problems or potential problems for future study.
6. Presentation of the major findings and demonstration of their contribution to knowledge.

14.7 Separation of art and design

One of the consequences of introducing professional doctorates appears to be an ultimate yet maybe unavoidable dissolution of the art and design marriage, which is not inauspicious. There is no need to mention that independence offers promises for both of them. The first indication is that separate titles for doctorates, such as DA (Doctor of Art), DFA (Doctor of Fine Art) or DDes (Doctor of Design), evokes the apparently still unresolved question of knowledge. I assume that we will be heavily involved with the question of knowledge in art and design over the next decade. With reference to Clive Dilnot's Ohio paper, I would argue that knowledge about art is different from art knowledge. Knowledge about art, such as art history and theory, is derived from artworks and the results of artistic actions. Art knowledge is derived from the process, means and artistic action itself. This is different from both knowledge about art and also knowledge of methods, techniques and materials. Whether it springs from invisible sources of inspiration, vision and interpretation, the art knowledge that generates artworks needs to be identified if we stick to the concept of knowledge developed by the scientific research tradition. If we don't, which is likely to be the case, we face the daunting task of defining art knowledge.

Of course, design is not exempt from this knowledge-defining process. Despite their cognitive characteristics, no one can convince me that art knowledge resembles design knowledge. Therefore, I speculate that C. P. Snow's famous book, *The Two Cultures*, may be rewritten as *The Three Cultures* at the beginning of the twenty-first century. While I may be a reader of this one day, I certainly will not be the author.

CHAPTER 15
A THRESHOLD WHERE THEORY AND PRACTICE CONGREGATE FORTUITOUSLY

This chapter was first presented as a paper at The UK Council for Graduate Education Annual Summer Conference 1999, 14–15 July, Leeds Metropolitan University.

As the previous two chapters indicate, the debate about doctorates in art and design has created great enthusiasm and interest, with particular attention to practice-based doctorate programmes in the last years of the twentieth century. This chapter is an attempt to clarify further the basic arguments concerning doctoral programmes.

Artists and designers who believe their practice is research, or incorporates a great deal of research, question the nature of PhDs, demanding academic recognition of their activities as the core aspect of their programme. In other words, the duality of theory and practice, and their balance or proportion, is the key issue dominating the dispute. The relationship between theoretical and practical work, and their composition and weighting, raise the question of whether they belong in the category of PhDs or professional doctorates. This question falls into the contentious area described by the booklet on practice-based doctorates, published by the UK Council for Graduate Education (UK Council, 1997). Having attended five conferences and delivered three papers on the subject in the 1998–99 academic year, I would like to attempt to present a coherent scenario.

First, I note that the desire to achieve a PhD with a substantial amount of practical work has led to an inflation of expressions, including the following, which are widely used today in the UK:

1. Art and practice-based research
2. Studio-based PhD
3. Practice-based PhD
4. Practice-led PhD

In Australia, the Ohio papers show that the following phrases are used, although they are also considering 'work-based learning programs at the doctorate level' (Caban, 1998).

1. Practice-based learning
2. Cooperative education
3. Work-based learning

However, this diversity is both confusing and considerably damaging to the concept of the PhD. Trying to introduce practice as the basis of research while renaming existing PhDs accordingly is problematic. Being aware of the problem and using existing practice in music as a precedent, the UK Council booklet suggests an 'inclusive' method, which is a strategy that accommodates practice-based art and design research for a PhD degree award. At first sight, this looks fine because all practice-based research is included under the single title of PhD by revising the concept in light of new developments, thereby avoiding the current proliferation of titles. However, despite seeming simple and workable, this strategy is detrimental in the long term because it jeopardizes the established understanding of a PhD. The reason is obvious: not all practice-based research proposals are appropriate within the scope of a PhD. Hence, their inclusion in such programmes creates unavoidable ambiguity as to what a PhD is. Instead, considering the balance of theory and practice, as well as the intention of the project proposal, may help to define a suitable structure for the highest level of study.

I believe that level eight, which comprises PhDs and professional doctorates, provides a good combination of degrees in which to locate the vast variety of research projects. For comparison, we can briefly list the following major attributes of PhD:

1. Advanced study programme
2. Mostly theory-based research
3. Theorization and/or contextualization of applied or practice-based research
4. Contribution to (mostly theoretical) knowledge of a discipline
5. For academic and research careers

A professional doctorate has a slightly different emphasis, including the following basic characteristics:

1. Advanced study programme
2. Mostly practice-based research
3. Theorization and/or contextualization of applied or practice-based research
4. Contribution to (mostly practical) knowledge of a discipline
5. For educational, professional and research careers

These concise definitions strongly prioritize the threshold where theory and practice congregate fortuitously. The PhD is the right programme if theory, theoretical research and the thesis form the main body of work. I believe practical work should not account for over 40 per cent of a reasonable work for a PhD, so the theoretical part should be 60 per cent. Although I do not like the idea of limiting and defining written and practical work with word counts and percentages, I am not courageous enough to deny their descriptive power. Thus, a PhD thesis should probably be in the region of 60–80,000 words, depending on the weighting of the practical work.

For professional doctorates, the ideal proportion can be 50 per cent practice and 50 per cent theory; this is because the principle of the equal participation of the equals should be applied here to give the right power to both parties. Within this spectrum, a thesis with substantial theoretical research appears appropriate for PhDs whereas a thesis balancing theory and practice represents the ideal duality for professional doctorates. The question is the minimum percentage of theoretical work essential for doctorates. It should probably not be less than 40 per cent while the word count should be about 30–40,000, as specified in the booklet mentioned above.

I think that allocating the PhD mostly for theoretical academic research without any suffix or prefix while allocating the doctorate scheme mostly for professional practice-based research with an identified subject specialism makes clear the differences besides incorporating many contentious areas within a simple and coherent structure. However, there are a few points to emphasize. First, both degrees are equal at level eight but designed to serve distinct functions, as required by various circles such as academia, business, industry and so on. Given the importance of equality, the worry is that one degree might be superior to another, which would lead to them being treated differently. Unfortunately, the booklet on practice-based doctorates does not take a clear stand, but in reading between the lines, this is the case: 'There is debate as to whether they (that is, professional doctorates) are superior or inferior to the PhD depending on the subject, institution and recipient' (UKCGE, 1997: 25).

One way of resolving this problem is to introduce clear definitions, a common understanding of PhD and professional doctorates, quality assurance and high standards. The QAA has published a booklet on the subject, entitled 'Code of Practice for the Assurance of Academic Quality and Standards in Higher Education'. However, the real test of quality and equality will emerge from the works of those graduates who set a precedent.

Second, degrees contribute to knowledge but not always with similar means. Professional doctorates aim at advancing the knowledge in/for/on/by practice for a particular discipline whereas PhDs are concerned with generic knowledge, as Professor Frayling explained at the Matrix Conference in 1999. Again, what I find unhelpful for this argument is, as mentioned in a previous chapter, a consultation paper circulated by the Quality Assurance Agency, which does allocate the doctoral title for those works not containing original research (QAA, 1998). Ensuring quality should not mean sacrificing the principle of contributing to knowledge or the originality of work at level eight, where PhDs and other forms of doctorates are situated by Sir Ron Dearing's Report.

Third, there has been concern about the proliferation of degree titles. In last year's Annual Summer Conference papers, Lucy Thorne, for example, listed fifty-one different doctoral titles awarded in the United States and commented that 'The American model of a plethora of doctoral titles did not augur well and this may lead to undesirable qualification inflation' (Thorne, 1998: 51).

Although I sympathize with her concern, I do not worry about the number of qualifications, providing that the work produced is sufficiently high quality. While the proliferation of degree titles will undoubtedly attract more people to apply for such programmes, this does not mean that the standard will decrease. Instead, it means that the areas of interest defined by these new titles are carefully tailored to the needs of specific industries and people. Hence, the real question does not concern qualification inflation but qualification quality, which should not be compromised at all. Hence, I insist that originality and contribution to knowledge should remain among the main criteria for a doctorate level.

Concerns about inflation can also be linked to the question of subject matter in doctorates. Will this possibility of launching doctorates under distinct titles lead to various subjects being proposed without solid ground? Or, are there currently unrecognized subjects, professions or disciplines that have accumulated sufficient knowledge in theory and practice to instigate substantial scrutiny at the doctorate level? Professor Hugh H. Genoways responded to these questions from his particular profession's perspective in 'Museum Studies Programs are not Prepared for the Ph.D.' (1996). One of his justifications for this judgemental title is that 'we have not created a body of scholarly knowledge sufficient to support a doctoral program' (Genoways, 1996: 7). The reasonable corollary of this is that investigating any body of scholarly knowledge requires a scientific method. This understanding corresponds to the second assumption of two controversial approaches, as identified by the UK Council booklet:

Every subject can give rise to a PhD award,

OR

Only those subjects where the 'scientific method' can be applied in reasonably direct form should give rise to a PhD.

(UKCGE, 1997: 9)

Again, one could argue that museum studies may have not created a body of scholarly knowledge yet. However, they have solid professional knowledge which may now need advancement thanks to the subject's growing significance, which professional doctorates could certainly address. Hence, I could stress, in line with the structure of the two options in doctorates, that the first assumption may well be addressed by professional doctorates whereas the second is reserved for PhDs, as suggested. To this end, assuming that many subjects can give rise to professional doctorates, there are a few reasons why professional doctorates should not use a general title such as DProf.

First, it reminds me immediately of the award of a PhD because it emphasizes generality. The generality and resemblance of these titles underestimate the different nature of professional doctorates and the characteristics of each individual subject specialism. Thus, I fear that DProf as a single degree title will be vulnerable to direct comparison with PhDs, and possibly based on criteria that are not applicable to both.

One of the reasons to identify the subject area within the title is that professional doctorates are linked to a discipline, so the practical research conducted should naturally reflect this. For example, the DDes, that is, Doctor of Design, perfectly represents the qualification level and subject specialism, as well as highlighting that this is a degree that combines practice and theory. The communication of the title is simple, clear and decisive.

Another reason is that professional doctorates are the ultimate extension of professional study programmes so it is not unusual to have as many professional doctorates as BA (Hons) degrees. If we deny this, we deny the discipline-oriented and profession – and practice-based approach of the doctorate programme, which is its essence, is it not?

There are other advantages worth mentioning. As opposed to the rigid academic research approach of PhD programmes, professional doctorates supply students with a flexible scheme within which a variety of projects can be launched. Especially in art and design, where personal projects have particular meaning and aspirations for their realization are high, it is essential that the programme is flexible and allows wider exploration of the subject.[1] Therefore professional doctorates operating on the intersection between theory and practice promise new perspectives in art and design that likely lead towards work that is both new and full of potential.

---

[1] Katy Macleod's paper reveals these when she states, 'What this study uncovered was the postgraduate Fine Art student's anxiety about centring the research firmly within his/her art practice' (1998: 33).

CHAPTER 16
INDUSTRIAL DESIGN IN TURKEY
A NEW AGENDA (REWRITTEN WITH AREN EMRE KURTGÖZÜ IN 2023)

The first version of this paper was published as 'Industrial Design in Turkey: Agenda', in G. Türkoğlu Akay, ed. (1988), Designers' Odyssey 98, exhibition catalogue, Istanbul: ETMK publication. This paper was revised, updated and rewritten with Aren Emre Kurtgözü in 2023.

16.1 The rise of industrial design

Industrial design in Turkey has advanced significantly since the beginning of the twenty-first century due to many factors. I make a list of them in no particular order of importance. The first is the significant increase in the number of designers, industrial design departments, graduate and postgraduate programmes, design offices and design competitions

Second, rising media diversity and expansion including conferences, fairs/exhibitions, design weeks, design publications, magazines, journals and TV programmes have all contributed to a growing interest in and awareness of design.

Third, the activities of the Industrial Designers' Society of Turkey (ETMK), established in 1988, have also raised design awareness and expanded recognition and appreciation of the profession through conferences, seminars, workshops, exhibitions and a design award scheme.

Fourth, the sector of design and design activities was growing at the beginning of the twenty-first century by the demand due to economic developments, such as an increase in per capita income, the emergence of a new middle class with substantial purchasing power and investment in housing, new interiors and furniture.

Fifth, changing shopping habits in Turkey have resulted in reliable domestic markets for mass-produced and high-quality consumer goods for those who can afford them. Supermarket chains and shopping malls, including international ventures, have opened across the country, changing the whole structure of the culture of purchasing and consumption. The products of global brands and designer goods have become available to the public in giant new shopping centres, where high-income groups can satisfy their consumption needs.

Sixth, newly enacted legislation due to the European Customs Union (1996) and the efforts of the Turkish Patent Institute (1994) ended the 'free' era of unlicensed production of designed goods (that is, copying). This has increased the demand for new designs. Meanwhile, Turkey's industry has penetrated international markets with globally competitive consumer goods and realized the importance of original design as an essential element of competitiveness.

Accordingly, growing numbers of industrial designers, including some recognized internationally, are confidently designing and producing in many sectors: white goods, electrical appliances, brown goods, electronics, communication systems, information technology, domestic and office furniture, packaging, ceramics and glass, textiles, leather, transport and automotive industries, lighting, kitchen apparatus and utensils, cutlery and so on. There are designers specialized in certain fields such as Alev Ebüzziya Siesbye in ceramics, Oya Akman in glass, Orhan Irmak and Gamze Güven in packaging design. Adnan Serbest, Aziz and Derin Sarıyer, Faruk and Koray Malhan are among those designers, well-known for their furniture works. There are also designers operating in various areas such as Ali Bakova, Can Yalman, Ece Yalım, Erdem Akan, Kunter Şekercioğlu, Meriç Kara, Şule Koç, Tamer Nakışçı and Ümit Altun to name but a few. A few highly regarded industrial designers live abroad with close links with Turkey such as Ayse Birsel, Defne Koz, Koray Özgen and Mirzat Koç. Obviously, this is an indicative list giving an idea about the dimensions and variety of industrial design practices in Turkey, which has interesting other features worth investigating briefly.

16.2 Industrial design departments

Industrial design (ID) as a discipline was first discovered by educationists and incorporated into academic programmes long before the industry realized its significance. One of the results of this early discovery was an unplanned burden on the ID departments that found themselves before the industry, arguing for the importance of industrial design and the potential benefits of adopting it. In their formation years, departments somehow felt responsible for the employment of their graduates and tried to secure strong ties with the industry. For industrial placement, summer practice in a factory was a good vehicle for students and industrialists to get to know each other. Departments also organized design exhibitions before design weeks were launched in 2002. The Italian Design Exhibition in 1980 was not a big one, but it was very effective in demonstrating what industrial design is. Designers' Odyssey 1994 and 1998 were two statement-making exhibitions and conferences where young Turkish industrial designers began to gain confidence in the quality of their work.

The first ID department was launched at the Higher School of Applied Industrial Arts (today's Mimar Sinan Fine Arts University, Istanbul) by Önder Küçükermen in 1971 (Küçükerman, 2021). Mehmet Asatekin is responsible for the establishment of the Department of Industrial Product Design, at Middle East Technical University, Faculty of Architecture, in Ankara, in 1979 (Asatekin, 2006; Hasdoğan, 2021). Chronologically speaking, two professors, Şermin Alyanak and Nigan Bayazıt, founded the third and the fourth departments. Alyanak established the Department of Industrial Product Design at Marmara University in 1985 while Bayazıt launched her Department of Industrial Product Design[1] at Istanbul Technical University in 1993 (Bayazıt, 2006).

---

[1] Many product design departments were established in the twenty-first century in Turkey. When established these departments were named as industrial design, industrial product design, industry design and so on. The Higher Education Council in Turkey stepped in 2020 and adopted industrial design as a generic title and asked the existing departments to change their names accordingly if needed.

Following these initial attempts, design education has flourished rapidly in this century as both state and private universities opened new programmes, with the number of ID departments today having reached thirty-three. As a result, this relatively new profession has been widely recognized, and thousands of designers began to operate in various fields as in-house designers, company owners, freelance designers and academicians. Some researchers have found opportunities to complete their PhDs abroad, while some designers worked overseas and got international recognition. Reputable names like John Heskett, Bruce Archer, John Langrish, Guy Julier and Clive Dilnot are among those who were somehow involved in Turkish design education through conferences, seminars and supervision of MA and PhD works of Turkish students, and later became important figures in the field of industrial design. In this respect, the following section is a short introduction to academic works demonstrating the changing trends in research.

16.3 Industrial design academia

Until the late 1980s, academic studies were pursued, and the degrees obtained by the ID graduates were mainly from MSc programmes in architecture and PhDs in building science. Most of these postgraduate studies were addressing such hard-science topics as ergonomics and user models, as well as some case-based explorations of particular design methods (such as scenario building) or materials. The rationale behind the choice of subject matter was not arbitrary. When the ID departments were first established, they were, and some still are, institutionally located within faculties of architecture. The well-established postgraduate programmes in architecture were the closest option available to the young staff of ID departments in need of academic promotion. Hence, those hard-scientific, positivist topics were probably considered the common ground between the two disciplines in the formative years. Some works of Asatekin (1975, 1976), Bayazıt (1984, 1987) and Küçükerman (1978) fall into this category.

The second decade of scholarship in ID, beginning in the early 1990s, was a period of expansion and discovery of new territories, new subjects and topics as well as newly identified issues coming to prominence. On one hand, we saw a considerable number of academics focusing on design management, design thinking and design methods in a very rigorous sense; on the other hand, an equal number of academics undertook graduate studies in such areas as semiotics (product semantics included), cultural studies, material culture and anthropology. In addition to this plethora of interests, a small number of academics broached a fresh concern with design history, theory and criticismas we see in the publications of N. Bayazıt (1984, 1987, 2006), S.B. Çelikel (2015), A. Er (1995, 1997, 2003), Ö. Er (1997, 2006) G. Hasdoğan (1994, 2009), A. O. İlhan (2016), H. Kaygan (2008, 2016, 2019) and so on. Overall, this was a decade characterized by an unbridled pursuit of interdisciplinary work, with academics crossing boundaries in order to find useful substance to be adopted and claimed for the newly emerging discipline of ID. Compared to the previous decades, this was also a period that saw the majority of ID academics acquiring their postgraduate degrees from abroad, that is, graduate programmes in Europe and the United States.

The period since the early 2000s has been one of disciplinary consolidation and full integration into the global ID academia. Firstly, academics pursuing postgraduate degrees in ID have found an array of available topics ready to be explored, which had become indigenous to the discipline. Contrary to the previous decade, these topics were not imported from different disciplines; they were, rather, born into the field of design in the first place and became specialist topics in the discipline of ID, such as designing for emotions, usability and user experience, and unprecedented attention given to the local histories of ID in the periphery. The works of N. A. G. Z. Börekçi (2015), F. Korkut, A. E. Kurtgözü (2003), A. C. Özcan (2009) and Ş. Timur (2009) are amongst good examples. Transdisciplinary crossings have not diminished, however. We have seen the growing popularity of ANT (actor-network theory) and phenomenological and post-phenomenological inquiries into design problems and user interactions. Secondly, the ID academia in Turkey has become an integral part of the global academic world through the international presence of Turkish academics as well as international events and conferences organized and held in Turkey.

16.4 The gender balance

One of the unusual aspects of industrial design in Turkey is the gender balance. Women industrial and product designers are rather rare in the Western world unlike in Turkey where the number of male and female designers are almost equal. Likely, the equilibrium is still the same when reputable designers are concerned. Roughly speaking, the number of famous women industrial designers is not less than that of men as is apparent in the list of designers given earlier. The high number of female students in ID departments results possibly from a misconception and misunderstanding that industrial design is a profession similar to architecture and interiors, and therefore suitable for women. The chief factor creating this prejudice is that ID departments have been institutionally set up either under the faculty of architecture or fine arts. Therefore, many students and their families do not notice the engineering aspects of the curriculum where metal workshops equipped with machinery are part of the course. Apparently, once registered, female students stick tightly to the programme and become as successful as male students. The research on gender balance in Turkish higher education indicates that the gap has vanished among undergraduates. The more interesting fact is that female students have lower drop-out rates than male students (Seskir, 2017).

We come across the same balance situation in educational institutions where female academicians are well-represented and, in some cases, even outnumber their male colleagues. This observation is also valid in some other design fields. For example, in the fashion world, famous female designers are well-represented despite a strong male presence. We encounter a similar situation in Turkey where designers like Arzu Kaprol, Bahar Korçan, Dice Kayek, İdil

Tarzi and Özlem Süer are some of the key female figures keeping the gender balance intact. I think the problem in gender balance surfaces when administrative and managerial posts are concerned. For instance, there are 131 state universities and only five of them are governed by female rectors. No need to say that none of them are designers.

16.5 The present situation

Despite many success stories, unfortunately, the economic and political situation has changed substantially in recent years. According to the World Bank, developing countries face a middle-income trap whereby per capita gross national product has remained between $1,000 and $12,000 at constant prices. The OECD's 2019 report also directed our attention to the squeezed middle class (OECD, 2019). Income inequality has increased, while, more recently, the Covid-19 pandemic has severely damaged small businesses. During the pandemic in Turkey, the government did not support the small industry with proper measures. Designers were among those hit most firmly.

During the revision of this chapter, on 6 February 2023, Turkey witnessed a devastating series of earthquakes in her southeast region where ten cities were hit severely and ruined almost totally. Thousands of people were killed and wounded, buildings collapsed one after the other and containers in the port of Iskenderun caught fire and burned emanating heavy smoke. While rescue operations are continuing, the state announced a week-long nationwide mourning for the victims of the earthquake. Although this is not the place to discuss it further, the dimensions of this disaster are immense. The issue from our viewpoint is that the southeast region has a well-established, traditional craft and design-based industry, which was definitely affected, and its negative outcomes are yet to be felt.

Although we can now talk about an established design culture in Turkey, we cannot ignore the consequences of natural disasters and current economic stagnation. In addition to the impact of the Covid-19 pandemic, sharp currency fluctuations, inappropriate economic measures, high inflation, corruption and political and economic turmoil seriously threaten Turkish designer initiatives and businesses just before the 2023 general elections. For example, the Design Week Istanbul, the Design Biennale and Turkey Design Award Scheme were cancelled in 2022. Based on these recent developments, one may say that the future of industrial design in Turkey is uncertain at present and less bright than a decade ago.

Nevertheless, it is necessary to forecast the future despite current negative circumstances although it may remain speculative until crucial economic and social problems are resolved. Instead, I would encourage all parties to prepare and participate in the following action plan to enhance design in Turkey, redrafted for today's conditions.

16.6 A draft action plan for the development of industrial design in Turkey

I have identified four key areas for the action plan and specified the subjects and problems, made suggestions and indicated potential actors. Needless to say, you can add, extract, cut, paste, correct, retype, copy and circulate this action plan as you wish. Whatever you do, however, please think about it, develop it, publicize it and fight for it. Many thanks.

Subjects	Problems	Suggestions	Actors
1. Institutionalization			
Design policy and strategy of Turkey	One of the main weaknesses is the lack of a clear-cut design policy and strategy applied by the state, known about and followed by the industry and businesses. Unsurprisingly, each party is currently trying to find its own way by trial and error.	As a first step, an independent committee of qualified members representing various interest groups and parties should be appointed to study and work on the subject with the purpose of developing a draft document to put before the public for further discussion.	Government Design associations Chamber of architects Business Universities Patent office Industry Research centres
Design Council (an organization promoting design)	There have been attempts to establish a design council in Turkey; a few meetings have been organized and ministers have delivered speeches. However, it has not been as effective as its UK equivalent, which promotes design, introduces it to the wider public, helps medium and small-scale firms to develop a design perspective, supports design projects, links industry with education, produces publications and so on.	The present Turkish Design Consultancy Council (Türk Tasarım Danışma Konseyi) must be restructured as a powerful and independent body run by an executive board reporting to a board of governors who represent designers and design associations, the government, universities, research centres, the patent office, industry and business.	Government Design associations Chambers of architects Business Universities Patent Office Industry Research centres
Design Museum (an organization collecting and presenting design among other related activities)	The lack of any design museums is a major problem, as these are essential to enhance design ideas, visions and perspectives, apart from their educational and archival functions.	An independent body should be formed to undertake this project, whether a private initiative or a consortium of related parties.	Government Patent Office Industry Universities Industrial designers' associations Individual sponsors and collectors
Design Association: Chamber of Industrial Designers (an organization representing designers)	While the ETMK's efforts are appreciated, they should be expanded by giving it legal authority and status regarding professional conduct and the formal representation of designers.	A more powerful, legally and financially well-established, professional and influential organization, with the support of the design community, is greatly needed. A Chamber of Industrial Designers must be seriously considered.	Designers Design associations

Subjects	Problems	Suggestions	Actors
Design libraries	There are a few design-oriented libraries belonging to private initiatives, design businesses and offices. More are needed in major cities, especially where local design is expected to flourish.	Municipalities may take the lead in their region to allocate a dedicated space for design libraries of any size. The main purpose is to promote design and innovation by making quality design more widely known to the public.	Municipalities Design businesses Design offices Designers (by donating archives, books, journals and so on)
Design literature	Although the level of academic and popular design publications is satisfactory, the inadequate number of Turkish design books on various aspects of design is concerning. Understandably, since the market is limited with little chance of making a profit, publishers mostly avoid design books.	Although consumption power is not currently promising, Turkish design books should be available for the public, educators and professionals as much as textbooks for students.	Academicians Researchers Writers Publishers
Design awards	Awards are essential to encourage designers and increase competition. Design Turkey's awards scheme is a successful project that must continue. However, more nationwide awards are needed on specific aspects of design. The other issue is the prestige of awards because there are weak or fake ones as well as internationally acknowledged excellent schemes around the world. It is therefore time to question the standard and quality of awards to identify the ones that are highly respected rather than those which are merely established to make a business out of an award scheme for which participants pay money to get their award.	Design industry and business can further expand the awards system and create a prestigious Best Design Award scheme. Competitions are currently announced across many areas while the awards are only given to participants. In contrast, the Best Design Award scheme suggested here would operate nationwide to identify the best designs regardless of whether the designers are applied. Although it would be hard to identify the best designs if their creators failed to submit their work to the jury, it is the only way to create a respectable and independent award-giving body.	Design business Municipalities Design associations

(Continued)

Subjects	Problems	Suggestions	Actors
2. Education			
Design education	While there are dedicated ID departments, the following areas require further curriculum development: new teaching and learning methods and techniques, including distance learning with or without online systems and self-assessment and quality assurance schemes, research, feedback mechanisms and collaboration.	Actions can include feedback mechanisms from graduates; integrated approaches between design departments, more collaborative and joint projects with other departments, institutions and industry; more live projects and intense dialogue with students, well-prepared project briefs and system designs; emphasis on creativity, innovation and design identity; further understanding of people and society as well as technology, methods, materials and communication.	Administrators Educators Academics Scholars Designers Graduates and students
Design awareness, recognition and appreciation	There is a need to educate industry, business and exporters since industrial design, while recognized, is not wholly appreciated or supported yet. Consolidation is the next stage.	Those sectors that are not sensitive to design and far from appreciating designers can be identified and a special awareness-raising programme can be implemented.	Government Patent office University design departments Professional bodies Other design associations
Design awareness, recognition and appreciation	There is a need to educate the state and other governmental and administrative authorities since design is not well recognized or exclusively valued and supported by local or regional councils, and many state authorities.	State offices and local councils should consider employing designers just as they employ architects.	Government Patent office University design departments Professional bodies Other design associations
Design awareness, recognition and appreciation	There is a need to educate the public. Although 'design', 'dizayn' and 'tasarım' are used in public, these terms are frequently worn out, flattened, misused or insufficiently impactful.	Precautions should be taken against overusing the term. One way is to continuously discuss the changing meanings of design, update the public and put the new use into practice.	Designers Media Institutions and associations

Subjects	Problems	Suggestions	Actors
Design awareness, recognition and appreciation	Clients need educating as many lack a clear design understanding or workable brief. Clients also prefer to reduce or avoid design costs, which leads to dissatisfaction and complaints from designers.	In addition to normal business meetings, designers should spend more time properly informing their clients about recent progress in design, design management, designer-customer relationships and so on.	Designers Design businesses Design offices Design consultants
Design awareness, recognition and appreciation	Children need educating, but there are no design-related teaching units in either primary or high school curricula.	A teaching unit should be incorporated into primary, middle and high school curricula to introduce design concepts with some practical elements. Handicraft lessons used to introduce the craft tradition, so why not design today?	Ministry of Education Design institutions Universities Industry Designers and other design pressure groups
3. Design profession			
Research and development	The research budgets of companies, institutions and businesses are inadequate while research and development are insufficiently focused on innovation, creativity and novelty.	R&D budgets should be increased; industry should be encouraged to prioritize R&D departments and employ more researchers, scientists and designers.	State departments Industry Design businesses Institutions Universities Research centres
Royalty, patent rights, contracts, client relations and other legal issues	Despite the wishes of designers, the designer-client relationship in business is still mostly informal rather than professional. Consequently, contracts are not well developed while royalties are not even considered in many cases. It will take time for small manufacturers to come to terms with designers' modern working methods. Unfortunately, although many producers now recognize that design is essential, they also consider it a financial burden. Therefore, they prefer to minimize the cost of design and designers which designers are not legally protected against.	Solidarity, strong professional associations and support from state departments and organizations are essential to convince those employing or working with designers.	Government State departments Municipalities Design associations Designers

(Continued)

Subjects	Problems	Suggestions	Actors
Job opportunities and expanding employment areas	There are fields where the significance of design has not been grasped yet.	The above-mentioned activities to raise design awareness will bring new job opportunities. In general, designers should seek work opportunities in any field that is related to design. That is, designers must identify new areas and direct their interest to them. For instance, Turkey's marble industry is growing and definitely in search of design ideas. Designers should take more initiative to create innovative products and systems, and develop new areas of work.	Government Design businesses Industry Designers Universities Associations of industrial designers
Design plagiarism	Many developing and developed countries, such as Japan, Korea and China, went through a copying period during their early industrial development. Turkey is no exception. Despite a significant decrease in copying, plagiarism still occurs.	Illegal and unethical behaviour needs to be identified and exposed publicly via the internet or similar means. If the designers who commit crimes are members of design associations, then their membership should be reviewed by the relevant authorities regardless of any legal actions taken against them.	Designers Design associations State departments Professional bodies Other design associations
4. Core issues			
Evaluation of design, and expansion of its scope in line with scientific, technological, social and economic factors	The world is changing faster than ever. We are now living with epidemics, new business methods, big data algorithms, internet shopping, working from home, distance learning, artificial intelligence, augmented reality, Zoom meetings, virtual reality, blockchain, 5G and new space exploration. These, and many other twenty-first-century innovations are forcing us to redefine the areas, content and meaning of design. These changes require immediate action in every field.	The Design Council should take the lead by establishing a scientific committee to monitor developments in design-related areas and advise industry, businesses, associations, universities and designers. All parties involved in design should consider the future of the discipline, their responses to changes and take action to adapt to the evaluation and transformation of design.	Design Council Design associations Design industry Design businesses Academicians Educators Designers

Subjects	Problems	Suggestions	Actors
New approaches and visions on design history, theory and philosophy	Design in Turkey needs a strong identity and perhaps a more coherent approach. The influences of Bauhaus, Modernism, Minimalism, Traditionalism and so on are clear while some work is patchy and hardly original. While there are exceptional, creative and innovative designs, they are not in the majority yet.	The continuously changing characteristics and meaning of design should be discussed, developed and applied to design for needs, the future, people, life, fun, pleasure and so on. Notions that need further study and evaluation include functional creative, innovative, politically correct, environmentally friendly, recyclable, technologically sound, sustainable, visually, aesthetically and intellectually pleasing, meaningful, communicative, global and/or local. These are essential for any serious work in design history, theory and philosophy.	Designers Academics Educators Theorists Thinkers Philosophers
Design critique	The nature of design critique is also changing. It was possible to write on new objects and systems in the early years of industrialization. However, in the era of consumption, when millions of objects are available, the axis of critique has shifted from individual items, and the form and function of systems towards more general issues and attitudes. The new criteria include environmentally and user-friendly approaches, universal design, sustainability and so on. Some Turkish designers claim that they have received no response and need critique to further develop their designs.	The issue of design critique should be considered together with the issue of design standards. The Design Council and design associations could set up a system, say a committee, to review the products and give feedback when required. An independent body as such can also respond to designers' individual applications to evaluate their work.	Design Council Design associations Design journal Academicians Researchers Writers

CHAPTER 17
REDESIGNING TURKISH CULT OBJECTS FROM TRADITIONAL TO 'MODERN'?

The first version of this chapter was presented as a paper at the 8th Conference of the International Committee for Design History and Design Studies in São Paulo, Brazil, 2012. It was published in the proceedings. Farias, P., Calvera, A. Braga, M. da C. and Schincariol, Z., eds. (2012), Design Frontiers: Territories, Concepts, Technologies, *130–134, São Paulo: Blucher.*

17.1 Introduction: Some problems

At the opening speech of the 4T (Design History Society, Turkey) conference in 2009, Jonathan Woodham asked the following question: 'Will Turkish products conform to aesthetic global markets or manage to retain some aspect of local, regional or national identity?' (Woodham, 2010: 17). Although Woodham's point is perfectly legitimate, global market trends appear to be encouraging diversity. In May 2011, the MoMA Design Store in New York introduced Turkish products under the title of 'Destination Istanbul'.[1] The heavy orientalist discourse of the store's advertisement was filled with clichés like 'East meets West.' It reads: 'The *Destination: Istanbul* product collection captures the aesthetic of a cultural crossroads where East meets West and ancient meets modern. Istanbul's celebrated design history is an amalgam of Byzantine and Ottoman influences, blending geometric patterns, rhythmic lines, and vivid colors' (BOH, 2011). Edward Said must have been turning in his grave.

'[A]n amalgam of Byzantine and Ottoman influences' and 'distinctive lifestyle products'! Here you are! This is what the global market has been waiting for from Turkish designers. The former stands for 'historical', (meaning of historical value) while the latter signifies 'exotic' (meaning attractive and appealing to you). What salesman-like language! We shouldn't blame the MoMA Design Store for this though, as they are not the only ones. In a recent example, *The Telegraph* published an article about Turkish design on 16 April 2012, with the title 'Modern Turkish design spreads across globe' (Cumming, 2012). What do we see on the cover page? The Blue Mosque! A mosque built 400 years ago. Although the text is about the work of Zeynep Fadıllıoğlu, a woman designer, the author falls into the trap of using old rhetoric by repeatedly mentioning

---

[1] After the project of selling Turkish products ended, the MoMa Design Store no longer published the relevant web page, although the information was still available on other web pages at the time this paper was rewritten.

Byzantines, Ottomans, the Grand Bazaar, sumptuous palaces and Çırağan Kempinski Palace in the essay's introduction. Therefore, answering Woodham's question, one can say that while these orientalist approaches still survive, perhaps, even predominantly, designers from Turkey will always have the opportunity to satisfy these expectations with products reflecting local, regional or national identity. Nevertheless, this is not without its price; on the contrary, it is very costly. Seeking 'local, regional or national identity' is often a strategy employed by designers operating with particular agendas and intentions, which could have worrying political consequences, as explained below.

17.2 The circumstances: Actors demanding design with identity

It is important to underline that the first debates on global versus local took place in the mid-1990s with a slightly different vocabulary but with great significance. 'Cultural identity' was advanced and strongly emphasized. It was recognized as a legitimate channel to deal with the objects of global markets as well as a vehicle of survival within globalization (Bayrakçı, 1996; Sezgi, 1996). Actually, it was felt at that time that globalization was perhaps forcing design towards the production of similar, mundane and monotonous objects; valid and functional worldwide, so universal, with no identity of belonging to a place. The suggested solution was cultural diversity. Some designers had already begun to use, refer to, or be inspired by Turkey's rich historical culture. Since then, aspects of 'cultural identity' within globalization have been studied regularly.[2] What interests us here is the shift within Turkish design in the last ten to fifteen years. A shift derived from a cultural approach and dispersed in many directions: Modernist, Islamist, Ottoman Revivalist, Nationalist and so on.

Since 2000, the Islamist right has flourished in Turkey, with the religiously-oriented Justice and Development Party (AKP) winning a large parliamentary majority in the 2002, 2007 and 2011 elections with almost half of the vote. Thanks to economic development, mostly due to measures taken by the previous government and money injected from abroad,[3] new right-wing and religious middle-class and high-income groups have emerged in Turkey. One such group is the 'Anatolian Tigers', a term borrowed from the expression attributed to East Asian countries. As a result, it is no longer unusual to see a young woman covered from top to toe wearing Gucci or Prada and driving the latest Porsche along Istanbul's main streets. If Italians have Armani, we have Armine in Turkey, where one can buy the latest fashion scarf in perfect congruence

---

[2]In one of these studies, tendencies towards local, regional, national, traditional and cultural designs were analysed, described and categorized as the neologistic approach, morphological application, topographical execution, formal interpretations, allegorical interpretations and conceptual inspirations. See Section One, Chapter 3.
[3]The sources of money coming from abroad into the Turkish economy have never been clearly identified and have always been a matter of discussion. Some of this cash injection has been labelled 'Green Money' in the book entitled *The Rise of Political Islam in Turkey* (Rabasa & Larrabee, 2008).

with religious rituals (see http://armine.com). The contradiction is obvious. On the one hand, modernization is equated with Westernization and resisted; on the other, the desire to become contemporary and civilized is expressed by Islamic fashion products, whereby fashion – a phenomenon generated by the West – is accepted! As Kaya writes, the search for originality in neo-Islamic design has not gone further than becoming an inferior version of Western material culture (Kaya, 2008: 102).

Naturally, the nouveau riche religious bourgeoisie needed various designs to represent their ideology and lifestyle: from fashion to decoration, from art to architecture. They have found a suitable atmosphere and many tangible examples in the work of those professing 'cultural identity'. Turkish culture is so rich that it could provide a basis for all ideologies to formulate their own design styles, identity and iconographies. Indeed, nationalists on the opposite end of the spectrum from political Islam have also utilized Turkish culture.

According to a Heinrich-Böll Foundation report, 'nationalism in Turkey has been on the increase' (Dufner, 2008: 1): 'Nationalism can be functionalised: in Turkey there is Islamic nationalism, left-wing nationalism, Ataturk-nationalism, even a liberal wing of nationalism' (Dufner, 2008: 2). Of course, this is not a definitive list; for instance, it omits Turkish right-wing nationalists. Nonetheless, this gives us an idea about the level of complexity.

All these actors are seeking a design style that reflects their identities and positions, and reproduces and disseminates their ideologies. Some are also training and educating young designers in accordance with their own ideologies. One example is the Istanbul Design Centre, established with the support of Istanbul municipality when it was controlled by AKP (see www.istanbultasarimmerkezi.org). Soon, we may witness polarization and confrontation between designers from various political and religious factions through their work and attitude. Under these circumstances, to what degree can designers be autonomous? Jeremy Aynsley asked the same question almost two decades ago: 'Can design resist straightforward alliances with a political regime to construct its own autonomous identity? Most commentators agree with the view that design, like other cultural manifestations, has a relative autonomy. It is sufficiently independent to define its own languages, but nonetheless represent broad tendencies within a political economy' (Aynsley, 1993: 14).

The relative autonomy underlined above has a limited territory, and this limited territory is becoming more limited than ever. Unsurprisingly, various left-wing designers who are committed to modernist principles and have applied them with integrity and success, have sometimes been commissioned by right-wing, religious or nationalist business owners. As Kaygan implies, some may have become the producers of a banal nationalist attitude, most likely within a context of orientalist prejudices (Kaygan, 2008).

17.3 The designer's dilemma

The designer's dilemma is thus clear. On the one hand, there is an inclination to benefit from Turkey's rich cultural heritage; on the other, there is the risk of being categorized as an Islamite, neo-Ottomanist or some kind of nationalist, depending on the work they create. Until recently, Turkey's designers have graduated from a modernist, strongly Bauhaus-influenced education. They are striving to define their own design character, identity and direction, and probably do not care how they are labelled as long as they feel they remain consistent with their own philosophy. However, while not yet clear-cut, there are now signs of political divisions among designers. Once each political group can educate and accommodate their own designers committed to a certain ideology, designers may also split into opposing groups. At present, designers are preoccupied with two vital issues as members of the global design community: design identity and direction. With these anxieties in mind, the last twenty years have witnessed an extensive increase of cultural references in the widest sense of the term, which have been well explored and documented. The ways in which designers use traditional objects, historical symbols, architectural forms and local values are innumerable. Recent trends suggest a predisposition towards redesigning what I call 'Turkish cult objects'.

17.4 Cult objects

Concepts like fetish, cult, icon, ritual and vintage began to appear in the literature of design after Karl Marx coined the term 'commodity fetishism' (Marx, [1867] 1983: 77). In design specifically, Clive Dilnot was one of the earliest commentators to relate the concept to mass-produced objects. He directly associates design with fetish:

> That is, the effects of advertising and design styling combine to make 'things' less things in themselves and more totems, or images or fetishes of other things. And the curious situation that has arisen now is that, amongst the values expressed or represented by design objects, are those of 'design' and 'style' themselves. Design itself has gradually become a fetish or a value.
>
> (1984a: 10)

John Walker makes a similar remark in his criticisms of design books that 'present industrial products as if they were precious works of art: isolated from people and the everyday environment, surrounded by a halo of light, the designed object becomes a fetish' (1989: 58). He thinks this is also supported by design history: 'In design history too a fetish is made of the designed object as indicated by books such as *One Hundred Great Product Designs* (1970) and *Cult Objects* (1985)' (Walker, 1989: 58). Actually, the author of *Cult Objects*, Deyan Sudjic, explores the notion and gives various examples in the context of product design. For instance, he describes the Jeep as a cult object: 'It belongs to a class of artifact which exercises a powerful, but mysterious fascination. By definition a cult depends on a group of insiders, tightly knit and linked by secret signs recognizable only to initiates' (1985: 11). For Sudjic, Jeeps, Barbour jackets and Mont Blanc pens are all cult objects 'appealing to small groups of aficionados' (1985: 11). However, there are also cult objects accepted by almost all people. Zippo lighters, for example, like 'other cult objects have exerted an immediate mass appeal'. According to Sudjic, 'in the nature of things, a cult object has to be a mass-produced, or at least has to be suggested in its shape and finish that it is produced by a machine even if it isn't' (1985: 16). In his remarks on fashion, he argues that even an old product like Levi's 501 is also a cult object because '[a] cult object is not necessarily a fashionable one' (1985: 18).

17.5 Cult objects in Turkey: Going in which direction?

The most typical and undisputed cult objects are widely used everyday items. These cult objects are an essential part of Turkish tea, coffee and raki[4] drinking, smoking habits and social addictions: teapots, tea glasses, tea trays, coffee pots, coffee cups, raki bottles, raki glasses, water pipes and so on. They are used daily, consumed and enjoyed. They are visible, attractive and the subject of common parlance and mundane conversations. They have a similar status to the Zippo lighter described by Sudjic. When people drink tea or coffee, they talk about it: its quality, how it is made, where to find the best one and so on. These are issues well-studied and published by Turkish scholars. Yet other issues have been ignored, such as why cult objects are redesigned, the effect of market demands and potential political motivations. Leading Turkish designers, design companies and companies generating and selling designs are, one after the other, providing us with new products and new versions of cult objects. Arçelik, one of Turkey's top white goods brands, launched an electric Turkish coffee machine. Soon after that, the typical traditional coffee pot, which is a simple pot with a handle placed on a hob to boil water and coffee, was redesigned. The electric kettle technology turned it into a self-standing object. Kunter Şekercioğlu, the designer of the Arzum Cezve, has remained faithful to the original form while adding a modern touch that somehow reminds us of the curvy lines in Philippe Stark's works (Figure 40A, 40B). On the shelves of a superstore, it conveys the message that it is still a cezve as we know it. Immediately, new versions emerged. Homend Pottoman 1803, designed by Ümit Altun, is one example. It looks very modern in line, shape and colour, as well as being nicely designed and well made. It has the feeling of a perfect German product, such as one from the days of Dieter Rams. While it is a Turkish product, its name uses a very clever play of English words by combining home and end, and pot and Ottoman: Homend, Pottoman. Despite its obviously modernist form, by referring to the Ottomans in its names, it claims a stake in tradition and history, as well as the associated status and power.

Ali Bakova appropriates a different perspective. He keeps almost everything the same but changes the material. Thus, the typical traditional copper coffee pot is now made of

---

[4]Rakı is a strong alcoholic spirit produced in Turkey. It is distilled from grape juice and flavoured with anise. Rakı, which tastes like French Pastis or Greek Ouzo, is considered the national Turkish alcoholic drink.

Redesigning Turkish Cult Objects

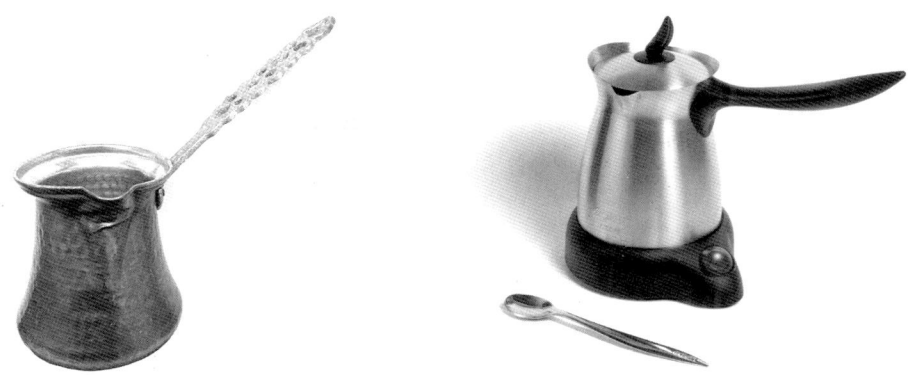

Figure 40A–B A Traditional coffee pot (40A), compared with Arzum Cezve (40B) designed by Kunter Şekercioğlu in 2005. Photo courtesy of Kunter Şekercioğlu.

Figure 41 Coffee pot made out of glass, designed by Ali Bakova in 2010. Photo courtesy of Ali Bakova.

transparent glass (Figure 41). While respecting the original form, he adds a new value: visibility. This helps the coffee maker to observe the process and decide the right time to remove the pot from the hob. Bakova's contribution is therefore an attempt to control and improve the quality of the coffee whereas the other designs try to simplify coffee making through elegant redesign.

17.6 Conclusion: Cult objects as an arena of the design battleground

How can we explain designers' propensity, aspiration and fondness for redesigning cult objects? Is this a challenge to history? Is this a desire to contribute to the country's modernization? Knowing that the Republic of Turkey and the early modernists wished to move the new state away from its Ottoman roots, are designers now settling their account with the past by revisiting cultural and local symbols, beliefs and canons? Or is this just another attempt to gain an identity and constitute differences in a world where diversity is more appreciated than ever? It is difficult to provide substantial evidence and respond to all of these questions within the limits of this paper. However, asking questions and speculating can be very revealing, especially at this particular stage of design development in Turkey since these issues have not yet been explicitly discussed.

Although the scene is not well-defined, there seems to be a discreet or hidden struggle regarding the redesign of cult objects. There are various areas of interest in this battleground of cult objects. One hidden actor is Turkey's current right-wing religious government. It is mostly interested in design iconography to disseminate its ideology while making its rule and presence strongly felt. Coins, for example, are cult objects. The government has altered their design by replacing the bunch of bay leaves symbolizing victory (derived from ancient Greek and Roman civilization) with a pattern resembling Islamic ornamentation. The current right-wing and religious stance aims to force design forms away from modernist, minimalist and mainstream styles towards traditional configurations almost in every field. It is not surprising that we see the traces of this policy in daily life, even a boiler in a typical Turkish tea house may reflect this tendency very successfully (Figure 42).

One of the characteristics of Turkish design circles is that many designers initiate their own projects: after identifying a niche, they develop a project and try to get it manufactured and sold by known companies. If this does not work, designers rely on their own means and capital to get their designs produced, usually in limited editions. Once produced, they try to promote and sell them through fairs, exhibitions, websites and marketing agents. Since designers control what they want to make, they understandably select the most popular, extensively used and widely purchased goods to redesign – which are inevitably cult objects. The economic aspect is not the only reason. Designing the most prevalent, commonly used things can quickly bring public recognition, even appreciation if the work is good enough. It is a prestigious thing to do. Wide publicity, respect, acknowledgement and hopefully good sales may follow an immediate success. It is also a defiant thing to do – a rebelliousness against the collective memory, norms, notions and practices. It is an intrusion and interference. Therefore, each new endeavour of redesigning a cult object is inherently risky simply because the result is – strangely enough – measurable. In other words, if your design does not sell well, you fail, you feel a failure or you are made to feel a failure. Given that cult objects are visible, known and followed by many, the risk is obvious. The competition is obvious too.

Let us take the case of typical tea glasses that everybody uses every day in Turkey. They are being mass-produced by Paşabahçe Glass Company, which is dominating the

Figure 42 Boiler providing hot water to make tea or coffee in traditional public Turkish tea houses. Photo courtesy of Cevdet Ankun.

Figure 43A–E A few examples of Paşabahçe tea glasses. From left to right: Aida (43A), Etnik (43B), Heybeli (43C), İncebelli (43D), Samanyolu (43E). Photos courtesy of Paşabahçe.

market (Figure 43). Paşabahçe has its own in-house designers but occasionally works with famous figures depending on the project. In addition to the variety Paşabahçe presents, numerous new tea glasses fill the shelves of shops, some of which are products of well-known designers such as (in alphabetical order) Ali Bakova (Figure 44A), Can Yalman (Figure 44B), Defne Koz (Figure 44C), Faruk Malhan (Figure 44D and 44E), Koray Özgen (Figure 44F) and so on.

If many renowned designers design a tea glass one after the other (Figure 44A-F), they not only challenge tradition but also defy each other with or without their own knowledge, discretely and in disguise. Each glass design deserves a separate analysis displaying similarities and differences as well as its relationship with the plate, which

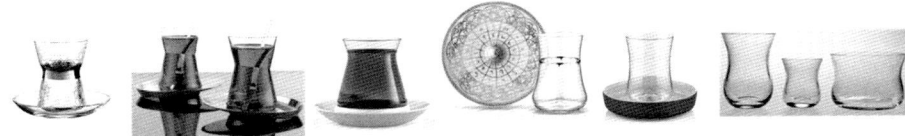

Figure 44A–F Tea glasses (from left to right): Ti Te Chai by Ali Bakova (44A), Hisar (two glasses) by Can Yalman (44B), Unnamed by Defne Koz (44C), Dervish (saucer and glass) by Faruk Malhan (44D), İstanbul by Faruk Malhan (44E) and İncebelli (three glasses) by Koray Özgen (44F) Photographs courtesy of the designers.

appears to be a prominent component in these days. Although it is intangible at the moment, it is possible that a hidden rivalry exists and has the potential to surface in due course. It is not easy to predict which side or which product will prevail in the battle for mainstream design. However, design concepts, thought and technologies are steadily maturing within this turmoil of variety, and one hopes that the number of good works will continue to grow.

REFERENCES

Turkish spelling is used when reference is made to Turkish names and publications. English spelling is used for Turkish names and references if the original source is in English.

Ağır, A. (2005), 'Balyanlar'ın Eğitimi Üzerine Notlar', in A. Ağır, D. Mazlum and G. Cephanecigil (eds), *Afife Batur'a Armağan. Mimarlık ve Sanat Tarihi Yazıları*, 65–71, İstanbul: Literatür.

Akcan, E. (2000), 'Orientalism and Melancholy: Bruno Taut in the East', in L. V. Wells-Bowie (ed), *88'th ACSA Annual Meeting Proceedings*, 263–72, Heterotopolis.

Akcan, E. (2012), *Architecture in Translation: Germany, Turkey and The Modern House*, Durham & London: Duke University Press.

Aldersey-Williams, H. (1992), *Nationalism and Globalism in Design*, New York: Rizzoli.

Appadurai, A. (1990), 'Disjuncture and Difference in the Global Cultural Economy', in M. Featherstone (ed), *Global Culture: Nationalism, Globalization and Modernity*, 295–310, London: Sage.

Archer, B. (1974), *Design Awareness and Planned Creativity in Industry*, London: Office of Design, Department of Trade, Industry and Commerce.

Archer, B. (1977), 'Some Tasks for Design History', *Art Libraries Journal*, 2 (2): 4–10.

Arseven, C. E. (1984), *Türk Sanatı* [Turkish Art], İstanbul: Cem Yayınevi.

Asatekin, M. (2006), 'ODTÜ Mimarlık Fakültesi, Endüstri Ürünleri Tasarımı Bölümü "BAŞLANGIÇ NOTLARI"', *Tasarım+Kuram*, (5): 28–32.

Asatekin, M. (1994), 'Turkish Design Facing the Global Market', in G. Hasdogan (ed), *Design, Industry and Turkey*, 3–8, Ankara: Middle East Technical University.

Asatekin, M. (1976), 'Postural and Physiological Criteria for Seating: A Review', *METU Journal of the Faculty of Architecture*, (1): 55–83.

Asatekin, M. (1975), 'Endüstri Tasarımı Ölçütlerine Bütünsel Bir Yaklaşım', *ODTÜ Mimarlık Fakültesi Dergisi*, (2): 247–63.

Ashwin, C. (1978), 'Art and Design History: The Parting of the Ways?', *Design History: Fad or Function?* 98–102, London: Design Council.

Aslanoğlu, İ. (1976), 'Dışavurumcu ve Usçu Devirlerinde Bruno Taut (1880–1938)', *ODTÜ Mimarlık Fakültesi Dergisi*, 2 (1): 35–48.

Attfield, J. (1985), 'Defining the Object and the Subject', *The Times Higher Educational Supplement (THES)*, 1 February, 26.

Aynsley, J. (1993), *Nationalism and Internationalism: Design in the 20th Century*, London: Victoria & Albert Museum.

Baker, N. (1990), *The Mezzanine*, Cambridge: Granta Books.

Balcioglu, T. (1993), 'A Review of the Emergence of the Term, Concept and History of Industrial Design and a Theoretical Analysis of the Major Elements Forming the Structure for a Prospective Historiography', PhD Thesis, Middle East Technical University, Ankara.

Balcioglu, T., ed. (1998), *The Role of Product Design in Post-Industrial Society*, Rochester: Kent Institute of Art & Design; Ankara: Middle East Technical University.

Balcioglu, T. (1999), 'Problematic of Local and Global Design: Identity in New Industrialised Countries with Special Emphasis on Turkey', in *Design Cultures: Proceedings of the Third European Academy of Design Conference*, 57–71, Sheffield: Sheffield Hallam University. It was also published in ArchiScope 4, March–April 1999, 61–65, in English and Turkish.

References

Balcioglu, T. and Emgin, B. (2014), 'Recent Turkish Design Innovations: A Quest for Identity', *Design Issues*, 30 (2): 97–111.
Banham, R. (1989), *Theory and Design in the First Machine Age*, Cambridge, MA: The MIT Press.
Barthes, R. (1976), *The Pleasure of the Text*, trans. R. Miller, London: Jonathan Cape.
Baudrillard, J. (1988), *Selected Writings*, ed. M. Poster, Cambridge: Polity Press.
Bauman, Z. (1998), *Globalization: The Human Consequences*, Cambridge: Polity Press.
Baxandall, M. ([1972] 1991), *Painting and Experience in Fifteenth-Century Italy*, Oxford: Oxford University Press.
Bayazıt, N. (2006), 'İtü'de Endüstri Ürünleri Tasarımı "DENEYİ'mim"', *Tasarım+Kuram*, (5): 41–53.
Bayazıt, N., Çorbacı, F. K. and Günal, D., eds. (1996), *Tasarımda Evrenselleşme*, İstanbul: İTÜ Mimarlık Fakültesi.
Bayazıt, N. (1987), 'Theoretical Basis of a Computer-Aided Design Education and Research Laboratory', *Design Studies*, 8 (3): 138–49.
Bayazıt, N. (1984), 'Scientific Design Decisions within a Changing Society', in R. Langdon and N. Cross (eds), *Design and Society*, London: Design Council.
Bayly, C. A., Beckert, S. and Connely, M. I. (2006), 'AHR Conversation: On Transnational History', *The American Historical Review*, 111 (5): 1441–1464.
Bayrakçı, O. (1996), 'Yerel Ürün Kimliği - Küresel Dış Pazar', in N. Bayazıt, F. K. Çorbacı and D. Günal (eds), *Tasarımda Evrenselleşme*, 93–103, İstanbul: İTÜ Mimarlık Fakültesi.
Becher, T., Henkel, M. and Kogan, M. (1994), *Graduate Education in Britain*, London: Jessica Kingsley Publishers.
Benjamin, W. ([1936] 1977), 'The Work of Art in the Age of Mechanical Reproduction', in *Illuminations*, 219–253, Glasgow: Fontana/Collins.
Benton, T. (1975), 'Past Should be Looked at Through Well-Designed Spectacles', *The Times Higher Educational Supplement (THES)*, 10 October, p. 7.
Bertram, A. (1938), *Design*, Harmondsworth: Penguin Books Limited.
BOH. (2011), 'MoMA's "Destination: İstanbul" Features Products from Turkey', Business of Home, 16 May. Available online: https://businessofhome.com/articles/1246/moma-s-destination-İstanbul-features-products-from-turkey (accessed 26 August 2022).
Bone, J. D. (1999), 'Institutional Positioning Following the Harris and Dearing Reports', in N. Watts (ed), *The International Postgraduate: Challenges to British Higher Education*, Lichfield: UK Council for Graduate Education – UKCGE.
Börekçi, N. A. G. Z. (2015), 'Usage of Design Thinking Tactics and Idea Generation Strategies in a Brainstorming Session', *METU Journal of the Faculty of Architecture*, 32 (2): 1–17.
Bozdogan, S. (1997), 'Against Style: Bruno Taut's Pedagocial Program in Turkey', in M. Pollak (ed), *The Education of the Architect: Historiography, Urbanism and the Growth of Architectural Knowledge*, 163–92, Cambridge: The MIT Press.
Braudel, F. (1980), *On History*, trans. S. Matthews, London: Weidenfeld and Nicolson.
Buchanan, R. (1995), 'Rhetoric, Humanism, and Design', in R. Buchanan and V. Margolin (eds), *Discovering Design: Explorations in Design Studies*, 23–66, Chicago: The University of Chicago Press.
Buchanan, R., Doordan, D., Justice, L. and Margolin, V. (1999), *Doctoral Education in Design: Proceedings of the Ohio Conference*, Pittsburgh: Carnegie Mellon.
Caban, G. (1998), 'Work-based Learning and Doctoral Education in Design', in R. Buchanan, D. Doordan, L. Justice and V. Margolin (eds), *Doctoral Education in Design: Proceedings of the Ohio Conference*, 131–43, Pittsburgh: Carnegie Mellon University.
Calvera, A., Woodham, J. and Barbosa, H. (2016), *Reflections on Design*, Aveiro: University of Aveiro Press.
Carr, E. H. (1964), *What is History?* Middlesex: Penguin Books.

References

Carrington, N. (1976), *Industrial Design in Britain*, London: George Allen and Unwin.
Çelikel, S. B. (2015), *Endüstriyel Tasarımda Paradigma Kaymaları: Bruno Latour'a Özel bir ilgiyle*, İstanbul: Nobel Akademik Yayıncılık.
Cerasi, M. (1988), 'Late Ottoman Architects and Master Builders', *Muquarnas*, (5): 87–102.
Chakrabarti, A. and Blessing, L. (2015), 'A Review of Theories and Models of Design', *Journal of the Indian Institute of Science*, 95 (4): 325–40.
Chermayeff, S. (1982), 'New Materials and New Methods', in R. Plunz (ed), *Design and the Public Good*, Cambridge, MA: The MIT Press.
Childe, G. ([1942] 1964), *What Happened in the History*, Middlesex: Penguin Books.
Cipolla, C. and Birdsall, D. (1979), *Technology of Man*, New York: Hold, Rinehart.
Cluster, I. D. (2016), *International Design Organisations: Histories, Legacies, Values*. Available online: http://arts.brighton.ac.uk/research/research-events/internationalising-design-history-events/international-design-organisations-histories,-legacies,-values (accessed 12 March 2017).
Cole, H. (1884), *Fifty Years of Public Work*, London: George Bell and Sons.
Conran, T. (1993), 'Forward' to *Industrial Design: Reflection of a Century*, ed. J. de Noblet, Paris: Flammarion/APCI.
Conway, H., ed. (1987), *Design History: A Student's Handbook*, London: Allen and Unwin.
Council, D. (1978), *Fad or Function*, London: Design Council.
Crane, W. and Day. L . F. (1903), *Moot points: friendly disputes upon art & industry between Walter Crane & Lewis F. Day*, London: B. T. Batsford.
Crane, W. (1887), 'The Importance of the Applied Arts, and Their Relation to Common Life', *Journal of the Society of Arts*, 35 (3): 717–732.
Cross, N. (1998), 'Editorial', *Design Studies*, 19 (1): 1–4.
Cross, N. (1999), 'Design Research: A Disciplined Conversation', *Design Issues*, 15 (2): 5–10.
Cumming, E. (2012), *Modern Turkish Design Spreads Across Globe*. Available online: https://businessturkeytoday.com/modern-turkish-designs-spread-across-globe.html (accessed 27 February 2022).
David, R., ed. (1966), *The Arden Shakespeare, Love's Labour's Lost*, London: Methuen.
Dearing, R. (1997), *Higher Education in the Learning Society: Summary Report*, The National Committee of Inquiry into Higher Education.
Deniz, Ş. (2006), 'Ortaköy Camii'nin İnşa Sürecinde Gayri Müslim Yönetici, Usta ve Tüccarların Rolü', in K. Kahraman (ed), *150. Yılında Dolmabahçe Sarayı*, 693–706, Ankara: TBMM Milli Saraylar Daire Başkanlığı.
Design Council. (2022), *Our History*. Available online: https://www.designcouncil.org.uk/who-we-are/our-history (accessed 1 September 2022).
Design Innovation Group. (1990), *The Benefits and Costs of Investment in Design: End of Award Report to the Economic and Social Research Council*, The Open University: UMIST, Working Paper WP-13.
Design Research Society. (2015), *Design Research Society*. Available online: https://www.designresearchsociety.org/cpages/history (accessed 2 September 2022).
DIA. (1915), *Pamphlet about the Establishment of DIA*, London: Design and Industries Association.
Diez, E. and Aslanapa, O. (1955), *Türk Sanatı*, İstanbul: İstanbul Üniversitesi Edebiyat Fakültesi Yayınları.
Diler, F. G. (2016), 'Devletin mimarlık tarihiyle imtihanı', *Agos*. Available online: https://www.agos.com.tr/tr/yazi/14478/devletin-mimarlik-tarihiyle-imtihani (accessed 6 August 2023).
Dilnot, C. (1984a), 'The State of Design History Part I: Mapping the Field', *Design Issues*, 1 (1): 4–23.
Dilnot, C. (1984b), 'The State of Design History Part II: Problems and Possibilities', *Design Issues*, 1 (2): 3–20.

References

Dilnot, C. (1999a), 'The Science of Uncertainty: The Potential Contribution of Design to Knowledge', in R. Buchanan, D. Doordan, L. Justice and V. Margolin (eds), *Doctoral Education in Design: Proceedings of the Ohio Conference*, 65–97, Pittsburgh: Carnegie Mellon University.

Dilnot, C. (1999b), 'Useful and Critical: The Position of Research in Design', *Conference Proceedings*, Helsinki: University of Art & Design UIAH.

Dormer, P. (1990), *The Meaning of Modern Design Towards the Twenty First Century*, London: Thames and Hudson.

Dufner, U. (2008), *Nationalism and the Turkey - EU relations: Perspectives from both sides*, Report, Heinrich-Böll-Stiftung.

Durling, D. and Friedman, K. (2000), *Foundations for the Future: Doctoral Education in Design*, Staffordshire: Staffordshire University Press.

EAD. (2017), *The European Academy of Design*. Available online: https://ead.yasar.edu.tr/ (accessed 2 September 2022).

EB: Encyclopaedia Britannica. (1771), *Encyclopaedia Britannica or A Dictionary of Arts and Sciences by a Society of Gentlemen in Scotland*, Edinburgh: A. Bell and C. Macfarquhar, first edition, 418–19.

Eldem, E. (2010), 'Discovering "Other" Architects', in H. Kuruyazıcı (ed), *Armenian Architects of Istanbul*, 12–17, Istanbul: International Hrant Dink Foundation Publications.

Elmas, D. (2008), 'Tarihi bir gerçek aydınlığa çıkıyor…"Balyanlar" mimar değildi', *Antoloji.com*. Available online: https://www.antoloji.com/tarihi-bir-gercek-aydinliga-cikiyor-balyanlar-mimar-degildi-mutlaka-oku-siiri/ (accessed 2 September 2022).

Elton, G. R. ([1967] 1984), *The Practice of History*, London: Fontana.

Enzensberger, H. M. (1990), 'Second Thoughts on Consistency', *Political Crumbs*, trans M. Chalmers, London: Verso.

Er, A. (1997), 'Development Patterns of Industrial Design in the Third World: A Conceptual Model for Newly Industrialized Countries', *Journal of Design History*, 10 (3): 293–307.

Er, A. (1995), 'The State of Design: Towards an Assessment of the Development of Industrial Design in Turkey', *METU: Journal of the Faculty of Architecture*, 13 (1–2): 31–51.

Er, Ö. (1997), 'Nature of Design Consultancy Work for Newly Industrialised Country Clients', *The Design Journal*, 1 (1): 30–40.

Er, Ö. and Er, H. A. (2006), 'Design Research in the Periphery: A Review of the Foundations and Development of Characteristics of Industrial Design Research in Turkey', *A/Z ITU Journal of the Faculty of Architecture*, 3 (1–2): 85–97.

Er, A., Korkut, F. and Er, Ö. (2003), 'US Involvement in the Development of Design in the Periphery: The Case History of Industrial Design Education in Turkey, 1950s–1970s', *Design Issues*, 19 (2): 17–35.

Erdem, C. (2003), 'Sadık Karamustafa: Grafik Sanatının Renkli Yüzü', *Art Decor*, Ocak, (118): 36–41.

Erdim, B. (2007), 'From Germany, to Japan and Turkey: Modernity, Locality and Bruno Taut's Transnational Details from 1933–38', *Lunch 2, Journal of the University of Virginia School of Architecture*, 103–115.

Erkmen, B. (1987), 'Yurdaer Altıntaş'la Sohbet', *Grafik Sanatı*, 3 (10): 25–48.

Erkmen, B. (1992), *Works From 91/92*, Istanbul: Ofset Yapımevi.

Erkmen, B. (1994), *Works From 93/94*, Istanbul: Ofset Yapımevi.

Erkmen, B. (1997a), *ISBN 975-342-142-7*, Istanbul: Metis Yayınları.

Erkmen, B. (1997b), *Works Around Art and Culture*, Mainz: Gutenberg-Museum.

Erkmen, B. (1997c), *Works From 95/96*, Istanbul: Ofset Yapımevi.

Erkmen, B. (1999), *Works From 97/98*, Istanbul: Ofset Yapımevi.

Erkmen, B. (2001), *Works From 99/00*, Istanbul: Ofset Yapımevi.

Erkmen, B., Ulay, F. and Altılar, T. (2000), *32 Büst: 32 Fotoğraf İçin Yazılmış Yalanlar*, Istanbul: Ofset Yapımevi.

References

Ertel, M. (1999), *Büyültmeler İçin Grafikler /Graphics for Blowups*, Exhibition Catalogue, 16–30 April 1999, Istanbul: Dolmabahçe Kültür Merkezi.

Evans, M., Veveris, M. and Wormald, P. (1994), 'Modelling Within Product Design Activity: Applications and Opportunities', in *PDE 94 Product Design Education*, Conference Proceedings, Bournemouth: Bournemouth University.

Featherstone, M. (1993), 'Global and Local Culture', in J. Bird, B. Curtis, T. Putnam, G. Robertson and L. Tickner (eds), *Mapping the Futures: Local Cultures, Global Change*, 169–87, London: Routledge.

Flusser, V. (1999), *The Shape of Things: A Philosophy of Design*, London: Reaktion Books.

Forty, A. (1986), *Objects of Desire: Objects and Society 1750–1980*, London: Thames and Hudson.

Forty, A. (1993), 'A Reply to Victor Margolin', *Journal of Design History*, 6 (2): 131–2.

Foucault, M. ([1969] 1974), *The Archaeology of Knowledge*, trans. A. M. S. Smith, London: Tavistock Publications.

Frayling, C. (1993), 'Research in Art & Design', *Royal College of Art Research Papers*, 1 (1): 1–5, London: RCA.

Frayling, C. (1998), 'Practice-Based Doctorates in the Creative and Performed Arts and Design', *UK Council for Graduate Education Newsletter*, n.17, February.

Friberg, K., Hilson, M. and Vall, N. (2007), 'Reflections on Trans-national Comparative History from an Anglo-Swedish Perspective', *Historisk Tidskrift*, 127 (4): 717–737.

Fry, T. (1981), 'Design History: A Debate?', *Block*, (5): 14–18.

Fry, T. (1988), *Design History: Australia*, Sydney: Hale & Iremonger.

Fry, T. (1995), 'A Geography of Power: Design History and Marginality?' in V. Margolin and R. Buchanan (eds), *The Idea of Design*, Cambridge: MIT.

Genoways, H. H. (1996), 'Museum Studies Programs are Not Prepared for the Ph.D.', *Curator*, 39 (1): 6–11.

Ghose, R. (1995), 'Design, Development, Culture, and Cultural Legacies in Asia', in V. Margolin and R. Buchanan (eds), *The Idea of Design*, 187–203, Cambridge: MIT.

Giedion, S. ([1948] 1955), *Mechanization Takes Command*, New York: Oxford University Press.

Ginzburg, C. ([1976] 1980), *The Cheese and Worms: The Cosmos of a Sixteenth-Century Miller*, trans. J. and A. Tedeschi, London: Routledge and Kegan Paul.

Ginzburg, C. (1980), 'Morelli, Freud and Sherlock Holmes: Clues and Scientific Method', trans. A. Davin, *History Workshop Journal*, 9 (1) March: 5–36.

Gloag, J. (1934), *Industrial Art Explained*, first edition, London: George Allen & Unwin Ltd.

Gloag, J. (1945), *Plastics and Industrial Design*, London: George Allen & Unwin Ltd.

Gloag, J. (1946), *Industrial Art Explained*, revised and enlarged third edition, London: George Allen and Unwin Limited.

Gloag, J. (1947a), *Good Design Good Business*, Edinburgh: Published for the Scottish Committee of the Council of Industrial Design.

Gloag, J. (1947b), *Self Training for Industrial Designers*, London: George Allen & Unwin.

Gloag, J. (1947c), *The English Tradition in Design*, London: King Penguin Books.

Gloag, J. (1950), 'Identity and Development of Industrial Design I', *Eidos*, no: 2, September-October: 34–43; part II, no: 3, November–December: 34–40.

Gloag, J. (1959), *The English Tradition in Design*, London: King Penguin Books.

GMK: Turkish Society of Graphic Designers. (1995), *Turkish Graphic Designers 1*, Istanbul: Alternatif Yayıncılık.

GMK: Turkish Society of Graphic Designers. (1998), *Turkish Graphic Designers 2*, Istanbul: Alternatif Yayıncılık.

GMK: Turkish Society of Graphic Designers. (1999), *18th Graphic Design Exhibition*, Istanbul: GMK.

References

GMK: Turkish Society of Graphic Designers. (2000), *19th Graphic Design Exhibition*, Istanbul: GMK.

Gönenç, T. (1985), 'Books and Illustrations 1: Master Münif Fehim', *Grafik Sanatı*, 1 (3), May-June: 51–3.

Goodwin, G. (1992), *A History of Ottoman Architecture*, London: Thames and Hudson.

GSD. (1999), *The Official Register 1998–1999*, Cambridge, MA: Harvard University, Graduate School of Design.

Guillerme, J. (1993), 'Design in the First Machine Age', in J. de Noblet (ed), *Industrial Design: Reflection of a Century*, Paris: Flammarion/APCI.

Gwynn, J. (1766), *London and Westminster Improved, Illustrated by Plans*, London: Printed for the Author.

Haller, S. and Fili, L. (1998), *German Modern: Graphic Design from Wilhelm to Weimar*, San Francisco: Chronicle Books.

Hannah, F. and Putnam, T. (1980), 'Taking Stock in Design History', *Block*, (3): 25–34.

Hanrahan, S. (1998), 'The Possibility of Dialogue: The Relationship between "Words" and "Art-making"', in Fine Art Research', *Drawing Fire*, Winter, 2 (2): 29–31.

Hasdoğan, G., Korkut, F. and Börekçi, N. A. G. Z. (2021), 'Orta Doğu Teknik Üniversitesi ve Endüstriyel Tasarım Eğitiminde 'Ortadoğu' Ekolü: Yerele ve Dışarıya Sınırdaş bir Türkiye Modernleşmesi Örneği', *Tasarım+Kuram*, 17 (Özel Sayı: 4): 29–64.

Hasdogan, G. (2009), 'The Institutionalization of the Industrial Design Profession in Turkey: Case Study – The Industrial Designers Society of Turkey', *The Design Journal*, 12 (3): 311–38.

Hasdogan, G., ed. (1994), *Design, Industry and Turkey*, Ankara: Middle East Technical University.

Haug, W. F. ([1971] 1986), *Critique of Commodity Aesthetic*, trans. R. Bock, Cambridge: Polity Press.

Haug, W. F. (1987), *Commodity Aesthetics, Ideology and Culture*, New York: International General.

Heskett, J. (1980), *Industrial Design*, London: Thames & Hudson.

Hill, T., Acker, S. and Black, E. (1994), 'Research Students and Their Supervisors in Education and Psychology', in R. G. Burgess (ed), *Postgraduate Education and Training in the Social Sciences: Process and Products*, London: Jessica Kingsley Publishers.

Hogben, C. (1983), 'Introduction', in *British Art and Design, 1900–1960: A Collection in the Making*, exhibition catalogue, London: Victoria & Albert Museum.

Holme, G. (1934), *Industrial Design and the Future*, London: Studio.

ICDHS. (2008), *International Conferences on Design History and Studies*. Available online: http://www.ub.edu/icdhs/index.html (accessed 5 September 2022).

Ilhan, A. O. and Er, A. (2016), 'Existential Antagonisms: Boundary Work and the Professional Ideology of Turkish Industrial Designers', *Design Issues*, 32 (1): 19–31.

Irwin, D. (1991), 'Art versus Design: The Debate 1760–1860', *Journal of Design History*, 4 (4): 219–32.

Jackson, F. G. (1894), *Theory and Practice of Design: An Advanced Text-Book on Decorative Art*, London: Chapman and Hall.

Jameson, F. (1998), 'Notes on Globalization as a Philosophical Issue', in F. Jameson and M. Miyoshi (eds), *The Cultures of Globalization*, 54–77, London: Duke University Press.

Kalman, T. (1991), 'Good History Bad History', *Design Review*, Spring, first Issue: 48–57.

Karamustafa, S. (1999), 'Türkiye'de Grafik Tasarımın Son Çeyrek Yüzyılı', in A. Ödekan (ed), *Cumhuriyet'in Renkleri, Biçimleri*, 82–90, İstanbul: Tarih Vakfı.

Karamustafa, S. (2002), 'Tasarım Eğitimi ve Grafist', *Arredamento Mimarlık*, (6): 120–6.

Karol, E., ed. (2001), *Grafist İnadına Afiş & Posters, Relentlessly*, 5th International Istanbul Graphic Design Week, International Poster Exhibition Catalogue, Istanbul: Mimar Sinan University.

References

Kart, U. (2002), 'Latif Ariş: Yitik Sanatçıya Saygı', *Art Decor*, September.
Katarina, F. M. H. (2007), 'Reflections on Trans-national Comparative History from an Anglo-Swedish Perspective', *Historisk Tidskrift*, 127 (4): 717–37.
Kaya, C. (2008), 'Bir Temsil Mecrası Olarak Türbanın Çağdaş Türkiye'de Dönüşümü', in T. Balcıoğlu and G. Baydar (eds), *Kim(lik)lerin Tasarımı*, 96–109, İzmir: İzmir Ekonomi Üniversitesi.
Kaygan, H. (2016), 'Material Semiotics of Form Giving: The Case of the Electric Turkish Coffee Pot', *Design Issues*, 32 (3): 78–90.
Kaygan, H. (2019), 'Performing Turkish Design in Products, Collections and Exhibitions: Expanding the Archive, Seeking Depth', in G. Julier, A. V. Munch, M. N. Folkmann, H.-C. Jensen and N. P. Skou (eds), *Design Culture: Objects and Approaches*, 189–202, London: Bloomsbury Visual Arts.
Kaygan, H. (2008), 'Tasarımda Milli Kimliğin Varoluş Koşulları', in T. Balcıoğlu and G. Baydar (eds), *Kim(lik)lerin Tasarımı*, 123–30, İzmir: İzmir Ekonomi Üniversitesi.
Khun, T. S. (1970), *The Structure of Scientific Revolutions*, Chicago: University of Chicago Press.
Kikuchi, Y. (2014), 'Transnational Modern Design Histories in East Asia: An Introduction', *Journal of Design History*, 27 (4): 323–34.
Kimmer, C. (1989), 'Ph.D. in Pastry', *Connoisseur*, March, 101–6.
Kinross, R. (1985), 'Design History's Search for Identity', *Designer*, November, 12–13.
Kinross, R. (1988), 'Herbert Read's Art and Industry: A History', *Journal of Design History*, 1 (1): 35–50.
Klem, F. (1964), *A History of Western Technology*, Cambridge, MA: The MIT Press.
Krippendorf, K. (1999), 'A Field for Growing Doctorates in Design?', in R. Buchanan, D. Doordan, L. Justice and V. Margolin (eds), *Doctoral Education in Design: Proceedings of the Ohio Conference*, 207–224, Pittsburgh: Carnegie Mellon University.
Kruft, H. W. (1994), *A History of Architectural Theory, From Vitruvius to the Present*, New York: Princeton Architectural Press.
Kuban, D. (2007), *Osmanlı Mimarisi (Ottoman Architecture)*, İstanbul: YEM Yayınları.
Kubler, G. (1978), *The Shape of Time: Remarks on the History of Things*, New Haven and London: Yale University Press.
Kurtgözü, A. E. (2003), 'From Function to Emotion: A Critical Essay on the History of Design Arguments', *The Design Journal*, 6 (2): 49–59.
Küçükerman, Ö. and Şen, S. M. Ö. (2021), 'Türkiye'de İlk Endüstri Ürünleri Tasarımı Bölümünün; İstanbul Güzel Sanatlar Akademisi'nden Mimar Sinan Güzel Sanatlar Üniversitesi'ne 50 Yıllık Serüveni', *Tasarım+Kuram*, 17 (Özel Sayı: 4): 1–28.
Küçükerman, Ö. (1997), *Endüstri Tasarımı: Ürün Tasarımında Adımlar*, İstanbul: YEM Yayınları.
Küçükerman, Ö. (1996), *Endüstri Tasarımı: Endüstri İçin Ürün Tasarımında Yaratıcılık*, İstanbul: YEM Yayınları.
Küçükerman, Ö. (1978), *Kişi-Çevre İlişkilerinde Çağdaş Gelişimler ve Oturma Eylemi*, İstanbul: DGSA Yayını.
Kuhn, T. S. (1970), *The Structure of Scientific Revolutions*, Chicago: University of Chicago Press.
Kuran, A. (2012), *Architecture in Turkey, from the Seljuks to the Republic*, İstanbul: Türkiye İş Bankası Kültür Yayınları.
Lakatos, I. (1970), 'Falsification and the Methodology of Scientific Research Programmes', in I. Lakatos and A. Musgrave (eds), *Criticism and the Growth of Knowledge*, 91–196, Cambridge: Cambridge University Press.
Lindbeck, J. R. (1995), *Product Design and Manufacture*, New Jersey: Prentice Hall.
Lucie-Smith, E. (1983), *A History of Industrial Design*, Oxford: Phaidon Press.
MacCarthy, F. (1979), *A History of British Design 1830–1970*, London: George Allen & Unwin Ltd.

References

MacCarthy, F. (1982), *British Design Since 1880*, London: Lund Humphries.

Macdonald, S. (2013), *Transnational History: A Review of Past and Present Scholarship*. Available online: https://www.ucl.ac.uk/centre-transnational-history/sites/centre-transnational-history/files/simon_macdonald_tns_review.pdf (accessed 6 September 2022).

Macleod, K. (1998), 'Research in Fine Art: Theory, Judgement and Discourse', *Drawing Fire*, 2 (2): 33–7.

Maden, S. (1985), 'Türk Grafik Sanatı Tarihi / History of Turkish Graphic Art', *Grafik Sanatı*, 1 (3), May–June: 58–62.

Maden, S. (1989), 'Ülkemizde Grafik Sanatının Dünü, Bugünü'/ Past and Present State of Graphic Art in Turkey', *Türk Grafik Sanatçıları /Turkish Graphic Artists*, Istanbul: Turkish Society of Graphic Designers.

Maden, S. (1999), 'Grafik Sanatının Dünü, Bugünü', in A. Ödekan (ed), *Cumhuriyet'in Renkleri, Biçimleri*, 74–81, İstanbul: Tarih Vakfı.

Maldonado, T. (1993), 'Industrial Design: Some Present and Future Queries', *Journal of Design History*, 1 (1): 1–7.

Manzini, E. and Susani, M., eds. (1995), *The Search for Consistency, A Changing World: The Solid Side, Projects and Proposals*, Netherlands: V+K Publishing.

Margolin, V. (1989), *Design Discourse*, Chicago: The University of Chicago Press.

Margolin, V. (1992), 'Design History or Design Studies: Subject Matter and Methods', *Design Studies*, 13 (2): 104–16.

Margolin, V. (1998), 'Design and the World Situation', in T. Balcioglu (ed), *The Role of Product Design in Post-Industrial Society*, 15–34, Ankara & Rochester: METU & KIAD.

Margolin, V. (1999), 'History, Theory, and Criticism in Doctoral Design Education', in R. Buchanan, D. Doordan, L. Justice and V. Margolin (eds), *Doctoral Education in Design: Proceedings of the Ohio Conference*, Pittsburgh: Carnegie Mellon University.

Marquard, O. (1989), *Farewell to Matters of Principle: Philosophical Studies*, New York: Oxford University Press.

Martin, H.-P. and Schumann, H. (1997), *The Global Trap: Globalization & The Assault on Democracy & Prosperity*, London: Pluto Press.

Marwick, A. (1976), *The Nature of History*, London: Macmillan.

Marwick, A. (1989), *The Nature of History*, London: Macmillan.

Marx, K. ([1867] 1983), *Das Capital*, trans. S. Moore and E. Aveling, ed. F. Engels, London: Laurence and Wishart.

Meikle, J. (1979), *Twentieth Century Limited, Industrial Design in America, 1925–1939*, Philadelphia: Temple University Press.

Meikle, J. (1992), 'On The Mezzanine', *Design History Society News Letter*, no: 54, July.

Miller, D. (1987), *Material Culture and Mass Consumption*, Oxford: Basil Blackwell.

Morris, W. (1969), 'Of the Origins of Ornamental Art', in E. D. Lemire (ed), *The Unpublished Lectures of William Morris*' (first recorded delivery of this speech: 1886), Detroit: Wayne State University Press.

Mumford, L. ([1934] 1947), *Technics and Civilizations*, London: George Routledge and Sons.

Mumford, L. (1960), *Art and Technics*, New York: Columbia University Press.

Naylor, G. (1985), *The Bauhaus Re-assessed: Sources and Design Theory*, London: Herbert Press.

Naylor, G. (1971), *The Arts and Crafts Movement*, London: Studio Vista.

OECD. (2019), *Under Pressure: The Squeezed Middle Class*. Available online: https://www.oecd.org/social/under-pressure-the-squeezed-middle-class-689afed1-en.htm (accessed 2 September 2022).

Ogut, Ş. T. (2009), 'Material Culture of Tea in Turkey Transformations of Design through Tradition Modernity and Identity', *The Design Journal*, 12 (3): 339–63.

References

O'Shea, T. (1998), 'How New Technology is Changing the Nature of the PhD', *Annual Summer Conference 15 & 16 July 1998*, UK Council for Graduate Education, pp. 2–7.

Özcan, A. C. (2009), 'An Overview of the Early Foundations and Development of Contemporary Industrial Design in Turkey', *The Design Journal*, 12 (3): 267–287.

Pacey, P. (1992), 'Anyone Designing Anything? Non-Professional Designers and the History of Design', *Journal of Design History*, 5 (3): 217–25.

Packard, V. (1964), *The Waste Makers*, Middlesex: Penguin Books.

Perec, G. (1990), *Things: A Story of the Sixties with A Man Asleep*, trans. D. Bellos and A. Leak, Glasgow: Harvill.

Pevsner, N. ([1940] 1973), *Academies of Art: Past and Present*, New York: Da Capo Press.

Pevsner, N. (1937), *An Enquiry into Industrial Art in England*, Cambridge: Cambridge University Press.

Pevsner, N. (1936), *Pioneers of the Modern Movement*, London: Faber.

Polanyi, M. ([1958] 1974), *Personal Knowledge: Towards a Post-Critical Philosophy*, Chicago: The University of Chicago Press.

Press, M. and Cooper, R. (2003), *The Design Experience: The Role of Design and Designers in the Twenty-First Century*, Hants: Ashgate Publishing Limited.

Pulos, A. (1983), *American Design Ethic*, Cambridge: MIT Press.

QAA: The Quality Assurance Agency for Higher Education (1998), *A Consultation Paper on Qualification Frameworks: Postgraduate Qualifications*. November.

Rabasa, A. and Larrabee, F. S. (2008), *The Rise of Political Islam in Turkey*, Santa Monica: RAND, National Defence Research Institute.

Read, H. ([1934] 1956), *Art and Industry*, London: Faber and Faber Limited.

Read, H. (1947), *The Future of Industrial Design*, London: Design and Industries Association.

Reilly, P. (1987), *An Eye on Design: An Autobiography*, London: Max Reinhardt.

Renzio, T. D. (1977), 'Mistaken Identities in the History of Design', *The Times Higher Educational Supplement (THES)* 11, 4 February.

Robertson, R. ([1992] 1996), *Globalization: Social Theory and Global Culture*, London: Sage.

Rodgers, P. A. and Bremner, C. (2021), *118 Theories of Design(ing)*, Wilmington: Vernon Press.

Rousseau, J. J. (1768), *Dictionnaire de Musique*, Paris: M DCC LXVIII (Chez la VEUE DUCHESNE, Libraire, rue Saint Jacques, au Temple du Gout.

Rousseau, Monf. J. J. (1779), *Dictionary of Music*, trans. W. Waring, London: Printed for J. French.

Sadık, N. (1928), *Türk Alfabesi*, İstanbul: Akşam Matbaası. Available online: https://tr.wikipedia.org/wiki/Türk_Alfabesi_(kitap) (accessed 25 February 2022).

Sâdullah, M. (1928), *Yeni Türk Harfleri-le İlk Alfabe*, İstanbul: İstanbul Tefeyüz Kitaphanesi. Available online: https://okumagunlugu.com/yeni-turk-harfleriyle-ilk-alfabe-midhat-sadullah/ (accessed 25 February 2022).

Segal, W. (1972), 'About Taut 1880–1938', *Architectural Review*, 151 (899): 25.

Seskir, Z. C. (2017), 'Türkiye'de Yükseköğretimde Nicel Cinsiyet Açığındaki Değişimin Olası Nedenleri ve Etkileri', *Yükseköğretim ve Bilim Dergisi*, 7 (2): 321–32.

Sezgi, O. (1996), 'Küresel Bir Dünya İçin Tasarım / Yerel Kimliğin Var Olma Hakkı', in N. Bayazıt, F. K. Çorbacı and D. Günal (eds), *Tasarımda Evrenselleşme*, 105–19, İstanbul: İTÜ Mimarlık Fakültesi.

Shakespeare, W. [16th C.] (1988), 'Love's Labour Lost', *The Complete Works*, London: Michael O'Mara Books.

Simon, H. A. (1998), *The Science of Artificial*, Cambridge: MIT Press.

Snow, C. P. (1995), *The Two Cultures*, Cambridge: Cambridge University Press.

Sudjic, D. (1985), *Cult Objects*, London: Paladin Books.

Szélpál, L. (2009), 'Transnational History: An American Perspective', *Americana: E-Journal of American Studies in Hungary*, 5 (2). Available online: https://americanaejournal.hu/vol5no2/szelpal (accessed 10 August 2023)

References

Taylor, F. W. (1906), 'On the Art of Cutting Metals', an address made at the opening of the annual meeting in New York, December, New York: American Society of Mechanical Engineers.
Teymur, N. (1981), 'The Materiality of Design', *Block*, (5): 19–27.
Teymur, N. (1982), *Environmental Discourse*, London: ?estion Press.
Tunstall, D. (2020), 'Decolonizing Design', YouTube video. Available online: https://www.youtube.com/watch?v=jjLV1vVm9bc (accessed 5 August 2023).
The World Bank. (1997), *World Development Indicators*, Washington: The World Bank.
Thelen, D. (1999), 'The Nation and Beyond: Transnational Perspectives on United States History', *The Journal of American History*, 86 (3): 965–975.
Thorne, L. (1998), 'Developing a Doctoral Framework-Middlesex Experience', Annual Summer Conference 15 & 16 July 1998, UK Council for Graduate Education, 50–2.
Turan, G. (2006), 'Türkiye'de Endüstri Tasarımı Alanındaki İlk Dernek Üzerine Bir Araştırma: Endüstri Tasarımı Derneği – ETD', *Türkiye'de Tasarımı Tartışmak*, III. Ulusal Tasarım Kongresi Bildiri Kitabı, 374–83, İstanbul: İTÜ.
Tyrrell, I. (2007), 'What is Transnational History?' Available online: https://iantyrrell.wordpress.com/what-is-transnational-history/ (accessed 15 September 2022).
Tyrrell, I. (2009), 'Reflections on the Transnational Turn in United States History: Theory and Practice', *Journal of Global History*, (4): 453–74.
UKCGE. (1995), *Graduate Schools*, UK Council for Graduate Education.
UKCGE. (1996), *Quality and Standards of Postgraduate Research Degrees*, UK Council for Graduate Education.
UKCGE. (1997), *Practice-based Doctorates in the Creative and Performing Arts and Design*, UK Council for Graduate Education.
Walker, J. (1989), *Design History and History of Design*, London: Pluto.
Walker, J. (1988), 'Design History: A Student's Handbook', (book review) *Journal of Design History*, 1 (1): 79–80.
Watts, N., ed. (1999), *The International Postgraduate: Challenges to British Higher Education*, UK Council for Graduate Education, Lichfield.
Wharton, A. (2010), 'Mosque Building in the Tanzimat Period', in H. Kuruyazıcı and H. Kuruyazıcı (eds), *Armenian Architects of Istanbul in the Era of Westernization*, 91–105, Istanbul: International Hrant Dink Foundation Publications.
Wharton, A. (2015), 'Armenian Architects and 'Other' Revivalism', in A. Lepine, M. R. Lodder and R. McKever (eds), *Revival: Memories, Identities, Utopias*, 150–67, London: Courtauld Books Online.
Wharton, A. (2016), 'The Balyan Family and the Linguistic Culture of a Parisian Education', *International Journal of Islamic Architecture*, 5 (1): 39–71.
Wood, J. (1990), *The BA Course in Design Studies (Total Design)*. Unpublished course outline, London: Goldsmith's College.
Woodham, J. (2010), 'Design History at the Periphery', in T. Balcioglu and G. Baydar (eds) *Tasarım Tarihinin Ötekileri (The Others of Design History)*, 6–23, İzmir: İzmir University of Economics.
Woodham, J. M. (1997), *Twentieth-Century Design*, Oxford: Oxford University Press.
Woudhuysen, J. (1998), 'Beyond the Dogma of Globalization', in T. Balcioglu (ed), *The Role of Product Design in Post-Industrial Society*, 93–112, Ankara & Rochester: METU & KIAD.

INDEX

4T Design and Design History Society 4, 143–54, 143 n.1
   design historiography, regional and institutional diversification in 150–3
   design organizations similar to 144–6
   development/maturation phases of 149–50
   with foreign design organizations 146–7
   foundation of 149
   framework 143–4
   future 153–4
   Inter-Cultural Forum for the Arts 147–8
   web of relations 146–7
5T (Türkiye Tasarım Tarihi Topluluğu Toplantıları) 149

Acıkan Taşlar (Tagore) 122, 126
active objects 24–6
actors demanding design with identity 201–2
Adam, Robert 7
advanced study programmes work
   artists and designers, demands of 46
   balance between 44
   changing nature of professions and practices, demands of 47
   concept of PhD 47–8
   individual identity 44
   new professional degree 47
   permanency 43
   practical part 41–2
   theoretical part 41
   timing/sequence of realization 41–2
   transferability 45
   unity 43
Aga Cooker 24
Ağır, Aygül 111–12
Akan, Erdem 190
Akcan, Esra 109–10
Akgün, Fikret 118
Akın, Özlem 173
Akman, Oya 190
Akpınar, Dudu 136–7
Aksu, Bora 61
Aktüre, Teoman 147
Alberti, Leone Battista 7
Alpan, Hüsnü 173
alphabets, Turkish 115–17
Altıntaş, Yurdaer 117–20, 127, 131, 133, 135
Altun, Ümit 190, 204

Alyanak, Şermin 190
Americanization 35–6
Amok (Zweig) 122, 125
Amygdalou, Kalliopi 150
anachronistic repetition 14
Ankara Castle 122
"an-other" model of knowing and doing 53
antiquity 13
Appadurai, Arjun 36
applied art 71
Arçelik 204
Archer, Bruce 54, 62, 99, 191
architecture within framework of design, FFAD 161–6
   academic staff employment policy 164
   awareness of being different 166
   common activities 165
   common courses 162–4
   common first-year studio 162
   gradual and controlled growth 165
   idea of being team 166
   research assistant employment policy 164–5
   shared offices 165–6
Armenian architects 111–12
Armenian Architects of Istanbul 111
Arseven, C. E. 111
art and design education 50–60
Art and Humanities Research Board 52
Art and Industry (Read) 80, 88, 91–2
artefacts 52–3
art knowledge 183
Art Nouveau 63
Arzum Cezve 204
Asatekin, Mehmet 190–1
Ashwin, C. 93
Aşkın, Cihat 148
Aslanoğlu, İnci 109–10
Association of Industrial Designers 144
Atatürk, Mustafa Kemal 109, 116, 122
Atkinson, Paul 145
Attfield, Judy 61, 95
awareness 34–5
Aybar, Sedat 147

BA (Hons) degrees 188
Bakova, Ali 190, 204–5
Balcıoğlu, Tevfik 147, 191
Balian, Agop 111

Index

Balian, Karabet 111
Balian, Nikogos 111, 112
Balian, Sarkis 111
Balians 111–12
Banham, Reyner 97, 110
Barın, Emin 119
Baroque 63
Batur, Afife 112
Baudrillard, Jean 10
Bauman, Zygmunt. 33–4
Bayazıt, Nigan 190–1
Baydar, Gülsüm 149
Bayly, C. A. 108
Belge, Murat 148
Bell, Quentin 70
Benjamin, Walter 9–10
Benton, Tim 91
Bertram, Anthony 67, 91
Beykoz Shoes 121–2
Bir Kadının 24 Saati (Zweig) 122
Birsel, Ayşe 190
Börekçi, Naz. A. G. Z. 192
Bozdoğan, Sibel 109–10
Braudel, Fernand 83 n.7
Breuer, Marcel 30
Brown, Gordon 35

CAD; *see* computer-aided design (CAD)
Calvera, Anna 146
Can, Selman 112
Canver, Nilgün 147
Carr, E. H. 82 n.6
Carrington, Noel 48–9, 71
Carter, David 62, 147
Çepoğlu, Gülizar 138–9, 141
Chalayan, Hussein 61
Chermayeff, Serge 71
Christie, James 147
Çırağan Kempinski Palace 111, 201
Cole, Henry 7, 70–1
colonization 62
combination furniture 26
combination of objects 26–7
commercial art 75–8
Commission for Architecture and the Built Environment (CABE) 8
commitments 56
commodity fetishism 203
commonalities, design 19–20
common objects 28–9
communication 34, 53
computer-aided design (CAD) 16
computer numerical control (CNC) systems 16
computers 16
connotative values of objects 20–1
Conran, Terence 66

consensus-based knowledge 58
consistency 80
Conway, Hazel 61, 96
Cooper, Rachel 145
cooperative education 58
Corbusier, Le 7
Council of Higher Education 156
Council of Industrial Design (CoID) 7–8, 89, 90
coups d'état, Turkey 118–19
Courtauld Institute of Art 148
Covid-19 pandemic 193
Crane, Walter 7, 71
Cross, Nigel 56, 181
cult objects 5, 20–1, 24, 157, 203–8
    as arena of design battleground 206–8
    in Turkey 204–5
Cult Objects (Sudjic) 203
cultural identity 36–7
cultural infiltration 37
culture, global 35–7
Curtius, Georg 107

Day, Lewis 71
Dearing, Ron 178–9
de Armado, Don Adriono 67
decolonization 62–3
decorative art 71
de Forest, Robert W. 71
del Renzio, Toni 91
dematerialization 18
Democrat Party 118
Deniz, Şerafettin 112
denotative values of objects 20–1
design
    commonalities 19–20
    conception of 65–6
    consciousness 66
    definition of 65–6
    denotative *versus* connotative values of objects 20–1
    Design History Society, Turkey 4, 143–54
    expansion of 3
    formal qualities, transformations in 21–31
    globalization of 2, 33–40
    graphic design in Turkey 3–4, 114–42
    historiography in UK 3, 61, 86–106
    history 61–3
    identities 2
    industrial design in Turkey 4
    Integrated design approach (IDeA) 4, 155, 159–73
    knowledge, nature of 2, 41–9
    one-directional transformation in 22–30
    personality 3
    principles of 19
    reproductions 1, 9–18

Index

in society 61, 143–54
technological transformation 2, 19–32
theory 7–8
transnational 3, 107–13
Turkish design transitions 5, 107–13
two-directional transformation in 30–1
in UK and its transformation 2–3, 61, 65–73
Design and Industries Association (DIA) 7, 49
Design (Bertram) 67
Design Council 8
design discourse 149 n.10
design education 88
designer's dilemma 202–3
Design for Today 72
design historiography
   regional and institutional diversification in 150–4
   research methods 150–1
   style of writing 151–2
   topics 152
   transnational 3, 107–13
   Turkish 3, 107–13, 153
   in UK (by end of twentieth century) 86–106
design historiography in UK 3, 61, 86–106
   in British higher education 90–2
   as dominant term/concept among other related nomenclature 88–9
   government's policy 92–3
   historical conditions 87–92
   historical consciousness, degree of 102–4
   identity formation 94–102
      aims and objectives 99–101
      content of design 96–8
      subject matter 95–6
      theoretical framework 101–2
   market-oriented strategy for design 92–3
   negligence, stage of 102–3
   official and formal titles, rise in 89–90
   overview 86–7
   as practice and profession, institutionalization of 87–8
   problems (in 1960s) of 93–4
   prospective 104–6
   recognition, stage of 103
   study, stage of 103–4
Design History: A Student's Handbook (Conway) 96
Design History and History of Design (Walker) 65, 103
Design History Society, Turkey 2, 4, 61, 63, 93, 144–54
design literature 96
Design Research Society 144
dessin 3, 69–71
Deutscher Werkbund 7
DIA; *see* Design and Industries Association (DIA)

Dilnot, Clive 52–3, 56, 61, 65–6, 95, 99–100, 102–5, 174, 181, 183, 191, 203
Diploma in Art and Design (DipAD) 91
disegno 68, 68 n.6
distribution of investment 34
Doctor of Art (D.Art) 48, 177, 181
Doctor of Design (D.Des) 48, 177, 179, 181, 187–8
Doctor of Fine Art (D.F.A.) 48, 177, 181
Doğan, Pelin 173
Dormer, Peter 23
DProf 187
Dreyfuss, Henry 72
Düben, İpek Aksüğür 138
Dyce, William 70

EAD; *see* European Academy of Design (EAD)
eclecticism 63
economic globalization 33–4, 34 n.2
Eczacıbaşı, Şakir 138
Eldem, Edhem 112
electric kettle technology 204
electric shaver 25–6
electronic production 16–17
   involvement of original 17
   original and its 17
Elton, G. R. 82 n.6
English Tradition in Design, The (Gloag) 78
Enzensberger, Hans Magnus 80
Er, Alpay 62 n.2, 191
Er, Özlem 62 n.2, 191
Erdim, B. 109–10
Erkmen, Aydın 119, 131
Erkmen, Bülent 119, 133, 135–6
Ertel, Mengü 118–19, 126–9, 131–2
Ertürk, İsmail 147
esthétique industrielle 67
European Academy of Design (EAD) 145–6
European Customs Union 189
Evans, M. 17

Faculty of Fine Arts and Design (FFAD) 159–73
   academic staff employment policy 164
   architecture within framework of design 161–6
   awareness of being different 166
   common activities 165
   common courses 162–4
   common first-year studio 162
   first year education 160
   fourth year education 161
   general education strategy 160–1
   gradual and controlled growth 165
   idea of being team 166
   IDeA on new FFAD building, reflections of 168–73

Index

integrated design approach, reflections on   161
overview   159–60
research assistant employment policy   164–5
second year education   160–1
shared offices   165–6
third year education   161
Fadıllıoğlu, Zeynep   200–1
Fallan, Kjetil   61
Falsificationism   53
Farhi, Musa   147
Fehim, Münif   117, 122
Ferebee, Ann   96
Feydeau, Georges   131
FFAD; *see* Faculty of Fine Arts and Design (FFAD)
Fiat Panda   16
film industry   36
Fine Art   71
Flusser, Vilém   54, 56
foreign food and cuisines   36
Forty, Adrian   14, 61, 95
Foucault, Michel   82–3
fragmentation   97 n.17
Frayling, Christopher   52, 186
Freely, Maureen   148
Friberg, K.   108
Fry, Tony   61, 100–1, 106
Fujita, Haruhiko   149
'Funded Consultancy Scheme' (FCS)   92

Gates, Bill   40
Geddes, Norman Bel   72
Gender Perspectives in Design: Turkish and Global Contexts   150
Genoways, Hugh H.   187
German fifty-Pfennig coin   126
Giedion, Sigfried   26
Ginzburg, Carlo   79 n.2, 85, 106
Glasarchitektur (Scheerbart)   110
Glass House   110
Gloag, John   61, 74–80
on acceptance of industrial design in UK   78–9
characteristics of method/survey   79–80
concept of industrial design   74–5
English Tradition in Design, The   78
Good Design Good Business   77
Industrial Art Explained   75–6
meaning of industrial design   75–8
Plastics and Industrial Design   76
Self Training for Industrial Designers   75, 77
global history   108
globalization   33–40, 106, 108
globalization of local design   2, 33–40
awareness   34–5
communication   34

culture   35–7
economics   33–4
Turkey   37–40
Göker, Selma   147
Golden Scarab, The   122
Good Design Good Business (Gloag)   77
Görey, İhap Hulusi   115
Grand Bazaar   201
graphic communication   138
graphic design in Turkey   3–4, 114–42
from 1923 to 1950   115–18
1960s, first coup d'état   118–19
1971, coup d'état   119
1980, coup d'état   119
abstract/integrative framework   131–3
after mid-1980s   119–20
analytic framework   120–39
conceptual/referential framework   133–9
Democrat Party (1950s)   118
historical perspective   114–20
realistic/representative framework   121–6
symbolic/illustrative framework   126–31
Great Exhibition (1851)   61
Griffin, Miranda   147
Gropius, Walter   7
Guillerme, Jacques   67
Güven, Gamze   190
Gywnn, John   69

Hasdoğan, Gülay   38, 190, 191
Height, Frank   62, 147
Heskett, John   61, 62, 147, 148, 191
Heynen, Hilde   149
higher education in UK   50–1
Higher National Diploma (HND)   50
Higher School of Applied Industrial Arts, Turkey   119
Hilson, M.   108
History of Design from the Victorian Era to the Present, A (Ferebee)   96
History of the World or World Architecture   97
History of Things (Kubler)   105
History of Western Technology, A (Klem)   15
Hitchcock poster (Altıntaş)   133, 135
Hogarth, William   69
Hollywood   36–7
Homend Pottoman 1803   204
Hulusi, İhap   116–17, 121–2

ICDHS; *see* International Committee of Design History and Studies (ICDHS)
ICFA; *see* Inter-Cultural Forum for the Arts (ICFA)
IDeA; *see* Integrated design approach (IDeA)
identicalness   16
identities, design   2

Index

IEU; *see* Izmir University of Economics (IEU)
İlhan, Ali O.   191
inclusive model   47–8, 47 n.6
inconsistencies   80–4, 81 n.3
   as emergence of conflict   82–3
   function within research   84
   in historiography   81–2
Incredible Stories (Poe)   122, 125
industrial architecture   75–8
industrial art   75–8
Industrial Art (Pevsner)   88
Industrial Art Explained (Gloag)   75–6
industrial design   7–8, 69 n.7, 72 n.11, 88–9
   acceptance in UK   78–9
   concept of   74–5
   divisions of   76–7
   inconsistency   81–4
   meaning of   75–8
   versus product design   76 n.1
   in Turkey   4, 189–99
   in UK   72
   in United States   72
Industrial Design Association   144
Industrial Designers' Society of Turkey
   (ETMK)   144, 189
industrial design in Turkey   4, 189–99
   academia   191–2
   departments of   190–1
   development, draft action plan for   193–9
   gender balance and   192–3
   present situation   193
   rise of   189–90
industrialization   2, 33–40
Industrial Revolution   15, 87
Integrated design approach (IDeA)   4, 155, 159–73
   emergence of   166–8
   features   159
   FFAD   159–73
   IEU   159–73
   on new FFAD building, reflections of   168–74
      collateral, transparent and open   170
      common areas   170–1
      corridors and open areas for critiques   169–70
      from specific to common   173
      studio locations   169
      zones by functions   171–2
   principle of   159
Integrated Design Curriculum   167
Inter-Cultural Forum for the Arts (ICFA)   147–8
International Committee of Design History and Studies (ICDHS)   146
International Council of Societies of Industrial Design (ICSID)   8

international history   108
international postgraduate students   51 n.1
International Prison Watch (Erkmen)   133, 135
Ionesco, Eugène   131
Iriye, Akira   107
Irmak, Orhan   190
Issigonis, Alec   61
Istanbul Film Festival poster (Karamustafa)   131–2
İzer, Ayşegül   74
Izmir Center of Architecture   153
Izmir University of Economics (IEU)   159–73

Jameson, Fredric   35–6
Japan Design History Forum   150
Japanese House   110
Julier, Guy   61, 191
Justificationism   53

Kalman, Tibor   95, 102, 191
Kaprol, Arzu   192–3
Kara, Meriç   190
Karamustafa, Sadık   119, 127–8, 131–2, 136–8
Karol, Esen   137–8, 140
Kaya, Cem   153–4, 202
Kayek, Dice   192–3
Kaygan, Harun   192
Kent Institute of Art and Design, Rochester, UK   148
Keşanlı Ali Destanı (Ertel)   131–2
Kikuchi, Yuko   107, 108
King, Philip   131, 133
Kinross, Robin   80, 84
kitchen tools   24, 24 n3
Klem, Frederick   15
knowledge   2, 43–9, 179
   about practice   44
   art   183
   in art and design practices   4, 50–60
   artefactual   53
   communication   53
   from language perspective   53
   by means of practice   44
   of object   12
   personal   55–6
   within practice   44
   in SAD   55
   scientific   55–7
   sensorial   53
   value and   56
Koç, Mirzat   190
Koç, Şule   190
Korçan, Bahar   192–3
Korkut, Fatma   192
Korvenmaa, Pekka   146
Koz, Defne   62, 148, 190

Index

Krippendorff, Klauss   174
Kubler, George   105
Küçükerman, Önder   190–1
Kuhn, Thomas   175–6
Kuran, Abdullah   111
Kurtgözü, Aren E.   156, 191–2

Labrouste, Alexandre   111
Labrouste, Henri   111
Lakatos, Imre   57–8
Langrish, John   62, 191
languages   53
Laugier, Marc-Antoine   7
Lees-Maffei, Grace   61
lemon squeezer   21
Lethaby, W. R.   7, 71
Levet, Füsün   148
Lewis, Bernard   148
Loewy, Raymond   72
Loos, Adolf   7
Lovegrove, Ross   61
Love's Labour (Shakespeare)   67, 67 n.2

Macbeth (Shakespeare)   137–8, 140
MacCarthy, Fiona   89–90
Macdonald, Simon   107
machine design   75–8
Macleod, Kate   45
Maden, Sait   117–19
Maldonado, Tomas   18
Malhan, Faruk   190
Malhan, Koray   190
Manioğlu, Mesut   118
Mansur, Cem   148
Manzini, Ezio   148
Margolin, Victor   56, 66, 95, 146, 148, 174
Marquard, Odo   19
Marriot, Michael   21
Marwick, Arthur   101
Marx, Karl   203
mass production   15–16, 29
   involvement of original   15–16
   original and its   16
mass transportation   31
material culture   105
Material Culture and Mass Consumption (Miller)   105
media   21
Mellor, David   20
memory   12
microcomputer   16
Miller, Daniel   105
Mills, C. Wright   8
miniaturization of components   18
mock-ups   17
modernisation   115

MoMA Design Store   200
Moot Points, Friendly Disputes upon Art & Industry between Walter Crane and Lewis F. Day   48
Morelli, Giovanni   79 n.2
Morris, William   7, 71, 79
mould-related techniques   13–14
moulds   13–14
multi-authorship   152
multi-functional objects   26–8
multiple production   13–15
   involvement of original   13–14
   original and its   14–15
Mumford, Lewis   11, 25
Musical Dictionary, A (Rousseau)   68
Muthesius, Hermann   7
Mutver, Cemalettin   119
Myerson, Jeremy   148

Nagel, Karl H.   23
Nakışçı, Tamer   190
National Advisory Council on Art Education (NACAE)   91
natural evolution of products   1–2
Nature of History, The (Marwick)   101
Naylor, Gillian   61
Neurotic Realism   176
New Relationship: Design History and Virtual Design Museum   150
Non-Reflective Transnational Dissemination of Impacts   108, 110–12
non-renewable objects   29–30

objects   1–2
   active   24–6
   combination of   26–7
   common   28–9
   connotative values of   20–1
   cult   5, 20–1, 24, 157, 203–8
   denotative values of   20–1
   from easy to difficult   21–2
   energy sources   25
   multi-functional   26–8
   from non-renewable to renewable   29–30
   one-directional transformation in   22–30
   in our life   98 n.18
   passive   24–6
   personal   28–9
   semi-active   24–6
   from single to various   29
   social status of   20–1
   transformation of   21–2
   two-directional transformation in   30–1
Oktay Aslanapa   111
one-directional transformation in design   22–30
   from common to personal   28–9

224

from functional to multi-functional 26–8
from non-renewable to renewable 29–30
from passive to active 24–6
from single to various 29
'one-dollar watch' campaign 28
One Hundred Great Product Designs 203
original 9–10
  in discourse of reproduction 10
  and its reproductions, relationship between 11–17
  meanings of 10
  in reproduction process 11
  and uniqueness 10–11
ornamental art 71
Ortaköy Mosque 111–12
O'Shea, Tim 179
Ottomans 63, 200–1, 204
Önal, Selçuk 118
Özal, Turgut 119–20
Özar, Mithat 117
Özbek, Rıfat 61
Özcan, A. Can 192
Özer, Adem 147
Özgen, Koray 190

Pacey, Philip 100
Packard, Vance 23, 23 n.2
Paker, Saliha 147
Palaeolithic scraper 12
Papaz Kaçtı (King) 131, 133
Parsons, Talcott 8
passive objects 24–6
Peel, Robert 69–70
personal knowledge 55–6
personal objects 28–9
Pevsner, Nikolaus 70, 88
PhD programmes 2, 4, 155, 174–88
  attributes of 185
  practice-based 41–9, 184–8
  research-based education 50–60
  work-based learning programs 184–5
Pioneers of Modern Design (Pevsner) 91, 97
Piranesi, Giovanni Battista 7
Plastics and Industrial Design (Gloag) 76
Poe, Edgar Allan 122
Polanyi, Michael 55
polytechnics 50
Popper, Karl 53
potter 12
practice-based learning 58
practice-based PhD programmes 4, 41–9, 174–88
  artists and designers, demands of 46
  balance between 44
  changing nature of professions and practices, demands of 47
  concept of 47–8

expectations 46 n.5
inclusive model 47–8, 47 n.6
individual identity 44
new professional degree 47
permanency 43
practical part 41–2
theoretical part 41
timing/sequence of realization 41–2
transferability 45
UK Council for Graduate Education (UKCGE) on 43
unity 43
prefiguration 12
Preston, Michael 62, 147
principles of design 19
private money 34
production 9
  electronic 16–17
  mass 15–16
  multiple 13–15
  repetitive 11–13
  versus reproduction process 9–11
product-oriented sophistication 30
product variety 29
professional degrees 47
professional doctorates (PD) 58–60, 178–88
  academic level of 180–1
  advantages of 181–2
  art *versus* design 182–3
  assessment of work 182
  characteristics 185
  knowledge 179–80
  PhD *versus* 179–80
  practice and research 181
Proficiency in Art 156
prototypes 16–17
Pugin, Augustus 7
Pulos, Arthur 71
Putnam, Tim 61

Quality Assurance Agency 180, 186

Rakı 204 n.4
Rams, Dieter 148
RCA; *see* Royal College of Art (RCA)
Read, Herbert 80, 88
renewable objects 29–30
repetitive production 11–13
  involvement of original 12
  original and its 13
reproduction process, industrial design 1, 9–18
  electronic production 16–17
  mass production 15–16
  multiple production 13–15
  original and its 11–17
  original in 11

Index

original in discourse of 10
overview 9
versus production 9–11
repetitive production 11–13
Research Assessment Exercise 50
research-based education at doctorate level 50–60
    background 50–2
    educational aspect 58–60
    epistemological aspect 52–4
    science, art and design 54–8
resemblance, levels of 14
Robertson, Roland 34
Rococo 63
Roden, Claudia 148
Rolex watches 20
Roman cameo glass 14
Roman Portland Vase 14–15
Rousseau, Jean-Jacques 68
Royal College of Art (RCA) 147
Ruskin, John 7

SAD; see science, art and design (SAD)
Said, Edward 200
Şakir, Cevat 117
Salinas, Oscar 146
sameness, original and reproductions 14
Sarıyer, Aziz 190
Sarıyer, Derin 190
Scheerbart, Paul 110
Schick, Irvin Cemil 112
Schools of Design, The (Bell) 70
science, art and design (SAD) 54–8
Science of Design, The (Simon) 8, 54
scientific knowledge 55–7
scissors 20
Segal, Walter 110
Şekercioğlu, Kunter 190, 204
self-referential writing 152
Self Training for Industrial Designers (Gloag) 75, 77
semi-active objects 24–6
Semper, Gottfried 7
Senan, Emre 139 n.7
sensorial knowledge 53
Serbest, Adnan 190
Siesbye, Alev Ebüzziya 190
similarity, original and reproductions 13
Simon, Herbert 8, 54
Smith, Edward Lucie 26
Snow, C. P. 54, 183
Society of Graphic Artists 119–20
Society of Industrial Artists (SIA) 90
Sokaklardan (Eczacıbaşı) 138, 140
The Solid Side project 30
Somerset House 148
Sony Walkman 28, 28 n.5

Sparke, Penny 61
Speidel, Manfred 109–10
Starck, Philippe 21, 204
Statism 115
Stone Age 11–12
Structure of Scientific Revolutions, The (Kuhn) 175
Sturt, George 88
Suavi, Ali 117
Suda, Orhan 148
Sudjic, Deyan 203
Süer, Özlem 192–3
sumptuous palaces 201
'Support for Design' (SFD) scheme 93
Susani, Marco 62, 148
Svengren, Elizabeth 145
Swatch 57
Swiss Army knives 27, 30–1

Tagore, Rabindranath 122
Tarzi, İdil 192–3
Tasarım Gazetesi (Design Newspaper) 139 n.7
Taut, Bruno 3, 108–11
Taylor, Frederick W. 15
Teague, Walter Dorwin 72
Teasley, Sarah 152
technologies 23, 36, 57
Temizan, Kenan 118
Teymur, Necdet 31, 148
Thatcher, Margaret 92, 92 n.11
Thelen, D. 108
Theory and Design in the First Machine Age (Banham) 91, 97
theory of uncertainty 52 n.3
third domain 60, 156
Thorne, Lucy 186
time measurement systems 28, 28 n.5
Timur, Şebnem 192
tools *versus* machines 25
Total Design 90 n.8
transformations of design 65–73
    in Britain/UK 67, 69–72
    design concept/definition 65–8
    with *dessin* 69–71
    expressions in field 72–3
    mass-produced objects, in context of 68–9
    technological progress 66–7
    in Western countries 67
transnational design history 3, 107–13
    Balians 111–12
    overview 107–8
    Taut, Bruno 108–11
    in Turkey 108–12
trans-national history 108
Tryyell, Ian 108
Tunstall, Dori 62
Türkali, Vedat 148

Turkey 37–40
    Arabic script replaced with Roman alphabet 115–17
    Armenian architects in 111–12
    Balians in 111–12
    cinemas 36–7
    coup d'état 118–19
    cult objects in 204–5
    Democrat Party 118
    design historiography 153
    design transitions 5, 107–13
    globalization of local design 37–40
    graphic design in 3–4, 114–42
    industrial design in 4, 189–99
    local culture for new design 39–40
    local designers 38–9
    overview 37–8
    Taut, Bruno 3, 108–11
    transnational design history 3, 107–13
Turkish graphic design 3–4, 114–42
    from 1923 to 1950 115–18
    1960s, first coup d'état 118–19
    1971, coup d'état 119
    1980, coup d'état 119
    abstract/integrative framework 131–3
    after mid-1980s 119–20
    analytic framework 120–39
    conceptual/referential framework 133–9
    Democrat Party (1950s) 118
    historical perspective 114–20
    realistic/representative framework 121–6
    symbolic/illustrative framework 126–31
Turkish Patent Institute 189
Turkish product 203–8
Turkish Society of Graphic Designers 120
Türk Mimarisinde İz Bırakanlar (Schick) 112
Two Cultures, The (Snow) 54, 183
two-directional transformation in design 30–1
    from large to small or vice versa 31
    from simple to complex or vice versa 30–1
typography 119, 138

UKCGE; *see* UK Council for Graduate Education (UKCGE)
UK Council for Graduate Education (UKCGE) 43, 155–6, 180, 184
Ünal, Erguvan 173
Ünal, Mahir 173
uniqueness 10–11

Vall, N. 108
Veveris, M. 17
Viollet-le-Duc, Eugène 7
virtual reality 18
VitrA, Turkish company 61, 61 n.1

Walker, John 65, 92 n.11, 94, 96, 103, 203
Wassily chair 30
Wedgwood, Josiah 14–15
Wegener, Claudia Maria 44 n.2
Westernization 63, 115
Wharton, Alyson 112
Wheelwright's Shop, The (Sturt) 88
Wood, John 90 n.8
Woodham, Jonathan 61, 146, 149, 200
work-based learning programs 58
World Bank 34
World Design Organization 8
world history 108
Wormald, P. 17
Woudhuysen, James 148
Wright, Frank Lloyd 7

Yagou, Artemis 150
Yalım, Ece 190
Yalman, Can 190
Yavi, Erkal 119, 129–30
Young, Michael Edward 173

Zeitgeist: Farewell to Matters of Principle (Marquard) 19
Zweig, Stefan 122

227